KINGDOM LEADERSHIP

SERVING YOUR GENERATION

SOLOMON OSOKO

KINGDOM LEADERSHIP:
Serving Your Generation

Copyright © 2011 by Solomon Osoko

All rights reserved.

The copyright laws of Switzerland protect this book.
No portion of this book may be copied or reprinted for commercial gain without the written permission of the author and publisher, with the exception of brief excerpts in articles, magazines or reviews.

The use of short quotation and occasional copying for personal or group study is permitted and encouraged.

Unless otherwise identified, all scripture quotations are from the King James Version of the Bible.

The first edition published **in 2011** © Osoko O. Solomon
ISBN -13: 978-3-9523844-6-6
Published in Switzerland.

Published **in 2019** by Amazon.com

For further information, contact:
Solomon Osoko Ministries
www.solomonosoko.com
sales@solomonosoko.com

Solomon Osoko

INDEX

INTRODUCTION 7

CHAPTER 1: LEADERSHIP CHALLENGES IN THE CONTEMPORARY WORLD 10

CHAPTER 2: WORLD THEORIES AND MODELS OF LEADERSHIP 27

CHAPTER 3: KINGDOM THEORIES AND MODELS OF LEADERSHIP . 37

CHAPTER 4: CALL TO VISIT THE WOES OF THE CHURCH 50

CHAPTER 5: BUILDING AN HONOURABLE CHURCH 62

CHAPTER 6: ROLES AND RESPONSIBILITIES 78

OF LEADERSHIP 78

CHAPTER 7: KINGDOM MODEL OF LEADERSHIP 95

CHAPTER 8: A CALL TO SERVICE 114

CHAPTER 9: WHICH TYPE OF SERVANT ARE YOU? 146

CHAPTER 10: PRINCIPLES OF SERVICE 172

CHAPTER 11: RENDERING SERVICE TO THE LORD 194

CHAPTER 12: PRINCIPLES OF LEADERSHIP 206

CHAPTER 13: CASE STUDY OF KINGDOM LEADERSHIP 214

CONCLUSION 248

FORWARD

Leadership is an all time important topic to mankind.
Many homes, businesses and countries have been ruined for lack of good leadership. All it takes for you to lose work, peace or life in the land God has given you is to have a reckless reign of bad leadership.

Though the topic of leadership universally concerns all men, different institutions have sought different definitions and approaches to the topic. I have watched how business schools take a business approach and political scientists barely take a political approach and Church institutions take a spiritual approach all to the same issue.

The fact however is that each of the approaches though relevant is as limited as its purview. There is a need for a bigger view.

God created man spirit, body and soul. Therefore, man has spiritual needs as much as he has social, political and economic needs. Trying to emphasize one part of the human need to the exclusion of another part is parochial and misguiding.

Leaders who ruled their nations as mere political entities have failed. The grave of history is filled with so many autocratic, despotic and dictatorial leaders who have ruined their people in their misrules. Spiritual leaders like Jim Jones have destroyed the destinies of their congregations as well, running them like spiritual freaks with no social or economic needs. Economic practices of man, be it communism, capitalism or socialism have also failed in many instances.

I have had a unique exposure to different types of leadership theories, structures and practice. I had my first university degree in Political Science, did my masters degree in Multicultural Management and my MBA in Business Administration.

Today, I practice as a Pastor. I have suffered under a millitary regime as well as experienced impacts of a budging democracy under a civillian regime in Nigeria. Today I live in one of the most stable and best democracies of the world, Switzerland.

Not only have I had in my leadership career, a privilege to serve in student organizations, private businesses, corporate world, and spiritual organizations, I have also had the opportunity to see the importance of leadership in these societal structures. No matter how great an organization is, her progress would be affected by the maturity, passion and corporate anointing of her leaders.

Incompetent leadership is disastrous for every organization.

That is why every concerned citizen of this world should pay special attention to this topic. God created man and gave him vital instructions to organize himself and his environment.

The first step to coming to grip with our systems is to come to grip with God's plan for leadership. Man needs to know who God created him to be and learn about God's instruction in order to become that person.

That is why I believe that the godly revelations and enlightened insights shared in this book will help you and your organization to enjoy every blessing of good leadership. Regardless of which organization you are, spiritual, political, economic or social; this book will enhance your leadership knowledge, ability and skill and help you to serve your generation with great impact.

If you are yet to become a leader, this book will expose you to ingredients of leadership that will make you assume honorable heights among your peer. If you are already a leader, this book will help to streamline and refocus you to your duties and enhance your leadership potentials and skills to deliver great values to your people and organization.

Since the greatest responsibility of leadership is to make leaders out of other people, this book will be a great daily companion to everyone wanting to offer great service to their subordinates in particular and their organisation in general.

May your generation rise up and bless God for your contributions to their well being. May you leave your organization and the world better than you met them. May your existence make a positive difference to this generation and those yet to come. Amen.

INTRODUCTION

And God saw everything that he had made, and, behold, it was very good. **(Genesis 1:31)**

And the LORD God said, It is not good that the man should be alone; I will make him an help meet for him. **(Genesis 2:18)**

God adjudged everything He created to be very good until He looked at the man He created in His own image staying alone. Then the Maker passed an instructive verdict on the sadness of loneliness. It is not good that the man should be alone!
God, who primarily created a man for fellowship with Himself thought it fair for a man to have another human being to relate with so his relationship with his Maker will not be out of compulsion but rather out of choice. God from the onset created man as a social and relational being. Not only did God cause His creature to have a relationship with Him and other mankind, He also chose relationship as an avenue of blessing mankind.

So God created man in his own image, in the image of God created he him; male and female created he them. And God blessed them, and God said unto them, Be fruitful, and multiply, and replenish the earth, and subdue it: and have dominion over the fish of the sea, and over the fowl of the air, and over every living thing that moveth upon the earth. **(Genesis 1:27-28)**

One person cannot be fruitful and multiply without inputs of others.
One person cannot have and enjoy dominion over all the other creatures and things God created alone.
God saw a life of loneliness as imperfect for man.
It is not good that a man should be alone!
God then created a platform for human progress; interdependence in a mutual relationship. God made two people out of one body even though He purposed the two to remain one body (Gen 2: 21-24). The express command of God for the man and woman (a womb man) to have joint dominion on the earth changed as the confusion of who to make responsible for the action of the couple emerged after they ate the prohibited fruit of evil and good knowledge.
The all-purposeful God of order then created clear orderliness for His equal creatures in order to guide their relationships and roles. The same way God remains the head of the man He created for

fellowship with Himself did He made man the head of the woman that He created to have fellowship with man.

> *Unto the woman he said ... thy desire shall be to thy husband, and he shall rule over thee.* **(Gen. 3:16)**
>
> *But I would have you know, that the head of every man is Christ; and the head of the woman is the man; and the head of Christ is God.* **(1 Cor. 11:3)**

Thus there has always being a need for a clear role of leadership from the beginning of the world even among equals. Any animal with two heads is a freak. God being no author of confusion but of order and peace, thus appointed man the head for this union of two equally blessed parts (1 Cor. 11: 11-12; 1 Cor. 14: 13) to avoid conflicts. Once there is a leadership crisis in our family, it will spill over to affect our society. As a divergent claim to leadership emerges among modern couples, we have seen an increase in marriage collapse and divorce. The bitterness, depression and rancor spilling out of such chaotic relationships have gone beyond the family boundary to affect our Churches, society and the world at large. In other cases, the lack of good leadership has led to the collapse of businesses, ministries and organizations. Countries are at war with each other and various tribes and races ensue in loggerheads as poor leaders wrongly guide their followers to avoidable troubles. Leadership has, in no doubt, become a great issue that needs attention in our society.

During my study for a Masters in Business Administration (MBA), I noticed with alarm how social man has sought for a working formula for leadership to no avail. While many of the leadership models in best business schools have borrowed greatly from biblical prescriptions, such models have remained ineffective having being diluted with other human philosophies.

As a Pastor, I have noticed with great awe that leadership problems also exist in the house of God. No wonder, every attempt to use a product contrary to the prescription of its maker will always result in abuse, chaos and confusion. There is however a perfect way God expects mankind to be governed. This book details and reviews God's provision for good leadership. Considering the pervasive leadership problems of today, God's prescribed leadership principles have not only proven most appropriate for the people of the past, but they also remain a relevant source of peaceful and progressive guidance for the modern day man so long finding peace and prosperity remains his objective desire.

CHAPTER 1: LEADERSHIP CHALLENGES IN THE CONTEMPORARY WORLD

While commercial enterprises are now operating in a business environment that is far different from the world of regulated domestic economies so characteristic of much of the past century, most are still trying to solve new problems with old prescriptions. As we enter into the information age, many theories propagated in the industrial age are still the ones forming the foundation of many management theories.

That is literally offering 20th century solutions for 21st century problems. Rather than responding with speed, dexterity and flexibility, many organizations are doggedly dragging with them the cultural and business baggage of the past, no wonder we continue to witness increasing problems' in our modern day businesses. Things have simply changed and we need to learn to change with time.

- ***Scorch of globalization.*** *The transcending growth of multinational businesses beyond national boundaries has necessitated the need to learn a global approach to regulation of business. Many businesses in Europe and the United States of America are now outsourced to Asia where the salary for workers and other costs of living is cheaper.*

- ***Communication advancement.*** *The advanced communication system has reduced the world to a global village where people can choose amongst various products and services options available in the increasingly unified global market. In a competitive world, specialization is increasingly the key to success, as only services where you have distinctive competencies have chances to survive. To remain abreast of competition, an average organization needs among other things versatile leader who knows the need of the contemporary man.*

- ***The threat of technology.*** *Modern technology has come with new knowledge that could be applied to improve productivity in our various organizations. Information sharing and social exchange between the management and the managed can be made faster than ever before. A major challenge for the leadership is not only to motivate members of the organization to share their knowledge and ideas with others but also to* *hold restrain in passing wrong information that might prove harmful to the well being of the organization.*

Every organization, in order to survive the contemporay challenges needs to educate her members to acquire relevant skill in modern technology especially in the areas of information organisation and management. While there is virtually every form of information freely available on the Internet, the main challenge remains how to secure those relevant to your need. We need people well trained in this area. Regardless of the amounts of money spent on the acquisition of technology and information, the effectiveness of such acquired technology will be dependent on the knowledge and attitudes of the personnel in charge. The most modern equipment will malfunction without sufficient human experience and know-how to use it.

As technology transforms the world into a global village where people can choose at ease which services or programs to patronize, only organization which know how to offer greater values at a lower price and faster delivery can stay ahead of the competition.

Most of our Churches are empty because Church leaders are still applying the same style used in the days of Jesus to witness to 21st century man. Many Churches are failing to use advance tools like emails, Internet services, Website, television and other mass media for propagation of the gospel.

Can you imagine how many rubbish unsolicited mails (Spam) you receive in a day? But many Churches are still waiting to make contacts with people just on Sundays. The entire world is now a second away with telephone, Internet and electronic mail systems so move out and make the best of the technological advancement.

The kingdom of darkness is misusing technology to bombard people with false information. We have the genuine message of life, love and salvation that the world needs. Let us wake up and make the best of this great time in civilization. Technology, like all products of godly wisdom and talents, is of the Lord and we must use it for His glory.

To what extent a leader can readjust his roles and relationship within the new reality without compromising the word of God or the values the Church offers her congregation will determine the continuous relevance of such body in the globalized world where service could be accessed from any part of the world with speed at ease.

DEFINING LEADERSHIP

Many ignorant people have taken the failure of man to use his God given ability to manage well his God given world, to mean a non-existent of God. What an irreverent way of disowning responsibility for our action and inaction. A world ruled in love according to the will of God could not have fallen in to failures we witness today.

The world's ever increasing problems of political crises, economic failure, civil unrest and marital divorce, among many other social ills, are major pointers to the failure of human leadership.

Various theories and practices of man over the age have not yet provided the long sought elixir for human leadership problems.

The progress we witness in areas of international co-operation, cultural integration, a stronger economy, dynamic markets, and ever changing technology has rather made the need for good leadership an urgent necessity. To know how to secure good leadership, we first need to have a clear understanding of what it is all about.

1) What is leadership?

There are diverse definitions of leadership out there as there are diverse people and interests offering them. On a good day, when you put on An Internet search machine, "what is leadership?" you will receive over half a million explanation - most of them with contradictory answers. My goal is to simplify things here.

Leadership generally refers to both the ability (skill) and the capability (position) to model, moderate, modify, move, motivate and mobilize members of a team to achieve a common mission. It is all about influence. The consensus among scholars is to view leadership as a process oriented influence toward achieving shared purposes.

That means, there must be a mutual goal and people to influence for an influential person to take the lead.

Quite often, leadership is confused with management. Though to be effective, leaders have to manage well their resources, the actual duty of a leader is far more than that. Leadership roles include:
- Inspiring vision, communicating goals, motivating actions
- Supervising processes and managing resources.

> **Kingdom leadership is not a pursuit of position but a passionate pursuit of becoming a person of great value.**

What is Kingdom Leadership?

*And he sat down, and called the twelve, and saith unto them, If any man desire to be first, the same shall be last of all, and servant of all. And he took a child, and set him in the midst of them: and when he had taken him in his arms, he said unto them, Whosoever shall receive one of such children in my name, receiveth me: and whosoever shall receive me, receiveth not me, but him that sent me. (**Mark 9:35-37**)*

*But Jesus called them to him, and saith unto them, Ye know that they which are accounted to rule over the Gentiles exercise lordship over them; and their great ones exercise authority upon them. But so shall it not be among you: but whosoever will be great among you, shall be your minister: And whosoever of you will be the chiefest, shall be servant of all. For even the Son of man came not to be ministered unto, but to minister, and to give his life a ransom for many. (**Mark 10:42-45**)*

Kingdom leadership is not a pursuit of position but a passionate pursuit of becoming a person of great value. Jesus Christ gave a radical definition and interpretation of leadership to His disciples by emphasizing the need for "serving attitude" above position.

Jesus Christ proved that point practically by serving His gifts and purpose even to the point of death and by so doing have become the greatest leader that ever lived. 2000 years later, 12 disciples following in His footsteps have increased Christ followership to over 2 billion people in this generation alone. Kingdom leadership is a style of leadership that influences life through serving attitude than control.

*Let this mind be in you, which was also in Christ Jesus: Who, being in the form of God, thought it not robbery to be equal with God: But made himself of no reputation, and took upon him the form of a servant, and was made in the likeness of men: And being found in fashion as a man, he humbled himself, and became obedient unto death, even the death of the cross. (**Phil. 2:5-8**)*

Kingdom type of leadership is the most influential with everlasting impact. It requires good understanding and practice because it has death and life impact on people's lives.

While human administration and organization focus on resources allocation and management, ministry of the word of God is about the management of the entire human destiny, be it physical, social, economic, political and spiritual. More than all these, the impact is eternal. Simply defined, kingdom leadership is about rendering valuable service to your community within your area of influence through efficient management of self, task and resources.

a) Leadership is about rendering valuable services

So he fed them according to the integrity of his heart; and guided them by the skilfulness of his hands. **(Psalm 78:72)**

Leadership is about effectively developing and efficiently serving your gift to your generation.
Foremost, you need to process both your gifts and skills in order to offer competitive service. David led the flock by the integrity of his heart and the skilfulness of his hand.
The integrity of heart without skill will only lead you to crises.
Skill is not a gift or an imparted virtue but rather an acquired virtue. You can not acquire skill without training.
You need self development training in leadership, communication, time management, resource management etcetera. Until you have processed well your gifts into skills, you have nothing to distinguish your service and put you in preeminent position. Only a man diligent in his business cans stand before kings (Prov.22:29). Leadership, in the end, is about serving your gifts in the best way possible.
A minister is a servant. A prime minister is the number one servant. Somebody needs to remind the despotic leaders of this world that what they are practicing is the antithesis to the notion of leadership.

> **Leadership generally refers to both the ability (skill) and the capability (position) to model, moderate, modify, move, motivate and mobilize members of a team to achieve a common mission. It is all about influence.**

b) Leadership is about influencing people not forcing or molesting them

For David, after he had served his own generation by the will of God, fell on sleep, and was laid unto his fathers, and saw corruption. **(Acts 13:36)**

Your education, experience, training, relationship, status and passion, among many other things have prepared you to influence some particular group of people than others. As a doctor, the best people apart from your peer that you can serve most are patients whose sicknesses fall within your area of specialty. If you are distinguished and successful in your field, there is no limit to what you can use your influence to achieve for the kingdom of God. Distance or age need no more restrict relationship among people in this information age.

Many youths are affected by the lifestyles of their pop role models living a generation or a continent apart. We can all influence some people falling within depth or breadth of our areas of influence.

You have a depth of influence for instance within your Church if it has different missions and ministries (outreach ministry, music outreach, books and media outlets etcetera) through which you can affect your society. You may also have a breadth of influence across your generation if you play several leadership roles across different level of authority in your society. In that case, you are not only recognized as a spiritual voice for your generation but also as a business leader, civil right activist, community leader, politician, motivational speaker, life coach, sports star, finance mogul etcetera.

> **Leadership is about taking the lead and setting the pace for others to follow. No doubt, failure of leaders at personal level can only lead to other social level failures.**

c) Leadership is about efficient management of self, task and resources

For if a man know not how to rule his own house, how shall he take care of the Church of God? Not a novice, lest being lifted up with pride he fall into the condemnation of the devil. ***(1 Timothy 3:5-6)***

Kingdom leadership begins with efficient management of self.

Leadership is about taking the lead and setting the pace for others to follow. No doubt, failure of leaders at the personal level can only lead to other social level failures. If the blind lead the blind, both shall fall into the ditch (Matt 15:14b). For if a man know not how to rule his own house, how shall he take care of the Church of God?

Many have been fooled with wrong indoctrination that you don't need any skill or education to be used of the Lord. That is partially true, but the fact remains that you cannot be useful beyond your skill and preparation. God most often uses skilled people, contrary to what many people will like to believe in this day that many see ministry of Jesus Christ as the only place to become leaders after failing in every other area of life. While God used fishermen disciples of Jesus Christ, none of them matched the performance of Apostle Paul, a well educated and highly skilled minister of the gospel.

What you put into your preparation in life will always determine how far God can use you. Moses was learned in all the wisdom of Egypt, so God used him to deliver his people.

Jesus Christ was already seeking skill and trading wisdom with most learned people of His days at the age of twelve (Luke 2:42-49)!

Kingdom leadership is also about the efficient management of tasks. When you study the lives of God appointed leaders, you will notice that quite often than not that they had distinguished themselves in one role or responsibility before they were elevated into the public field. Train yourself to focus on managing well your tasks if you want to be great and influential in life.

No one takes ignorant people seriously.

When tasks are not properly managed, there would be a limitation to your accomplishment. Without a good organizational and management structure no organization has a future.

Lastly, leadership concerns the efficient management of resources. Nothing puts a man above and ahead of his peer like a demonstrated ability to make most out of available resources. Jesus Christ set up 12 disciples in a way to manage ministry tasks efficiently.

God rewards faithful management only!

Only those who are faithful in little are considered faithful in much.

Adam and Eve's leadership commission in Eden to have dominion over other creatures of God (Gen 1:26) came with a management mandate to tend the garden and keep it well. (Gen 2:15).

Major differences between worldly and kingdom leadership

> *Calling them to Himself, Jesus said to them, "You know that those who are recognized as rulers of the Gentiles lord it over them; and their great men exercise authority over them. "But it is not this way among you, but whoever wishes to become great among you shall be your servant.* **Mark 10:42-43**

The relationship of Jesus Christ to his disciples was obviously that of a master to his follower. They called Him master and Teacher and made obeisance to Him without any biblical proof of His refusing them. He sent them on errands which they carried out and the relationship was never the opposite.

In essence, Jesus was never against the position of leadership *per se*. What He was against was the way leadership was practiced in His time. He only taught His disciples new views of leadership that was radical to that practiced in their age. Contrary to what we see around us today, Jesus teaches the following concerning leadership.

a) Leadership is a position of responsibility not superiority

And God hath set some in the Church, first apostles, secondarily prophets, thirdly teachers, after that miracles, then gifts of healings, helps, governments, diversities of tongues. Are all apostles? are all prophets? are all teachers? are all workers of miracles? Have all the gifts of healing? do all speak with tongues? do all interpret? **(1 Corinthians 12:28-30)**

Everyone in the kingdom of God is foremost a king and priest (Revelation 5:10). Everyone is equally relevant and respectable.

However God has given some people additional gifts to make perfect the body of Christ. Those in these positions of authority are placed there by God for responsibility not superiority.

While a man carrying a special gift of the Lord may be specially honored, carrying such a gift does not make him superior to others. His gift has been given to him, rather to serve others.

b) In leadership, service has priority over status and position

And when he had removed him, he raised up unto them David to be their king; to whom also he gave testimony, and said, I have found David the son of Jesse, a man after mine own heart, which shall fulfil all my will. **(Acts 13:22)**

Kingdom leadership is different from worldly leadership on one count; emphasis is placed more on your serving attitude than your service, status, skill and position. Your serving attitude comes first!

In essence, every office and service is honorable.

Your service creates, validates and maintains your position.

What however distinguishes a man is not what he is serving but how he is serving it. There are choir leaders and youth leaders that are more valuable and far popular than Church pastors. It all depends on how they serve their callings. While King Saul was still ruling, God made a new choice in a shepherd boy called David because of his favorable attitudes. God is more concerned about how you are serving more than your qualification and what you are serving.

> *Moreover it is required in stewards, that a man be found faithful.*
> ***(1 Corinthians 4:2)***

To God, your availability and faithfulness in service are as important as your skill. He lifts up and qualifies those He calls. However in the world, office and position is placed before service. You better not be on the road when a leader in the third world is travelling amidst riotous entourage. You can also see the same in some developed nations where status and position are rated higher than service.

c) Leadership is a position to empower and not to oppress

> *And he gave some, apostles; and some, prophets; and some, evangelists; and some, pastors and teachers; For the perfecting of the saints, for the work of the ministry, for the edifying of the body of Christ: Till we all come in the unity of the faith, and of the knowledge of the Son of God, unto a perfect man, unto the measure of the stature of the fulness of Christ.* ***(Ephesians 4:11-13)***

Many leaders in the world are rulers. Their duty is to lord it over others. The word Lord comes from a 13th century word called "laverd or loverd" meaning "master of a household, ruler, superior."
Most dictionaries describe a Lord as a person who has power or authority over others, such as a monarch. Leaders in the kingdom are however called servants and their duty is to serve others.
The word servant has its origin from the 12th century word called "servir" meaning "to render habitual obedience to or to be a slave."
While leaders in the world oppress their people and dispossess them of their possessions, kingdom leaders are to empower people and like Jesus Christ, serve them to the point of death.
The misunderstanding of the purpose of leadership is the reason worldly people manipulate their ways to enter the office and then go ahead to use it to defraud their people and disintegrate their society.

d) Kingdom leadership is about principles not whims

> *But the LORD said unto Samuel, Look not on his countenance, or on the height of his stature; because I have refused him: for the LORD seeth not as man seeth; for man looketh on the outward appearance, but the LORD looketh on the heart.* ***(1 Samuel 16:7)***

While worldly leaders lay claim to victory and legitimacy through popularity, in the kingdom of God, good character is the major requirement. While worldly leaders resort to politics, scheming, coercion, manipulation and other means of controlling people, kingdom leadership commands obedience through influence by showing exemplary conducts (Mark 10:42-43).

Though they looked pretty princely, all the brothers of David were disqualified for they lacked the serving attitude and integrity to ascend the throne. It takes an excellent character to rightly ascend the throne of leadership over God's people.

e) Kingdom Leadership is a ministry of a higher power

Let every soul be subject unto the higher powers. For there is no power but of God: the powers that be are ordained of God. Whosoever therefore resisteth the power, resisteth the ordinance of God: and they that resist shall receive to themselves damnation. **(Romans 13:1-2)**

While worldly leaders are solely responsible to the human constitution, kingdom leaders in addition to being responsible to their congregation and Church authority are also responsible to God.

While politicians enter the office through election and employment, you can only enter kingdom leadership by God's calling and godly appointment (Heb. 5:4; Rom. 11:29). While a politician can easily lie his way through in the front of people, a pastor or Church leader has all knowing, all present and all seeing God to deal with.

f) Kingdom Leadership is about influence not coercion

Be ye followers of me, even as I also am of Christ. **(1 Corinthians 11:1)**

Obey them that have the rule over you, and submit yourselves: for they watch for your souls, as they that must give account, that they may do it with joy, and not with grief: for that is unprofitable for you. **(Hebrews 13:17)**

Spiritual leadership is a place of influence where spiritual leaders are expected to lead by example. Kingdom leadership is delicate and dangerous because of the ability to influence people's lives.

While other types of leadership have limited effect only on the earthly existence of people, the effect of spiritual leadership is eternal.

That is why only serious and genuine people should be permitted to occupy Church leadership. I personally refuse to be pressurized to promote or appoint people. For all you know, you may be partaking in the misconduct of such people if they abuse their positions in dealing with people that have come to trust and depend on such because of their Church appointments and positions (1 Tim. 5:22).

The judgment over bad leaders is also not what anyone should look for. Lawyers may intercede for you in the court of man but who will intercede for you if you fall into the hand of God?
Pastors' duties are grave, delicate and dangerous and people need to support and co-operate with them to make their duties easier.

g) Leadership is a place of honor not dishonor

Let the elders that rule well be counted worthy of double honour, especially they who labour in the word and doctrine. For the scripture saith, Thou shalt not muzzle the ox that treadeth out the corn. And, The labourer is worthy of his reward. **(1 Timothy 5:17-18)**

It is a common thing to hear people slight, insult and ridicule people in a position of authority. The general reaction to political leaders is that of dishonor and disrespect. Most social leaders are distrusted correctly because of their dishonorable lifestyles. However in the Kingdom of God, the divine instruction is to give double honor to leaders who are noted to labor in the word and doctrine. That is because they add value to our lives in this world and the one to come! I have seen ignorant people complaining about people honoring their pastors. If the Queen or Prime minister or President of your country, village or club will attend your occasion, wouldn't you honor them?

> **However in the kingdom of God, the divine instruction is to give double honor to leaders who are noted to labor in the word and doctrine. That is because they add value to our lives in this world and the one to come!**

The work of God is more honorable that all those offices.
Let the elders that rule well be counted worthy of double honour!
How will you honour your business, political or traditional leader? Treat your pastors to double honours. Servants of God are honorable servants. That is why we call them, "reverend ministers"!
House of God is a house of honor. Work of God is a work of honor. Once you take honor away from the house of God, nothing is left. Worship of God becomes empty and dry. Service of God becomes powerless – missing in healing and breakthroughs.

> *And when he was come into his own country, he taught them in their synagogue, insomuch that they were astonished, and said, Whence hath this man this wisdom, and these mighty works? Is not this the carpenter's son? Is not his mother called Mary? And his brethren, James, and Joses, and Simon, and Judas? And his sisters, are they not all with us? Whence then hath this man all these things? And they were offended in him. But Jesus said unto them, A prophet is not without honor, save in his own country, and in his own house. And he did not many mighty works there because of their unbelief.*
> *(Matthew 13:54-58)*

Despite the astonishing ministry of Jesus Christ – filled with power, His own people cannot profit much from Him. Familiarity made them dishonor the anointing He was carrying. Dishonor will make you thirst amidst ocean and make you starve amidst plenteous harvest. You can only receive from a minister you honor.

Europe and America, like other developed nations are losing to dishonorable lifestyle in the Church where pastors are called first names and treated like another member of the congregation.

"Joe, pray for me." That is a Church member talking to his pastor.

Familiarity has brought standards and expectation concerning men of God so low that it has become a common sight to see pastors sharing cigarette, wine and beer with members of their congregations.

No wonder, there is hardly faith in the office of such pastor or within such member to receive miracles. For same people, it is a taboo to call a medical doctor or such professionals by the first name. Familiarity has brought standards and expectation concerning men of God so low that it has become a common sight to see pastors sharing cigarette, wine and beer with members of their congregations.

House of God has become a social club or a political arena where people slug it out among themselves. We need to restore honor back to our Churches if we want to see a mighty move of the Holy Spirit.

Recognition is the birth cradle of all followership

Recognition predates position when it comes to leadership.

Quite often, a man can lead by recognition without a position. How?

By simply creating recognition and acceptance among the people through distinguished service.

While in the worldly realm there is always a position of leadership to be contested and occupied and such position attracts leadership authority, in the kingdom of God, everyone is a reigning king and all that is required to reign is to generate recognition through your service. Late Pastor Kenneth Hagin (Senior) had no office or position of leadership established for him when he came into ministry as a teenager. His service created international recognition for him and though he never travelled out of America most of his lifetime, the whole world recognized and accepted him as a leading authority in faith ministry. Till today, you have Word of Faith Bible colleges and Churches all over the world.

Mother Theresa became a household name all over the world through her service to the poor segment of Indian society.

Many transformational and charismatic leaders that changed societies and business mostly came out from nowhere to assume the position of recognition and authority among their people. Of great example are a trio of Nelson Mandela, Indira Ghandi and Martin Luther King Jnr. Whosoever will be great among you, shall be your servant!

The emphasis of kingdom leadership is on service and serving attitude! In fact, your serving attitude comes before your service and your service comes before position and recognition in the kingdom of God. It is your ability to serve well your skills and talents that generates recognition and creates for you your position!

2) What leadership is not?

If any man desire to be first, the same shall be last of all, and servant of all. **(Mark 9:35)**

But so shall it not be among you: but whosoever will be great among you, shall be your minister: And whosoever of you will be the chiefest, shall be servant of all. **(Mark 10:43-44)**

Many ignoramus and anarchists are misusing Jesus Christ Statement on leadership to generate disorderliness in the house of God. God of order however is not the author of confusion or disorderliness.

I have seen both types of people misquote the above scriptures to back their wrong stands and despise Church authorities.

To solve our leadership problems, we first have to change our notions about leadership. Only then can we put the right people in the right position. Let's see the right way to see leadership position.

a) Leadership is about your action more than a position

As each has received a gift, employ it in serving one another, as good managers of the grace of God in its various forms. (1 Peter 4:10 WEB)

The position of leadership is available in every organization.
The means of attaining that position is however through your service and not manipulation, coercion or oppression. Great leaders don't oppress people. They just offer distinguishly their services.
When you stop adding value to other people through your service, you start to lose value and position.
Whosoever of you will be the chiefest, shall be the servant of all!
Jesus Christ didn't talk against the position of leadership, most of the time. He was only emphasizing the means of filling it.
Though you do not need a title or position to serve your gifts and skills, it takes excellent service to secure recognition and promotion to ascend leadership position among your people.
Have you seen a man that is diligent in his business? He shall stand before kings; he shall not stand before mean men (Prov. 22:29).
To occupy a position of leadership, you need to serve with passion.

b) It is about your serving attitude more than your service

For David, after he had served his own generation by the will of God, fell on sleep, and was laid unto his fathers, and saw corruption. **Acts 13:36**

Being a leader is more than what you serve.
It concerns much more how you serve.
When it comes to kingdom leadership, your attitude weighs more than your skill. What use is a wicked king, corrupt leader, fraudulent accountant or insincere counselor?
Holy Spirit chose to inspire the documentation of King David as a servant and not a ruler. You see, leadership is an attitude more than skill, service or position. Though King David was a King, he was a servant of his people. He led with a serving attitude.
Your serving attitude is more required in the kingdom of God than your gifts and service.

I have often had to let talented and skilled people leave our departments because of prideful and sinful conducts. It is expected of a steward to be found, foremost, faithful not skillful (1 Cor.4:2)!

Your attitude comes before your skills and talents, when it comes to the service of God. You can be a street cleaner and have a bossy attitude and you can be a king and have a serving attitude.

King David did not oppress but served his people.

c) It is about your obsession not oppression

> *No man taketh it from me, but I lay it down of myself. I have power to lay it down, and I have power to take it again. This commandment have I received of my Father.* **(John 10:18)**

> *For though I be free from all men, yet have I made myself servant unto all, that I might gain the more.* **(1 Corinthians 9:19)**

Jesus' life was a great example of faithful service to the Lord.

He was not only faithful to the Father but was also faithful to His assignment on earth. He willingly gave His life for the cause He believed in. You can only become great in a ministry you live and die for. Apostle Paul also gave himself fully to his ministry. David moved from being a shepherd boy to becoming a king because he was a servant not a ruler (Acts 13:36). He was a man obsessed with serving.

No kingdom leader has the right to lord it over other people. Mankind is given dominion over animals and not over people (Genesis 1:28-31).

You should exercise your authority over your skill and gift.

Your authority is rooted in finding the area of service that the Lord has given you to operate.

Dominion is about mastering something not people.

You are meant to be a benefactor of your service.

When you master a thing, people will seek you out.

When you help a man to get what he wants, you will always get what you need. As your service attracts compensation and appreciation, the one who serves will become the greatest of all.

> **No kingdom leader has the right to lord it over other people. Mankind is given dominion over animals and not over people. You should exercise your authority over your skill and gift.**

d) Leadership and extremism

Many extremists for lack of in-depth Bible knowledge tend to make a doctrine out of every word and line in the Bible. One extremist group says that because Jesus' disciples and other people worshipped Him and called him Lord, leaders are meant to be despotic figures.

The other extremist group misquoted Jesus Christ's washing his disciples' feet as a doctrine for leaders to become shoe cleaners for their people.

No leader can claim to be Jesus Christ; neither can anyone attach Jesus' greatness to His "once in a lifetime" washing of disciples' feet. That feet washing act was not meant to be a doctrinal principle otherwise He would not just have done it only once in His lifetime. Kingdom leadership needs not to be despotic or subservient but productive! It is about serving with the humble attitude your perfected gifts and talents in the best means possible.

> No leader can claim to be Jesus Christ; neither can anyone attach Jesus' greatness to His "once in a lifetime" washing of disciples' feet. That feet washing act was not meant to be a doctrinal principle otherwise He would not just have done it only once in His lifetime. Kingdom leadership needs not be despotic or subservient but productive!

e) Can you become a leader?

> The kingdom of heaven is like to a grain of mustard seed, which a man took, *and sowed in his field: Which indeed is the least of all seeds: but when it is grown, it is the greatest among herbs, and becometh a tree, so that the birds of the air come and lodge in the branches thereof.* **(Matt. 13:31-32)**

The fact that there are people who seem to be naturally endowed with leadership skills has made some experts conclude that leaders are born not made. I personally believe that people can learn leadership skills like any other skills vital to human existence.

And even though virtually every man has the potential to become a leader, only very few can become leaders due to tests and processes that must be endured and completed.

Like everything in the kingdom of God, becoming a leader is a process that requires persistent and patient training.

> *"But it is not this way with you, but the one who is the greatest among you must become like the youngest, and the leader like the servant.*
> *(Luke 22:26 NASU)*

Leadership is an excellent service that requires an excellent attitude of a servant. That implies that the one who humbly serves as a child among others will be the greatest.

A child serves without asking a question or waiting for rewards.

A child is willing to serve others at no cost and doesn't think of title or position. A child sees in every situation an opportunity to learn.

Can you submit yourself under other people to learn?

Good leaders are good learners!

Can you submit yourself under other people to learn? Good leaders are good learners!

Can you be a leader without a position?

A leader is a recognized center of co-ordination, motivation and direction. Leadership consists of both the person and the position. However, while the position is much more emphasized in the world (thereby leading to all forms of competition to ascend such position), in the kingdom of God, the emphasis is placed on your service. In the Kingdom of God, it is your service that determines your position! Servants end up mostly as leaders either in the political, spiritual or business and corporate world. When you think of people like Indira Ghandi, Benny Hinn, Bill Gates and Tiger Woods, they are all servants serving their gifts at the highest level.

However that does not make position insignificant.

In fact, I do not personally appreciate any leadership definition that tries to separate leadership position of authority (leadership status) from the occupant of that office (carrier of service and skills) because both hardly make sense without each other.

No matter how powerful, influential and respected an office may be, a vacant position cannot translate to leadership without any occupant. And while it is true that you may lead without formal title or office, the status to lead, however short-lived it might be, must be recognized or accorded to you by the the member(s) of your group.

Leadership everywhere requires both what you serve and the public position or recognition to serve it.

Expecting otherwise is like trying to separate life from a body.

Regardless of how a person assumes a position of authority be it democratic, autocratic or theocratic, the two elements of official service and recognition of position are necessary. Even despots, who do not go through a legitimate election, still make people recognize their position, basing their recognition not on service but sheer use of force. Until your people accord to you, a recognition to lead by virtue of your valuable contribution, you are not a leader but a mere pretender.

> **No matter how powerful, influential and respected an office may be, a vacant position can not translate to leadership without any occupant. And while it is true that you may lead without formal title or office, the status to lead, however short-lived it might be, must be recognized or accorded to you by member(s) of your group.**

CHAPTER 2: WORLD THEORIES AND MODELS OF LEADERSHIP

Various theories of leadership have evolved over the last four decades to help find out the best procedure to locate productive and effective leaders. It is instructive to observe some of these theories and how they affect our concepts of leadership. It is relevant here to take a cursory look at the evolution and the present stage of both worldly and kingdom leadership.

WORLD THEORIES AND MODELS OF LEADERSHIP

1) Situational Theories

This theory believes that situation rather than status determines who becomes a leader. It therefore focuses on what knowledge and skill a leader need to perform in a different situation.

Since a leader needed in a time of plenty and peace will not be relevant in a time of war and lack, the theory has difficulty in pinpointing requirements needed for leadership. Social sciences do not pay much attention to this theory for lacking predictability.

It is not practical to allow a situation to determine the leader of an organization.

2) Trait Theories

The trait theory suggests that individual personalities are made up of various traits. When describing a friend for instance, you may list some traits like honesty and kindness.

A trait can be thought of as a relatively predictable characteristic that causes individuals to behave in certain ways.

Many systematic studies in the past have been carried out to compare bishops and clergymen, sales managers and sales men, and railway presidents and station agents in order to find out if there are salient difference between leaders and followers. The idea was to find out if leaders have special traits that distinguish them from their followers.

Apart from a few traits that the studies find that differentiate the two groups; they seem to share the same ability most of the time. In fact

the study was not sure how many of the few differences found in areas of intelligence, adjustment, dominance and self-confidence are traceable to the occupation of leaders. Many people simply as a matter of necessity had to learn to carry out duties expected of them.
An average man can learn to play any role a situation places upon him. While the theory fails to prove beyond a reasonable doubt that people are born as leaders or with leadership traits, its exponents argue that except a person has some leadership traits, no amount of leadership training could make a leader out of him.
Some of the traits the theory uses to identify potential leaders include intelligence, enthusiasm, perseverance, courage and broad vision.
Trait theories have since evolved into two opposing groups.

Who I am versus what I do

> *Beware of false prophets, which come to you in sheep's clothing, but inwardly they are ravening wolves. Ye shall know them by their fruits. Do men gather grapes of thorns, or figs of thistles? Even so every good tree bringeth forth good fruit; but a corrupt tree bringeth forth evil fruit.*
> ***(Matthew 7:15-17)***

Since there seems not to be stable personality characteristics that distinguish leaders from non leaders, contemporary theories have mostly directed their searchlight on the style of leadership.
This situation has led to the emergence of functional and situational schools of thought in behavioral science.
Functional and contingency theories sought to see the role of functional and situational variables surrounding leaders in the performance of their roles.
While the functional theory believes that leaders tend to function according to their job requirements, the situational theory says it is a situation that determines what people do.

3) Style and Personality Theory

What matters most in leadership, the personality of the leader or his character? To rephrase the question, "What is more important; talking politically correct or talking genuinely from your heart?"

To style and personality theory, talking correctly is more important than talking honestly from your heart. The theory believes that good leadership is a direct result of attitudes, behaviours and personality. This seems to be the stand taken by many companies where recruitment focus concentrates more on how people look, talk and carry their bodies more than what characters they possess. Personality approach believes that culture and experience among many other things form the mindsets and frame of reference that determines the general way people perceive and interpret information. Such collective perception determines the behavior considered correct in such an environment.

Success in such setting is attributed to attitudes (mindset) and behaviors (skills, education and techniques). This line of thought has led to the popularity of public relations where skills like communication, strategic relationship, influential reactions etceteras are taught. The goal is to promote mental attitude like positive thinking, body talks (firm handshake, bold eyes contact, bold voice) etceteras. For this school of thought, your skills and techniques are simply more important than your commitment and honesty.

It is common to hear this group mention, "Your attitude determines your altitude." Believe anything and act like it and you are going to get it. This group believes that it is the attitudes (styles of leadership) with which a leader performs his duties rather than his character that make for effective leadership. Personality and observable behaviors, in terms of how you react to circumstances, are to this group of paramount importance than your moral make-up.

It is all about what people do rather than who you are!

You could be a liar and a messiah so long you can act out as occasion demands. Rather than look for godly and morally upright people that will selflessly work for the good of all, modern societies that apply this model mostly choose immoral men of a great personality who end up ruining same people they are supposed to lead. For this group the following traits will be the greatest focus in selecting a leader.

a) Skill and charismatic approach to situations.
b) Self assurance, independent minded and proactive attitudes.
c) Self motivating and commitment to group excellence.
d) Educated (formally or informally) and totally aware of human differences.
e) A flexible and spontaneous personality who can quickly diagnose a situation and offer a befitting response.

4) Character Theories

Character theory emphasizes the importance of moral and mental qualities of a man than skills and personalities. While skills and styles of leadership can be learned or transferred, living life of fidelity, temperance, justice, courage and simplicity has to be cultivated by individuals. To character theorists, basic principles of effective living include integrity, humility, patience, honesty, modesty and empathy. Powerful leaders like Pharaoh in the Bible and Hitler in recent human history though possessed great charisma and personality but have nonetheless committed atrocities against the human race for lacking morals and human empathy for the lives of others.

The nature of a leader will always affect what he does!

A leader with no fear or knowledge of the Lord, at his best, could only offer fair leadership to his followers. The woe of many societies is based on the fact that they have substituted needs for great characters with great personalities and after the excitement and uproar following the appointment of charismatic leaders, the people end up suffering from misuse and abuse of power.

To find great leaders that will not destroy the destiny of their people, character theorists believe that society needs to review its criteria for choosing her leaders. After all, everything will once boil down to who a leader truly is and not what he says or how he says it. An important requirement for leadership for this group will include:

a) God trusting, god-dependent and virtuous person.

b) Morally and mentally upright, possessing integrity, sincerity, humility, modesty, patience, honesty, proactivity etcetera.

c) Strongly determined yet gentle, vocal but fair, considerable but non- compromising.

d) Industrious, just, temperate and sincere and friendly team player who is persistent and enduring in the pursuit of the public good.

The woe of many societies is based on the fact that they have substituted needs for great characters with great personalities and after the excitement and uproar following appointment of charismatic leaders, the people end up suffering from misuse and abuse of power.

THE EVOLUTION OF CONTEMPORARY LEADERSHIP STYLES

The continuous search for perfect leadership theory is a reflection of man's restless desire to find an appropriate model of leadership that can bring the best out of our organizations.

In a technologically advanced age where daily changes have become a permanent reality, no leadership can afford to remain the same.

Many cultures and organizations in the world have unsurprisingly witnessed their leaders changing from "greater than thou" controllers to "mentors-leaders" who motivate their subordinates to perform.

Even many military regimes have civilianized their approaches by exchanging their uniforms for civilian clothes and leaving behind dictatorial styles for democratic approaches. Our social organizations also seem to have come of age to stop treating workers as machines.

1) TWO STYLES OF MANAGEMENT STYLES

The realization is dawning on us all that people, as the sole repository of the human ability to think, learn and effect all the required changes necessary for the ultimate good of our organizations, need to be treated well in order to get a good response from them.

No matter how much money you invest in materials, technology and structures, people will still determine the success of your business.

The leadership style everywhere has continuously evolved from an authoritarian style to a democratic one where individual opinions are respectfully treated as relevant.

Autocratic management style

This is the first type of management style that emerged in the agricultural and industrial eras. This management control evolved in order to ensure homogeneity in the processing of information, consistency in products and services, and standardization of general measurement and control. Compliance to rigid rules is used to ensure the fulfillment of pre-defined actions with pre-specified outcomes and the compliance of workers to the management policies.

It was the need for strong and firm handling of organization in the earlier economic dispensation especially in the industrial age that gave birth to an authoritarian system where a leader holds the authority to give orders and force obedience on the subordinates.

Expectedly, this style has led to human abuse as autocratic leaders use their positions to depress, oppress and repress oppositions.

Not only does the autocratic system subjected people to work with fear and intimidation under their superior leaders, but it also hindered creativity and initiative of followers especially in a competitive environment where survival depends upon the ability to question existing assumptions and find innovative ideas to do things better.

Democratic management style

Modern organizations in order to ameliorate the oppressive nature of the authoritarian system have tended to practice the democratic type of leadership. This less coercive system permits subordinates more say in the performance of their duties and the running of their organisations. Democratic management model created a co-operative and participative environment where people are empowered to involve in the making of decisions affecting areas of their responsibility. The extent a system is truly democratic, however depends on the situation at hand, the issues at stake and the personality of the leader involved.

In essence, it is more realistic to talk of participative or autocratic situations than talking of it as a style of management. For even with the worst autocrat, there is a time that it will be quite profitable to be democratic. Also, in general, leaders will most of the time take the decision alone when the decision in point is easy, not affecting or needing inputs of subordinates or when the decision to be taken is against the personal interest of their subordinates. Most modern governments practice democracies. The USA and other Western European nations offer the world good examples of democracy.

> No matter how much money you invest in materials, technology and structures, people will still determine the success of your business.
> The leadership style everywhere has continuously evolved from an authoritarian style to a democratic one where individual opinions are respectfully treated as relevant.

2) THREE MAJOR TYPES OF LEADERSHIP

Three major types of leadership that can be easily noticed around us are transactional, charismatic and transformational.

a) Transactional leadership

Transactional leadership, far more common than other leadership types, is built on the belief system that people are motivated by reward or punishment. These leaders therefore basically give clear instructions to followers concerning their expectations. Those who fulfill the expectations are rewarded with carrot and those who do not are beaten with a cane. The purpose of leaders here is to boost general performance and the management of resources.

Transactional leadership focuses more on a series of "transactions" between leaders and subordinates. The major problem here is that leaders mainly treat workers or followers as a means to an end rather than as an end in themselves. It is easy in such an environment to have people physically working with you without commitment and dedication for their minds are somewhere else. People are more motivated when they know you care for them specially.

b) Charismatic leadership

Charismatic leadership is based on the leader's emotional ability to inspire and motivate followers to achieve a mutual goal. Such leaders possess the ability to communicate in a very powerful way.

The problem and danger with this type of leadership are that people may follow them blindly not realizing in them lack of other vital leadership traits like skill and integrity. What a great havoc Stalin, and Hitler unleashed on their blind followers. Also noticeable is the problem of finding succession for such leaders who lead out of personal style than principles.

c) Transformational leadership

Transformational leadership style is closer to the biblical model than the other two leadership styles, discussed above.

This leadership style is uniquely different from earlier transactional or charismatic leadership for leaders here are not in office to maintain the status quo but are rather free moral agents who create necessary changes and reinvent meanings for work and live.

This type of leadership mostly seeks to transform the lives of people in ways beyond the existing standards. Such leadership seeks to empower people by sharing decision-making duty with them in such a way to mobilize them to accomplish the corporate goals together.

Leaders under this system are expected to earn the respect of their subordinates through teamwork and consensual decision-making. Though such leaders and their people have their areas of independence and responsibility where they are accountable for, they are nonetheless mutually interdependent. The focus shifts from autocratic authority to participative one where "our" views rather than "my" views carry the day.

Transformational leaders play among many other, nine great "E" roles of:

- ***Envisioning*** *the organization with insightful goals and principles to chart a clear direction.*

- ***Enlightening*** *the body through the gathering, processing and dissemination of relevant information.*

- ***Enabling*** *organizational process through the creation of structures, system and infrastructures.*

- ***Enlisting*** *followership through recruitment, development and appropriate allocation to fitting roles.*

- ***Encouraging*** *the effectiveness of the organization by providing necessary supports and motivation.*

- ***Empowering*** *members to perform duties efficiently and effectively.*

- ***Emancipating*** *members from destructive enemies, competition, invasion, division and detraction.*

- ***Enduring*** *in team spirit both good and bad weathers necessary to ensure the continuation of the body.*

- ***Ensuring*** *unity and interdependence of efforts in order to achieve corporate goals.*

Leaders like Martin Luther King Jnr., Mother Teresa and Nelson Mandela are examples of transformational leaders.

The distinctive traits of such leaders include a commitment to inspiring others to become part of the leadership process.

In essence, such leaders are expected to form a vision and commit people to accept and achieve it.

One major problem with this type of leadership system is the lack of formal procedures to formalize or reproduce such leadership. Scientific researchers have not been successful in finding sufficient similarities among the noticeable transformational leaders to help one formulate a standard theory or performance measurement, which could help to transfer the attributes to others. For instance, Mother Teresa, Mandela and Martin Luther Jnr. shared no cultural, ethnic, professional, intellectual or gender similarities!

> **Transformational type of leadership mostly seeks to transform lives of people in ways beyond the existing standards. Such leadership seeks to empower people by sharing decision-making duty with them in such a way to mobilize them to accomplish the corporate goals together.**

# CHAPTER 3: KINGDOM THEORIES AND MODELS OF LEADERSHIP

The heaven, even the heavens, are the LORD's: but the earth hath he given to the children of men. **(Psalm 115:16)**

And God blessed them, and God said unto them, Be fruitful, and multiply, and replenish the earth, and subdue it: and have dominion over the fish of the sea, and over the fowl of the air, and over every living thing that moveth upon the earth. **(Genesis 1:28)**

From the beginning, God created the earth for human dominion the same way He created Heaven for His own reign. God in His supreme plan, created both female and male equally to have dominion over the world and its entire creatures. Both Adam and Eve (the first man and the first woman on earth) had equal authority. There was no need to dominate or be dominated.
They were not to have control over each other but over the other creations of God. They were not to be subjected to themselves but only to the divine control of God, their Creator.

The genesis of leadership among mankind

Male and female created he them; and blessed them, and called their name Adam, in the day when they were created. **(Genesis 5:2)**

*And he said, I heard thy voice in the garden, and I was afraid, because I was naked; and I hid myself. And he (**God**) said, Who told thee that thou wast naked? Hast thou eaten of the tree, whereof I commanded thee that thou shouldest not eat? And the man said, The woman whom thou gavest to be with me, she gave me of the tree, and I did eat. And the LORD God said unto the woman, What is this that thou hast done? And the woman said, The serpent beguiled me, and I did eat.* **(Genesis 3:10-13)**

While under God's control, there was no room for pain, sorrow, failure, fear, inequality, accusation, hatred, and other products of sins. All those were to change as soon as man chose to place his trust in the serpent than in God. The immediate fallout of the fall of man was the birth of fear, nakedness, self-consciousness and accusation.

The selfish man, not wanting to take responsibility for his failure began to seek someone else to blame. That was not all. Sorrows, pain and laborious living also came to life (Gen 3:17-19).

Losing complete dependence on God forced man to fall on himself. His knowledge of evil and good now robbed him of complete faith and confidence in God. Trust in God is now replaced with fear of the known and unknown. Man is not only affected by the mighty things God can do, but he is also now exposed to the evil that the enemy could inflict upon him. Because of sin, man's past of blissful innocence has now been replaced with guilt and fear of divine punishment. Now disposed of his dominion over the earth, the man now begins to fear both the devil and the earthly creatures he was created to reign over. Having lost a direct connection to divine guidance, there now emerged a need for man to create an institution of orderliness and control. The fallen man needed an earthly form of leadership in order to ensure godly order on earth!

It was in this light that the re-order of the human relationship among each other became essential. Though the woman remains an equal partner of her male counterpart in dominating the earth, she is now subjected under the control of her man.

> *Unto the woman he said, I will greatly multiply thy sorrow and thy conception; in sorrow thou shalt bring forth children; and thy desire shall be to thy husband, and he shall rule over thee.* **(Genesis 3:16)**

As mankind began to live outside the presence of God, crime and all forms of misconduct grew. Immediately after the story of creation in Genesis, tales of human woes began with a murder.

> *And Cain talked with Abel his brother: and it came to pass, when they were in the field, that Cain rose up against Abel his brother, and slew him. And the LORD said unto Cain, Where is Abel thy brother? And he said, I know not: Am I my brother's keeper?* **(Genesis 4:8-9)**.

> *And Lamech said unto his wives, Adah and Zillah, Hear my voice; ye wives of Lamech, hearken unto my speech: for I have slain a man to my wounding, and a young man to my hurt. If Cain shall be avenged sevenfold, truly Lamech seventy and sevenfold.* **(Genesis 4:23-24)**

The need to have man held responsible for his misconducts and ensure peace and orderliness amongst each other led to the evolution of the institution of monarchy and priesthood. Not only has emerged the need for man to lead his wife, there now exists the necessity for man to lead other men and women in order to ensure law and order on earth. Man's disobedience and lack of dependence on God and his need for self dependence have led to the creation of human leadership over humans. In the beginning it was not so.

The spiritual man, self-controlled, was only subject to God!

The fallen man however needs not only to be accountable to God but also to human authority on earth in order to ensure peaceful co-existence. First it began with spiritual judges, prophets and priests and then kings as the children of Israel chose to be led like other nations. Institution of the monarchy had since evolved to autocratic and democratic leadership styles in the modern time.

> **Man's disobedience and lack of dependence on God and his need for self dependence has led to the creation of human leadership over humans. In the beginning it was not so.**

Important however is the fact that whatever the nature of human leadership is, it remains God's plan to continue to rule His creatures through such human institution. That is why it is necessary for us to always pray for people in the position of authority to govern us according to God's will and not their own whims and caprices.

> *I exhort therefore, that, first of all, supplications, prayers, intercessions, and giving of thanks, be made for all men;For kings, and for all that are in authority; that we may lead a quiet and peaceable life in all godliness and honesty. For this is good and acceptable in the sight of God our Saviour.* **(1 Timothy 2:1-3)**

God has given us all the duty of praying for our leaders if we want to enjoy a quiet and peaceful life!

Human history is filled with great tragedies and crimes resulting from the reign of ungodly men. Though many ignorant people have chosen to blame God for such human misconducts committed against the principle of God, the fact of the matter remains that God has given the dominion of the earth to man. It is our responsibility to keep it sane and orderly. If we fail in our responsibility, we are the one to suffer for it (Psalm 115:16).

The original and eternal plan of God however remains that man should only have dominion over other creatures and not over each other. The system of human dominion over humans is a direct result of the fallen nature of man. A non spiritual man wants to lord it over others and greedily keep to himself what belongs to all.

A carnal man places himself over others by force while a spiritual man exercises leadership influence on others through his distinguished and unrivalled services. Though human history has seen improvement in human leadership (from an autocratic and dictatorial regime to the present day democracy), we are however still a long way from God's expectation.

> **The original and eternal plan of God however remains that man should only have dominion over other creatures and not over each other. The system of human dominion over humans is a direct result of the fallen nature of man.**

From autocracy to democracy

Then all the elders of Israel gathered themselves together, and came to Samuel unto Ramah, And said unto him, Behold, thou art old, and thy sons walk not in thy ways: now make us a king to judge us like all the nations. But the thing displeased Samuel, when they said, Give us a king to judge us. And Samuel prayed unto the LORD. And the LORD said unto Samuel, Hearken unto the voice of the people in all that they say unto thee: for they have not rejected thee, but they have rejected me, that I should not reign over them. **(1 Samuel 8:4-7)**

And he said, This will be the manner of the king that shall reign over you: He will take your sons, and appoint them for himself, for his chariots, and to be his horsemen; and some shall run before his chariots. And he will appoint him captains over thousands, and captains over fifties; and will set them to ear his ground, and to reap his harvest, and to make his instruments of war, and instruments of his chariots. And he will take your daughters to be confectionaries, and to be cooks, and to be bakers. And he will take your fields, and your vineyards, and your oliveyards, even the best of them, and give them to his servants. And he

> *will take the tenth of your seed, and of your vineyards, and give to his officers, and to his servants. And he will take your menservants, and your maidservants, and your goodliest young men, and your asses, and put them to his work. He will take the tenth of your sheep: and ye shall be his servants.* ***(1 Samuel 8:11-17)***

From the excesses of the monarchy (listed above), it was not a good form of leadership neither was it meant to be. God never intended to give children of Israel monarchy but for their nagging to become like other nations. The shortcomings of that system had led philosophers and political scientists alike to continue to search for better models.

For some of the early political theorists, the institution of monarchy in which they grew was the most effective form of government.

The organized government was suspected for fear of ending up in the hands of dangerous people that could derail or monopolize the destiny of nations. Middle age political theorists like Plato and Aristotle mainly studied natural man and concentrated on essential human nature that inspires human passions. They also held open prejudices towards having an organized system of government.

Newer sets of political theorists like Machiavelli, Montesquieu and Burke soon emerged concentrating mainly on the political psychology of man. This group was fascinated by the social man's tendency to participate in government. The group believed that monarchy is good only for corrupt people who are better subjected under a single powerful leader. The ultimate for man is a popular government that involves free participation of all the members of society.

Machiavelli like other great political theorists of his time believed that before law and government were established, that man was a creature of passion and reason and was neither moral nor immoral.

For him, it is the discipline of law that forces men to be just and honest. The institution of popular government, he believed, was important than monarchy and other forms of oligarchy since people can only enjoy greater independence when they are involved in their own governance.

This new stand has grown into a leadership system of democracy.

Democracy, which derives from the Greek word "demos," or "people," has been defined by President Abraham Lincoln as the, "government of the people by the people and for the people."

The major problem with the theory of democracy is that true democracy can only be practiced in small cities and republics. Rousseau in fact rightly observed that real democracy couldn't be claimed to be practiced in vast societies where important business of government is made by the elected few.

To him, representative democracy is a mere illusion where the majority abdicated their political rights to the minorities that they could at best occasionally control at election period. Though the advantage of democracy seems to outweigh other systems created by man so far, it does not take away the fact that the system is over laden with its own disadvantage. Frankly speaking, democracy is an imperfect human system created by imperfect man to please himself.

Democracy or demon-crazy?

The human heart is the most deceitful of all things, and desperately wicked. Who really knows how bad it is? **(Jeremiah 17:9 NLT)**

Bible's verdict is that no human idea of government can ever be used to perfectly govern people. The nature of an unbeliever is wicked. The heart of human is the most deceitful of all things.

Though we have evolved into a better system, no amount of efforts by an unsaved man could provide a perfect system. Democracy, at its best could be seen as a perfect system for imperfect people. Democracy is created purposely to protect man against man. In its worst form, it can be used to remove God from human existence.

Nowadays, it is a recurring issue to debate if the name of God should be removed from our constitutions, currencies, national properties and institutions in the name of tolerance. Many states have banned religious study and worship in their schools in the name of neutrality. No wonder that kids are turning to violent lives of drug addiction and immorality in order to fill the vacuum left by the removal of religious training in our schools.

Our societies are now replacing terminologies like integrity, honor and respect with liberation, liberality and tolerance. Nothing seems to be fundamentally right or wrong anymore in a society where spiritual core values are increasingly eliminated and replaced by the judgment and verdicts of the majority. All it takes to pass an immoral decision in our democratic institution is to have a majority of immoral people in our legislative and decision-making institutions vote for it.

What a dangerous future for Christianity and the entire mankind in a world where the population of Christians especially in our political institutions continue to witness an alarming decrease!

Clear moral issues like the sin of homosexuality are now being contested in many democratic states and Churches where Lesbians and homosexuals are being granted the blessing of Bishops to live together as partners. Such atmosphere also tolerated popular approval for homosexual priests who now ride through the popular votes of their congregation to preside over godly institutions.

What shocks me is the extent that man can go to do the work of God using his own conviction rather than following God's instruction!

> *Not every one that saith unto me, Lord, Lord, shall enter into the kingdom of heaven; but he that doeth the will of my Father which is in heaven.* **(Matthew 7:21)**

What a wasted effort to try to work for God without walking with Him. Such services can only end us in frustration and hell.

That is what leadership by "majority will" rather than by the "will of God" can do. Two bad heads can never function well as a good one directed by God!

Have you considered once why we tolerate great riches in one part of the world and penury in another? Have you wondered why it is considered correct to have some individuals amassing trillions of dollars in the same country where some could hardly survive a day?

Democracy is like a prison wall that protects good people from bad ones. While in the short run, it may prove great for those benefiting from it, in the long run it is bound to fail woefully and destroy the same people it is created to protect. That is because every system devoid of the presence of God soon becomes a system for Satan.

> *In whom the god of this world hath blinded the minds of them which believe not, lest the light of the glorious gospel of Christ.* **(2 Cor. 4:4)**

The world is in a tragic form because Satan has blinded people who now consciously or unconsciously work for him. Democracy without God is the crazy manifestation of demons. Demon-crazy!

Communism with all its perfect ideologies and projections failed because it removed God from the system. Capitalism will fall into the same grave if it doesn't stop alienating God from the lives of citizens. The nature of an unbeliever is desperately wicked!

What will happen where word of God and that of man carry equal weight? What will happen where parents and their children have equal rights to their opinions and decisions? What will happen in a democratic setting where we are all reduced to figures and numbers?

What does man expect to enjoy after removing God from the heart of the people in the name of democracy? What has democracy - devoid of the fear of God- gotten to offer mankind?
Evil. Penury. Disaster. Unlimited reign of evil.
See how the enemy is misusing democracy already.
It is Satan that is behind government protected rights to abortion, homosexualism, suicide and other ills of the society we have come to accept as normal in a democratic society. While poor people are dying all over the world, great democracies especially in Europe and North America are busy throwing foods into the sea so that the price of food will remain stabilized, all in order to maintain a system of capitalism that thrives on equal demand for products. What is the equality between a poor man that has no penny and an affluent man with millions in saving? Only capitalism sacrifices love and human feeling for disadvantaged people on the altar of greed, selfishness and democracy. That is what the spirit of Mammon can do. That is why you cannot serve God and Mammon at the same time (Matt. 6: 24-25). I wonder what we will have left after the world has removed core Christian values like love, honesty, peace, mercy, patience, kindness, integrity and forgiveness from our social system and replace them with principles of tolerance in the name of democracy.

Theocracy or democracy?

While democracy could be considered a good system for the fallen man when compared to other forms of human government, it is clearly not a perfect form of governance for a saved and rejuvenated man. Thank God that He has provided for believers laws and instructions which when obeyed protect us from the evil of the world. While Satan may be responsible for the evil situation in the world, God is in control of what finally happens to everyone be it a man or Satan himself in this life and in the one to come.
Thank God that the kingdom of heaven is under complete responsibility and control of God!
It would have been a shame if heaven were run like Satan runs this world. While every man and spirit is permitted to do and determine what they obtain in life, God will finally judge and reward all according to their conducts. Only obedient observation of God's instruction can guarantee man of just reward in this word and in the one to come. Thank God that when we walk in His laws, we are protected from the condemnation of this world.

> *There is therefore now no condemnation to them which are in Christ Jesus, who walk not after the flesh, but after the Spirit. For the law of the Spirit of life in Christ Jesus hath made me free from the law of sin and death.*
> ***(Romans 8:1-2)***

In a theocracy, God is the sole authority and all leadership conducts, especially in the house of the Lord is ordered by His words.

The human constitution is the ultimate source of orderliness in a democracy. While in a theocracy, Godly authority flows from the top down (be it in Churches or family), in democracy authority flows from down up. It is presumed in a democracy that everyone has equal knowledge and influence regardless of age, mental stage, knowledge, experience or anointing.

In a democracy, freedom is believed to thrive on controversy and competition for power between rival parties rather than godly obedience and mutual co-operation among people. So long arguments and other competitions are made within bounds of societal law; democracy permits every rude act of disobedience either to God or man. Freedom of man has paramount importance in democracy over the injunction of God. Also, while democracy as a system of government invested power collectively on the majority, theocracy is based on the supreme law of God through the offices of the priests. The divine laws rather than human rules take pre-eminence as the invisible God rules through the visible man occupying a leadership position in the house of God.

Theocracy depends on human leaders only so long they uphold the principles and injunctions of God.

Does that mean that democracy and theocracy are incompatible? No! I am a trained political scientist and in my study and political activities during and after graduation, I saw many areas where godly men can operate effectively in politics. It is a matter of choosing to be led by godly principles rather than human instincts. There are many Christians in political positions today performing wonderfully to the glory of God. Thank God that most of the constitutions of the world democracies are not averse to godly life and existence.

The point I am boldly making here is that democracy and theocracy can work together so long human rules are not upheld against godly injunctions. Many countries in fact based their constitution, labor laws and other social principles on biblical principles.

To a large extent, many democracies borrow most of its terminologies and structures from theocratic practice in the Bible.

After carrying the burden of leadership over millions of his countrymen for many years, God instructed Moses to select 70 elders to partake in his leadership duties. That began the practice of delegated authority. Jesus also delegated his authority to 70 disciples. The apostles of Jesus Christ continued this practice by recruiting some members of the Church to cater to the need of the congregation when their population exploded beyond their ability.

> **Does that mean that democracy and theocracy are incompatible? No! I am a trained political scientist and in my study and political activities during and after graduation, I saw many areas where godly men can operate effectively in politics. It is a matter of choosing to be led by godly principles rather than human instincts.**

God is a God of order

And when they went from nation to nation, and from one kingdom to another people; He suffered no man to do them wrong: yea, he reproved kings for their sakes. ***(1 Chronicles 16:20-21)***

God's orderliness is the utmost source of enduring peace and prosperity. While following His orders, the millions of the children of Israel that migrated out of Egypt were kept alive, healthy and strong. Obedience to His orderliness ensures freedom from every disaster and crisis. Wherever democracy clashes with theocracy, we as believers need to uphold the law of the Creator over that of His creature. If you have anything against my stand, why don't you start unlimited democracy at your home? Begin by permitting your children to vote if they should bath, eat or go to school!

Of course, you will claim you know better than them and reserve the right to act for their good till they are mature. How mature and intelligent are you compared to your heavenly Father, your Maker?

God does not want you to lead Him.

He does not want you to lead yourself by your limited knowledge either. He wants to lead the world through those who obey His will.

As a pastor, I consider it recklessly foolish to put it to the vote if we should fast, pray and evangelize in a Church for instance. I will not even put it to vote if we should be regularly attending Church on

Sunday, refuse to commit immorality and other clearly stated principles and commandments of God.

That would be contesting God and doubting His words.

For every true believer, the word of God should simply be the final authority in any issue of life. There are things I know from the Bible and I do not discuss with my assistants in the ministry before I carry out in the Church. Some of the things we call democratic are simply doubt of God's personality and instructions. If the Bible says a man must pray always, you need not table that under discussion anymore. As a godly leader you only need to create an avenue for your Church to follow God's instruction.

Wherever inputs of others are necessary to arrive at a richer and better decision, seek it so long it does not result in contesting instructions of God. Many Churches have left the leading of the body under wills and caprices of the human committee of elders in the name of democracy. No wonder that many homosexuals have been voted to preside as ministers in many Churches. If it is against the will of God, I will go all the way to contest any committee.

A pastor's duty is to offer service to people based on his submission to the will of God. It is not to relate to God based on his submission to the will of people. A pastor's job is to look up and serve down. God is the head of His kingdom not people.

Theocracy is God's leadership style not democracy.

The word of God is supreme over our feelings and emotions and regardless of how painful it could be, we just have to do it.

It is not always that it is exciting to fast, pray at all night meetings or organize big conference or convention in Churches but they are great avenues of evangelism, revival, growth and divine blessings.

If you put such issues to vote you may lose. If you follow peoples' vote, you may lose God's own. Get your priority right!

While democracy tries to do things right, only the law of God does the right thing. To be an effective leader, one has to abide by the constraints of divine injunctions. It doesn't matter what your people, peer or elders say, the word of God is the truth and the life.

Living outside it leads to death!

King Saul rated the voice of his people above that of God and lost the kingship in his household forever. King Herod was eaten by worms for permitting himself to be equalized to God.

We all need to learn the instructive lesson from the builders of the tower of Babel in the Bible. Whenever the united voice of democracy comes against the powerful voice of God, the voice of man will fail and lead to great frustration and torment.

God is not a democrat but a theocrat. The word of man can fail but only the word of God abides forever more (Isaiah 55: 10-11).

CHAPTER 4: CALL TO VISIT THE WOES OF THE CHURCH

For the leaders of this people cause them to err; and they that are led of them are destroyed. **(Isa. 9:16)**

Let them alone: they be blind leaders of the blind. And if the blind lead the blind, both shall fall into the ditch. **(Matt. 15:14)**

Every organisation needs good leaders to be effective and productive. Many countries, organizations, businesses, Churches, family and clubs have been ruined for bad leadership. Your future is inexplicably attached to the type of leadership you serve under. That is why citizens of great nations naturally enjoy the security of a high standard of living while their contemporaries living under wicked leaders are subjected to poverty, corruption and other social ills.

Many spouses fail to see how their lives can be totally affected by their marriage choice.

Women, your future depends on the type of man you marry!

Marry a liar and lies will never be lacking in your marriage.

Marry a criminal and police case will never leave your door.

Marry a king and you become a queen overnight.

In the same way, every organisation is a reflection of its leadership.

In essence, every organization begets the leadership it deserves.

Birds of the same feather easily flock together. Every individual, history has proven over and over again, is a mirror image of the organization s/he belongs to. So if you are progressive minded, you will soon get attracted to a progressive organisation where the leadership is preoccupied with effecting progressive policies.

Whoever you are, your destiny will be determined by the quality of your leadership the same way the destiny of all passengers in an airplane depends on the quality of their pilot.

That fact applies more to the Church than any other organisation.

In fact, the impact of your spiritual leader is not limited to earthly existence as it is with other leaderships. The impact is eternal.

Both the quality of your life now and in the eternity are all attached to the type of influence you secure from your spiritual leadership.

DIMINISHING MORALITY IN CHURCH
The diminishing morality in Church communities resulting from incompetent leadership has become an issue of great concern for every believer. There are significant proofs of decadence everywhere.

1) Churches are losing focus of the great commission
The Church is preoccupied with so many things that she hardly has time to leave her comfort zone to perform her sole duty of winning souls for the Kingdom of God. We are called to evangelism as much as we are called into discipleship. In fact these are two sides of the same coin. A living Church has to balance both responsibilities well.

I have heard many self-righteous preachers complaining against Churches using hotels, clubs and other unconventional halls for worship. The claim of sucha group is that sharing the same place with unbelievers is evil. But you are sharing the same world with them already. What a shameful proof of complete misunderstanding of the calling of God. Can you imagine Jesus Christ refusing to come to the world to save mankind? God has called us to go into the world and reach out for the lost souls. We have to go to wherever Satan is illegally withholding lost souls and break them loose.

What a great advantage to live so close to your clients!

What a powerful opportunity to share the same hall with the people you are sent to bring back. You can pray and anoint such hall and follow up to invite such people to your service since they feel comfortable coming to the hall already. Christianity is about doing God's will not your will. If Jesus comes back today, I guess that you will find Him in clubs, pubs and social corners that many self-righteous Christians will find very difficult to go.

> *The Son of man came eating and drinking, and they say, Behold a man gluttonous, and a winebibber, a friend of publicans and sinners.*
> **(Matthew 11:19)**

Whose Church are you building?

I have heard of Churches where Pastors send away racially different people from their services for fear that some important members of the congregation may stop attending.

I have had department leaders complained to me personally of the unrighteous status of their potential members. They would prefer not to have such sinners in their groups. I have had to take my time to explain that the Church is meant for the bad, the good and the ugly.

Thieves, prostitutes, drunkards, addicts etceteras belong by right also to the Church. It is those that are sick that need treatment!

While Church is not meant to promote sin, it is meant to collect sinners and separate them from their sins. The Church's duty is to expose sinners to the power of God and the ministration of the Holy Spirit in a gradual process that converts the bad and ugly members to good and righteous children of God.

2) Believers' faith and moral standards have fallen

> *Beware lest any man spoil you through philosophy and vain deceit, after the tradition of men, after the rudiments of the world, and not after Christ.* ***(Colossians 2:8)***

> *Making the word of God of none effect through your tradition, which ye have delivered: and many such like things do ye.* ***(Mark 7:13)***

Many Christians are led by their cultures and traditions rather than biblical instructions. This is resulting in confusion and frustration in many Churches. I have to teach my people that we stand for kingdom culture not any form of human culture. We are not just Africans, Asians, Americans, Australians or Europeans but Christians. We are all one family under one culture of Christianity. That is what is important in heaven not nationalistic or denominational affiliation. Heaven is not divided.

Bible is our constitution and our code of conducts.

We are all *bona fide* children of the Lord.

3) There is an increase in immorality among believers in the name of civilization and tolerance

> *But now I have written unto you not to keep company, if any man that is called a brother be a fornicator, or covetous, or an idolater, or a railer, or a drunkard, or an extortioner; with such an one no not to eat.* ***(1 Cor. 5:11)***

Cohabitation and divorces among believers have become normal as the population of single parents explodes. The self-fulfilling prophecy concerning easy divorce is breaking homes. The higher the cohabitation we have before marriage the higher the divorce rate. Psychologists have found out that practicing infidelity before marriage increases the rate of distrust and divorce after marriage.

How often does our human culture prove to be the enemy of the kingdom culture? The word of the Lord is our final authority.

There shouldn't be any compromise on that by any genuine Church.

If the Bible says homosexualism is an abomination, it remains so until the second coming of Jesus Christ. Strict adherence to God's instruction has nothing to do with intolerance. We need to agree with the word of God at all time if He is truly the Lord over our lives. We need exemplary leaders who practice what they preach from the word of God. In the absence of godly leaders whose lives are a practical demonstration of God's love and power, many find it easier to follow local heroes whose conducts are considered good.

Beware that many things we consider good are dangerous and deadly. As a believer, choose godliness over goodness at all time!

Don't just do a good thing, do a God thing. Be godly! God is the ultimate standard of all goodness and not the opposite. Being sincere is not just enough for many times, man can be sincerely wrong when acting on his limited knowledge and information.

We have an everlasting word of God as a guide. What else do we need? Do not permit pride to ruin your life. No generation or person can claim to know it all. For all you know, you may know nothing.

> **Don't just do a good thing, do a God thing. Be godly! God is the ultimate standard of all goodness and not the opposite.**

4) Extreme religious practice devoid of godliness

> *They profess that they know God; but in works they deny him, being abominable, and disobedient, and unto every good work reprobate.*
> *(Titus 1:16)*

Out of ignorance or sheer pride, some believers just want to remain extremely independent of the Church without being responsible or committed to the body of Christ. They move from one Church to another enjoying the permanent status of visitors that share in all the excitement without partaking in any of the responsibilities.

This generation is witnessing the explosion in the growth of pseudo-Church clubs and groups ruining the Kingdom of God under the pretext of building the kingdom. There are so many choirs, prayer and intercession groups, cell groups; outreach groups etceteras operating not only outside the walls of churches but also with no affiliation or connection to any church. No wonder that many

churches are emptied of musicians and instrumentalists because of the cancerous existence of such freaky groups. The hall mark of Christianity is discipline, accountability and belongingness among the body of Christ. There is no way you can lay claim to having a relationship with the head without having a relationship with His body. God is God of order and accountability. No person drops from the sky! Each one is placed in a family at birth from where one grows up to join different organizations. It is the same with Christianity, everyone is meant to belong to a body of Christ.
That is a basic requirement for every believer.

And he is the head of the body, the Church. **(Colossians 1:18)**

Now therefore ye are no more strangers and foreigners, but fellowcitizens with the saints, and of the household of God. **(Ephesians 2:19)**

The relationship between the Church and Christian organizations is like that between a country and companies operating within it.
It is required that you belong to a country in order to start or work in any company or organization within that country.
Not only that, whatever you do in your company; you do it on behalf of your country. That is why workers like the company herself have to pay tax to the government.
It is the same thing with Christian organisations and the Church. The same way citizens take identity from their country does every Christian take identity from the body of Christ, the Church.
Until you belong to Jesus Christ and His body (the Church), you have no business doing anything on behalf of the Church.
You can claim to do it for kindness, business, and other personal reasons but do not claim to do it on behalf of the Church.
There is a difference between good work and God's work.
Many things we think are good are quite deadly!
I hear some Christian organisations and clubs lay claim to the tithes of their members. That is deadly wrong. Every believer should be paying tithe to their church not to their Christian clubs. Will you pay your tax to your club or business organisation rather than goverment? In fact such clubs should rather be tithing to the Church they are affiliated to rather than robbing people of their tithes and the blessing attached to it. Many people with good intention are being ruined for lack of adequate scriptural knowledge. Every pastor needs to take that duty of teaching God's people very serious if we want to see an end to wrong religious practices. Only the truth known can set free.

*There is a way that seemeth right unto a man, but the end thereof are the ways of death. **(Proverbs 16:25)***

*For God is not the author of confusion, but of peace, as in all Churches of the saints. **(1 Corinthians 14:33)***

Do not get me wrong, as a member of the Church, you can form any group with the goal of evangelizing or reforming area of your influence for the Lord (be it in the field of politics, education, culture, sport etceteras). There is nothing wrong with belonging to a choir club or prayer and intercession group outside your congregation provided such club and its members are affiliated to a church. What is wrong is having groups of independent people, belonging to no church and accountable to no authority, laying claim to the commitment of the body of Christ. Nothing can be more damaging to the orderliness of the body of Christ than that. It is like having countries submit to a bunch of people not belonging or accountable to any national or international authority for direction and instruction. That is a recipe for catastrophe. We all need to submit under authority for the purpose of accountability.

*Let every soul be subject unto the higher powers. For there is no power but of God: the powers that be are ordained of God. **(Romans 13:1)***

It is only by submitting and belonging to a church that you can have access to support and coverage of that church where you worship. If you suffer spiritual attacks or loss, you have a family to run to for back up.

Until you belong to Jesus Christ and His body (the Church), you have no business doing things on behalf of the Church.
You can claim to do it for kindness, business, and other personal reasons but do not claim to do it on behalf of the Church.
There is a different between good work and God's work. Many things we think are good are deadly!

The day you gave your life to Jesus Christ, you ceased to be master of your life. You should submit yourself under a church and serve there. Jumping from one church to another is a childish and parasitic act of irresponsibility. Such parasitic groups only enjoy being babied forever by the sacrificial service of mature Christians.

Also watch out for the other extreme group who wants the Church to stick rigidly to the practice of old. Such do not want to change to modern songs, or have flexible service. They believe the time of tongue speaking and baptism of the Holy Spirit is gone.

They believe God only understands and appreciates old hymns and religious practice.

They think God cannot tolerate new songs from a new generation. What a self-centered view that makes churches look outdated, insensitive, judgmental and insignificant.

While I believe the gospel should be preached uncompromisingly in its original form, there is nothing wrong in changing the strategy and approach to reach people. Trying to use 18th century approach to reach a 21st century man is like trying to ride your horse to the end of the world. In this computer age, the the Church can make use of the Internet, computerized music, beamers and other modern innovations to attract modern people especially the youths to the Church.

5) Adulterated belief system

For the time will come when they will not endure sound doctrine; but after their own lusts shall they heap to themselves teachers, having itching ears; And they shall turn away their ears from the truth, and shall be turned unto fables. But watch thou in all things, endure afflictions, do the work of an evangelist, make full proof of thy ministry. **(2 Timothy 4:3-5)**

Many people do not believe anymore in the existence of absolute truth but rather in relative truth. For such people nothing is right or wrong. For such people, it means there is neither sin nor the need for salvation through Jesus Christ. Carnal values are increasingly invading churches as many non-compromisable issues like obedience, adultery and church commitment become to be subjected to individual interpretation. People tend to decide what they do, not according to God's instruction but according to their personal situation and needs. To make things worse, churches are increasingly making decisions based on the voting system rather than the consultation of the Bible. The end product is a mix of human ideas and selected divine instruction considered acceptable.

> Many people do no more believe in the existence of absolute truth but rather in relative truth. For such people nothing is right or wrong. For such people, it means there is neither sin nor the need for salvation through Jesus Christ.

6) **Alternative belief**

No man can serve two masters: for either he will hate the one, and love the other; or else he will hold to the one, and despise the other. Ye cannot serve God and mammon. ***(Matthew 6:24)***

Increase in the practice of alternative religions is a direct result of dwindling manifestation of God's power in our churches. Many, in the absence of genuine encounter with God, have decided to make their own gods out of career, health and sports.

Others just devote themselves to seeking all forms of spirituality after their pursuits of materialism, new age religion and sex have failed them. Some merely worship money (Mammon) and will do anything to amass it. People in this group believe that spending time in the presence of God is a waste of time.

DIMINISHING NUMBERS OF TRAINED LEADERS.

All scripture is given by inspiration of God, and is profitable for doctrine, for reproof, for correction, for instruction in righteousness. That the man of God may be perfect, throughly furnished unto all good works. ***(2 Tim. 3:16-17)***

The imperfect stage of the Church is a direct reflection of the imperfect stage of her leadership. At a closer look at many church structures, one can easily understand why we end up where we are today. Many churches operate without Sunday school, Bible school and Leadership training and expect their leaders and congregation to function effectively. Wisdom does not just fall from the sky; it is acquired on earth through training and practice!

Some congregations not knowing the value of such training, show no interest to attend such courses where available. Another problem is the diminishing number of available teachers. The result of all these situations is a poor understanding of the basic tenets of Christianity and the diminishing faith level of the body of Christ.

At congregation level, absent of private Bible study at homes has created a vacuum in peoples' hearts (now filled with human philosophy and societal values). Many believe biblical instructions are outdated and that Church needs to accommodate modern concepts like trial marriage, multiple dating and so on.

At the leadership level, numbers of vibrant church leaders continue to reduce. The few that exist are not well trained in biblical principles. Many Church leaders today cannot recite Ten Commandments.

Every serious and God fearing church needs to invest in the training of her leaders. It is a bad mistake to expect people to function well without any form of training. Nothing just happens by accident.

> Many Churches operate without Sunday School, Bible school and Leadership training and expect their leaders and congregation to function effectively. Wisdom does not just fall from the sky; it is acquired on earth through training and practice!

WHY LEADERSHIP TRAINING?

And the things that thou hast heard of me among many witnesses, the same commit thou to faithful men, who shall be able to teach others also.
(2 Timothy 2:2)

It is important to have a well planned training directed at equipping people of God with sufficient knowledge and hand-on experience to tackle the spiritual, emotional, administrative and other social needs of the congregation. Such training, among many others, will achieve the following:

1) To prepare self to become worthy of the service of God

But in a great house there are not only vessels of gold and of silver, but also of wood and of earth; and some to honor, and some to dishonor. If a man

therefore purge himself from these, he shall be a vessel unto honor, sanctified, and meet for the master's use, and prepared unto every good work.
(2 Timothy 2:20-21)

2) To acquire sound doctrine background for ministry

Study to shew thyself approved unto God, a workman that needeth not to be ashamed, rightly dividing the word of truth. **(2 Timothy 2:15)**

O Timothy, keep that which is committed to thy trust, avoiding profane and vain babblings, and oppositions of science falsely so called: Which some professing have erred concerning the faith. Grace be with thee. Amen.
(1 Timothy 6:20-21)

3) To learn how to minister as a servant of the Lord

But shun profane and vain babblings: for they will increase unto more ungodliness. **(2 Timothy 2:16-17)**

Preach the word; be instant in season, out of season; reprove, rebuke, exhort with all longsuffering and doctrine. **(2 Timothy 4:2-5)**

4) To learn to become a graceful servant of the Lord

The Lord GOD hath given me the tongue of the learned, that I should know how to speak a word in season to him that is weary: he wakeneth morning by morning, he wakeneth mine ear to hear as the learned.
(Isaiah 50:4)

Let your speech be alway with grace, seasoned with salt, that ye may know how ye ought to answer every man. **(Colossians 4:6)**

5) To learn necessary ministerial etiquette and values

For a bishop must be blameless, as the steward of God; not selfwilled, not soon angry, not given to wine, no striker, not given to filthy lucre; But a lover of hospitality, a lover of good men, sober, just, holy, temperate.
(Titus 1:7-8)

And the servant of the Lord must not strive; but be gentle unto all men, apt to teach, patient. In meekness instructing those that oppose themselves; if God peradventure will give them repentance to the acknowledging of the truth. **(2 Timothy 2:24-25)**

6) To learn the Kingdom type of leadership

And he sat down, and called the twelve, and saith unto them, If any man desire to be first, the same shall be last of all, and servant of all.
(Mark 9:35-36)

But Jesus called them to him, and saith unto them, Ye know that they which are accounted to rule over the Gentiles exercise lordship over them; and their great ones exercise authority upon them. 43 But so shall it not be among you. **(Mark 10:42-45)**

7) To learn to cater to the social needs of others

For we preach not ourselves, but Christ Jesus the Lord; and ourselves your servants for Jesus' sake. And whosoever of you will be the chiefest, shall be servant of all. **(2 Corinthians 4: 5)**

And whosoever of you will be the chiefest, shall be servant of all. For even the Son of man came not to be ministered unto, but to minister, and to give his life a ransom for many. **(Mark 10:44-45)**

8) Not to lose your reward in the Lord

Not every one that saith unto me, Lord, Lord, shall enter into the kingdom of heaven. **(Matthew 7:21-22)**

It is important to have a well planned training directed at equipping men of God with sufficient knowledge and hand-on experience to tackle the spiritual, emotional, administrative and other social needs of the congregation.

CHAPTER 5: BUILDING AN HONOURABLE CHURCH

Be kindly affectioned one to another with brotherly love; in honor preferring one another. **(Romans 12:10)**

An end time victorious church will be a church that has mastered how to live in honor among each other. Whatever you honor thrives. An honorable church thrives greatly as the best in every member is encouraged to come out and each shining talent continues to ignite and complement another. Once you take honor away from the Church, there is nothing left to distinguish it from other social organizations. It is in the interest of the Church that great honor should be given to God and to each member of it.

1) Honor for God

A son honoureth his father, and a servant his master: if then I be a father, where is mine honor? and if I be a master, where is my fear? **(Malachi 1:6)**

He answered and said unto them, Well hath Esaias prophesied of you hypocrites, as it is written, This people honoureth me with their lips, but their heart is far from me. Howbeit in vain do they worship me, teaching for doctines the commandments of men. For laying aside the commandment of God, ye hold the tradition of men, as the washing of pots and cups: and many other such like things ye do. **(Mark 7:6-8)**

A triumphant church is one that worships God in spirit and in truth. True honor for God is reflected in deep worship of His person both in our private and public services.

Why will you go skating, jogging or strolling with the dog during your church meeting time if you truly believe God is King of Kings and Lord of Lords? Will you do the same thing if you have an appointment with the governor of your state?

God promises to be where two or three people gather to meet in His name (Matthew 18:20). It is your responsibility to wait expectantly for Him on every meeting day.

Honor for the day of the Lord

> *And he came to Nazareth, where he had been brought up: and, as his custom was, he went into the synagogue on the sabbath day, and stood up for to read.* **(Luke 4:16)**

Jesus Christ, our Lord and Savior, while on earth attended the synagogue always on the Sabbath as a matter of custom. Oxford advanced learner's dictionary describes custom as, "usual and generally accepted behavior among members of a social group. It is a particular way of behavior which, because it has been long established, is observed by individuals and social group." Jesus Christ who brought us salvation found it important to honor the commandment of God that many believers commonly break in the name of freedom from the law. I mean if you genuinely love God, shouldn't you seek His face more than the law required? If a law permitting you to visit your lover once in a week is suddenly removed, will you visit more or less? The painful truth is that many people attend the Church services more for a religious reason rather than as a pure expression of their love for God or the body of Christ. The fact however remains that Jesus Christ has not brought anyone liberty to disobey the commandment of God.

He has in fact come to fulfill God's commandments.

> *Think not that I am come to destroy the law, or the prophets: I am not come to destroy, but to fulfil. For verily I say unto you, Till heaven and earth pass, one jot or one tittle shall in no wise pass from the law, till all be fulfilled. Whosoever therefore shall break one of these least commandments, and shall teach men so, he shall be called the least in the kingdom of heaven: but whosoever shall do and teach them, the same shall be called great in the kingdom of heaven.* **(Matthew 5:17-19)**

The day is so important that God Himself observed it (Gen. 2:2). Jesus Christ honored it. The apostles honored it (Acts 17:2; 18:4).

Purpose of Sunday Services

> *Remember the sabbath day, to keep it holy. Six days shalt thou labor, and do all thy work: But the seventh day is the sabbath of the LORD thy God: in it thou shalt not do any work, thou, nor thy son, nor thy daughter, thy manservant, nor thy maidservant, nor thy cattle, nor thy stranger that is within thy gates.* **(Exodus 20:8-10)**

God rested on the seventh day of His work (no day has a name then) and we and everyone within our household are expected to do same. Sabbath or Sunday celebration services separate true worshippers from nominal worshippers. While we are free to choose a day of rest to worship God, such a day should be regularly observed.

The scriptural purpose to regularly observe Sabbath day includes:

1. **It is a proof of obedience. (Ex. 20:8; Luke 4:16; John 20:19)**
- This is demanded in both the New and Old Testament. In the Old Testament, defiling the day is punishable (Exodus 31: 14).

2. **It is a sign between God and His people(Ex.31:17; Ez. 20:12)**
- It is proof of faith in the biblical account of creation and the fact that God remains our creator and source (Exodus 31:13).

3. **It is proof of discipleship. (John 8:31; John 13:35)**
- It is a means of advertising His presence to unbelievers.

4. **It is a holy day, sanctified for the Lord (Ex. 20:8)**
- It is a day dedicated to honoring God in our lives.

5. **It is a day to worship God for His faithfulness. (Ex. 20:10)**
- It is a day of fellowshipping among believers. Heb. 10:25

6. **It is a day of rest. (Exodus 20:8-10)**
- It is a day meant to escape the care of the world and meditate the word of God. After service is a good time to go home and rest.

7. **It is a way of receiving God's blessings. (Isaiah 58:13-14)**
- Honoring Sabbath bestows God's blessing on you (Is.58:13-14).

If thou turn away thy foot from the sabbath, from doing thy pleasure on my holy day; and call the sabbath a delight, the holy of the LORD, honorable; and shalt honor him, not doing thine own ways, nor finding thine own pleasure, nor speaking thine own words: Then shalt thou delight thyself in the LORD; and I will cause thee to ride upon the high places of the earth, and feed thee with the heritage of Jacob thy father: for the mouth of the LORD hath spoken it.
(Isaiah 58:13-14)

It pays you to honor God and to observe His Sabbath!

The very least expected of any genuine Christian is to attend the Church services every Sunday. I wonder what such people are taught in their Sunday Schools as kids. God's expectation concerning worshipping Him in honor remains forever more. He is God of honor. Another question of honour is how you conduct yourself during church gatherings and meetings? Are you one of those that enjoy discussing your own issues while service is still going on?

Some people can hardly sit down throughout the service though they can sit down for hours at office time.

Do you honor God with your tithe or you believe God has changed His mind concerning the need to finance His kingdom on earth?

If Church members would not support the work of God with their finance, who should? God expects us to honor him with all our substance (Prov.3: 9). The Church is about God and doing His will. Christianity becomes barren when it is practiced without due honor and consideration for God's will.

2) Honor for servants of God

Let the elders that rule well be counted worthy of double honor, especially they who labor in the word and doctrine. **(1 Timothy 5:17)**

Honour for our leaders is one of the spiritual recipes for growth in the body of Christ. Since most of us will never see God come down physically, the only way to measure your honour for Him is through your treatment of His servants among us. When our church started newly, we had some insolent wolves parading themselves as God's defendants in their bid to corrode recognition of Church leadership and unleash confusion over the congregation. With statements like, "We are not here to worship any man" and "God shall not share His glory with any man", they started creating an atmosphere of intimidation where no one can honour any leader in the church for fear of being tagged worshipper of men.

The main goal of this group was to disrupt the orderliness in the church. I need not tell you that the atmosphere of disorderliness is the best place for evil to thrive. There, anyone can do anything without any hindrance. Thank God that no form of darkness could withstand the illuminating brightness of His words.

That you love God is no reason not to love your parents, your spouse or even your friends. God wants you to honour Him, your parents, leaders, friends and other human beings. The type of love you give to God is different from the one you share with His creatures.

The type of honour you give to your Creator is different from the one you give to your parents, pastors, spouse or boss. You are expected to love God and still love your parents, spouse and neighbours. That you honour God is no reason not to honour your parents, leaders, spouse and other people that may deserve it.

It took me some time of detailed teaching on this issue to restore the church back to normalcy.

Reasons why the enemy wants dishonor in Church

I. **Disorderliness**

> *For God is not the author of confusion, but of peace, as in all Churches of the saints.* **(1 Corinthians 14:33)**

God is a God of order and not the author of confusion.

Orderliness is a godly virtue. Every institution of God has clear leadership. Every family has a single leader. Every country and every human institution has a clear leader. The clarity of the hierarchy of leadership is paramount to the survival of any human organization since every block that falls out of position in the wall becomes an obstruction in the house. Orderliness prepares the room for growth. A double headed animal is a monster. A freak!

God defenders or equalizers?

> *But what I do, that I will do, that I may cut off occasion from them which desire occasion; that wherein they glory, they may be found even as we. For such are false apostles, deceitful workers, transforming themselves into the apostles of Christ. And no marvel; for Satan himself is transformed into an angel of light. Therefore it is no great thing if his ministers also be transformed as the ministers of righteousness; whose end shall be according to their works.* **(2 Corinthians 11:12-15)**

> *Verily, verily, I say unto you, He that entereth not by the door into the sheepfold, but climbeth up some other way, the same is a thief and a robber. But he that entereth in by the door is the shepherd of the sheep.* **(John 10:1-2)**

Apostle Paul warned the Church of falling prey to false workers who enter the body of Christ to cause confusion by usurping authority by way of projecting themselves as defenders of God's kingdom.

If you are able to form a doctrine and pastor a congregation, why not establish a new ministry instead of going to an existing ministry to usurp responsibilities or prove that you know it better than the man God has placed there? No disorderly act could be attributed to God. That is only a carnal urge to accrue authority where you are not called by God or man to lead. Such unedifying way of climbing to the sheepfold through the windows is the exclusive preoccupation of thieves. The shepherd always goes through the main door.

Until you are led in a ministry, you have no right to force yourself upon others as a leader. If you have an an honest intention, you will have the godly humility to submit yourself under the leadership of the house. Only usurping spirit of an equalizer will project a man to stand above and against the established authority only to promote personal image and status.

And Miriam and Aaron spake against Moses because of the Ethiopian woman whom he had married: for he had married an Ethiopian woman. And they said, Hath the LORD indeed spoken only by Moses? hath he not spoken also by us? And the LORD heard it. **(Numbers 12:1-2)**

Now Korah, the son of Izhar, the son of Kohath, the son of Levi, and Dathan and Abiram, the sons of Eliab, and On, the son of Peleth, sons of Reuben, took men: And they rose up before Moses, with certain of the children of Israel, two hundred and fifty princes of the assembly, famous in the congregation, men of renown: And they gathered themselves together against Moses and against Aaron, and said unto them, Ye take too much upon you, seeing all the congregation are holy, every one of them, and the LORD is among them: wherefore then lift ye up yourselves above the congregation of the LORD? **(Numbers 16:1-3)**

The children of Korah, filled with pride and a great sense of self worth, like Miriam and Aaron, began to equalize themselves with their leader, Moses who they claimed was merely ascribing authority to Himself. They did not know that the powers that be, are ordained of the Lord. They saw areas where they were physically and socially better than Moses and understood not why he should be accorded exclusive leadership over them. Each time a man's self righteousness put him against God's righteousness; he falls to the lowest ebb of unrighteousness where divine condemnation and wrath is the order of the day. Aaron and Miriam were rebuked and the earth swallowed up the children of Korah. The problem with children of Korah was that they were pumped up by their tabernacle service.

They forgot that God resists the proud, and gives grace to the humble (1 Peter 5:5). There is another lesson to learn from the story. It is great misconduct to follow confusionists for one will partake in their calamities. The children of Korah died with 250 followers made up of princes and the famous people among the congregation.

Many of these men died ignorantly not knowing why they supported the uprise against Moses. Refuse to gang up against God's people!

Beware of confusionists and equalizers

> *For to one is given by the Spirit the word of wisdom; to another the word of knowledge by the same Spirit; To another faith by the same Spirit; to another the gifts of healing by the same Spirit; To another the working of miracles; to another prophecy; to another discerning of spirits; to another divers kinds of tongues; to another the interpretation of tongues: But all these worketh that one and the selfsame Spirit, dividing to every man severally as he will.*
> *(1 Corinthians 12:8-11)*

> *For I say, through the grace given unto me, to every man that is among you, not to think of himself more highly than he ought to think; but to think soberly, according as God hath dealt to every man the measure of faith.*
> *(Romans 12:3)*

No tree is a forest and no man is an island.

No one man can make up a church or fulfill all the works required to lead a church. That is why God will not pick a person to start any mission without supplying him with those to support him.

Moses needed Aaron the same way Elijah needed Elisha and Jesus Christ Himself needed His disciples.

However everyone has different roles to play in bringing the same goal of establishing God's kingdom on earth.

There is no reason for the confusion of roles and duties. Even a 50 thousand member church begins with a man, then another and another. Everyone is expected to find his role and play it soberly according as God hath dealt with every man the measure of faith.

Every part, in order to function effectively, needs to know its role and stick to it. That we are co-workers with God does not make us

His equal (**1 Cor. 3: 9**). That we are co-workers in Christ do not make everyone in the Church equal worker (**1 Cor. 3: 9-15**).

If you are not equal with your leader at home, at the club, at work and other social organization, what makes you think you are equal to your spiritual leaders that God has given to guide you in your journey of life? The tendency to disregard or dishonor Church leadership is mostly a product of pride. Many people, considering their affluence and career status may consider themselves too big to submit to the leadership of men of God they consider are of lower social status to them. Such people, after equalizing themselves with every authority end of questioning God for giving them such authority.

Remember, it is the authority behind a man that makes him not his look or achievement. We honour policemen and executive leaders in government not because they are better or stronger than us but because of the authority they represent. When we question them in the exercise of their roles, we simply question the authority behind them. Questioning spiritual authority is simply questioning God that instituted such authority.

If in other social organizations, the office of leadership is never questioned, why should it be questioned in the house of the Lord? Why would God provide for pastors, prophets and other ministers of the gospel if they are not necessary? Why did God call the Levites to minister to Israelites in the Old Testament and gave some, in the New Testament, the offices of apostles, prophets, evangelists, pastors and teachers (Eph 4:11-12)?

God Knew His people could not be perfected and edified without such leaderships. Leaders are given to bless His people!

The church is not a democracy but a theocracy guided by biblical laws. Every church is to follow this model. A church that refuses to follow the order of God will soon fall into a pit of distraction and destruction designed by the enemy to divide and destroy.

First come disunity and discomfort that soon culminate to division and destruction.

I. Disunity

Behold, how good and how pleasant it is for brethren to dwell together in unity! It is like the precious ointment upon the head, that ran down upon the beard, even Aaron's beard: that went down to the skirts of his garments; As the dew of Hermon, and as the dew that descended upon the mountains of

Zion: for there the LORD commanded the blessing, even life for evermore. **(Psalm 133:1-3)**

II. Discomfort

But Jesus said unto them, A prophet is not without honour, but in his own country, and among his own kin, and in his own house. And he could there do no mighty work, save that he laid his hands upon a few sick folk, and healed them. **(Mark 6:4-5)**

III. Division

For ye are yet carnal: for whereas there is among you envying, and strife, and divisions, are ye not carnal, and walk as men? For while one saith, I am of Paul; and another, I am of Apollos; are ye not carnal? **(1 Cor. 3:3-4)**

IV. Destruction

And they said, Hath the LORD indeed spoken only by Moses? hath he not spoken also by us? And the LORD heard it. And the anger of the LORD was kindled against them; and he departed. And the cloud departed from off the tabernacle; and, behold, Miriam became leprous, white as snow: and Aaron looked upon Miriam, and, behold, she was leprous. **(Numbers 12:2,9-10)**

The Church is built on strong foundations of faith, discipline, honor, love, etceteras. When you tamper with these values, indiscipline takes over and the enemy can sneak in to destroy the unsuspecting people. Familiarity with Moses almost caused his senior sister Miriam her life. Gehazi was not that lucky for he died with leprosy and passed it over to his children (2 Kings 5: 25-27). When Saul trivilised his relationship with Prophet Samuel, he lost his throne forever (1 Sam. 15:23). That is because God always resists the proud!

Likewise, ye younger, submit yourselves unto the elder. Yea, all of you be subject one to another, and be clothed with humility: for God resisteth the proud, and giveth grace to the humble. **(1 Peter 5:5)**

How art thou fallen from heaven, O Lucifer, son of the morning! how art thou cut down to the ground, which didst weaken the nations! For thou hast said in thine heart, I will ascend into heaven, I will exalt my throne above the stars of God: I will sit also upon the mount of the congregation, in the sides of the north: I will ascend above the heights of the clouds; I will be like the most High. **(Isaiah 14:12-14)**

3) Honor for the body of Christ

Be kindly affectioned one to another with brotherly love; in honor preferring one another. **(Romans 12:10)**

Let every one of us please his neighbour for his good to edification. **(Rom. 15:2)**

God expects the body of Christ to honor each other by completely caring for and loving each other. Everyone has the duty to give love to others in other to ensure adequate flow of love supply in the body. Love is like to Church what blood is unto the body.

The life of a body is in its blood. The life of a church is in love shared among the congregation. Once the blood is dried up the body will die out. Sometimes you hear people complaining in the Church that they are not loved enough.

Mostly such people are concerned with receiving from others rather than giving. True love is in giving even to those you consider not deserving it. The world hated and crucified Jesus Christ but He was still interceding for His killers while on the cross.

When last did you make an excuse for people that offended you? Genuine love does not seek its own nor is it provoked. It doesn't rejoice in the calamity of others nor does it scheme to revenge.

It believes all things, hopes all things and endures all things.

> *Love is patient, love is kind and is not jealous; love does not brag and is not arrogant, does not act unbecomingly; it does not seek its own, is not provoked, does not take into account a wrong suffered, does not rejoice in unrighteousness, but rejoices with the truth; bears all things, believes all things, hopes all things, endures all things. Love never fails.* **(1 Corinthians 13:4-8 NASU)**

> *A new commandment I give unto you, That ye love one another; as I have loved you, that ye also love one another. By this shall all men know that ye are my disciples, if ye have love one to another.* **(John 13:34-35)**

Jesus endured the entire cross experience because He unconditionally loved us. It is easier to treasure and honor the person you love. Hatred in the other hand leads to dishonor.

> *For, brethren, ye have been called unto liberty; only use not liberty for an occasion to the flesh, but by love serve one another. For all the law is fulfilled in one word, even in this; Thou shalt love thy neighbour as thyself. But if ye bite and devour one another, take heed that ye be not consumed one of another.*

> *(Galatians 5:13-15)*
>
> *Let all bitterness, and wrath, and anger, and clamour, and evil speaking, be put away from you, with all malice: And be ye kind one to another, tenderhearted, forgiving one another, even as God for Christ's sake hath forgiven you.* **(Ephesians 4:31-5)** *Also Colossians3:13-15; 1 Peter 1:22*

It is easier to forgive the person you love. Jesus by dying for our sins has given us a perfect example to follow.

We can only prove ourselves to be His true followers when we love each other (John 13:35).

Our faith in the Lord could only bear fruits with love (Galatians 5:6). That is because love is the fulfillment of all laws (Rom. 13:10; Matt. 22:37-40). It is our first duty to love each other as the body of Christ for that is what makes us His genuine children.

> *Beloved, let us love one another: for love is of God; and every one that loveth is born of God, and knoweth God. He that loveth not knoweth not God; for God is love.* **(1 John 4:7-8)**
>
> *Beloved, if God so loved us, we ought also to love one another.*
> *No man hath seen God at any time. If we love one another, God dwelleth in us, and his love is perfected in us.* **(1 John 4:11-12)**

Our duty is to provoke each other to love God, to love ourselves and even our neighbors. We are God's ambassadors of love on earth. God is love and as His genuine children, we should be a manifestation of love among ourselves and the people of the world. People should remember you with only one world, love!

> *And let us consider one another to provoke unto love and to good works:*
> *Not forsaking the assembling of ourselves together, as the manner of some is; but exhorting one another: and so much the more, as ye see the day approaching.* **Heb 10:24-25** *(Also 1 John 4:20).*

You are a member of God's spiritual family with other Christians.

You prove your conviction as a child of God by being planted in the local Church where you are recognized as a regular member.

How can one claim to be part of a body when one is completely detached from that body? Unity is a vital ingredient that makes a Christian's life fruitful. That is why believers' entire relationship should be built on sharing mutual honor. We should walk in love, talk in love, live in love, correct in love and abide in love.

WINNING TOGETHER AS A CHURCH

For the body is not one member, but many. If the foot shall say, Because I am not the hand, I am not of the body; is it therefore not of the body? And if the ear shall say, Because I am not the eye, I am not of the body; is it therefore not of the body? If the whole body were an eye, where were the hearing? If the whole were hearing, where were the smelling? But now hath God set the members every one of them in the body, as it hath pleased him. **(1 Corinthians 12:14-18)**

And he gave some, apostles; and some, prophets; and some, evangelists; and some, pastors and teachers; For the perfecting of the saints, for the work of the ministry, for the edifying of the body of Christ: Till we all come in the unity of the faith, and of the knowledge of the Son of God, unto a perfect man, unto the measure of the stature of the fulness of Christ: **(Ephesians 4:11-13)**

God has distributed His spiritual gifts to different members of the Church for the united purpose of edifying the whole body.
We are one body created for co-operation not competition.
We are meant for collaboration not segregation!
God's gifts are not personal. It is not what the gifted person uses for himself or herself. You are not expected to preach or prophesize or evangelize yourself. The gifts are corporate properties. They are meant to unite our faith and make us all perfect like Christ.
God distributes His gifts among us so we can depend on each other in unity and in love. Anytime anybody fails to use his or her gifts well or just choose to walk away with it, we all lose together.

> **How can one claim to be part of a body when one is completely detached from that body? Unity is a vital ingredient that makes a Christian's life fruitful.**

The attributes of a winning Church

1. Godliness

Seek ye first the kingdom of God, and his righteousness; and all these things shall be added unto you. **(Matthew 6:33)**

Seeking God first is the priority of every genuine Christian.
Doing the will of God is the overiding desire of a winning body of Christ. This is reflected in the uncompromising dedication to winning the lost souls, sharing the love of God among each other and the world and establishing the kingdom of God on earth as His ambassadors.

2. Unity of purpose

Endeavouring to keep the unity of the Spirit in the bond of peace.
There is one body, and one Spirit, even as ye are called in one hope of your calling; One Lord, one faith, one baptism, One God and Father of all, who is above all, and through all, and in you all. **(Ephesians 4:3-6)**

You're not an island.
Your destiny is interrelated to those of other men.
You need a deep relationship with mankind as much as you need with God to live a fulfilled life. We are like a football team, judged by the total of all our efforts together. To win together, we need to unite our efforts to pursue a united purpose. We need to fight against our common enemy, the devil in order to enjoy the blessing of our common heavenly Father. Since we share the same name, same destiny in Christ and the same hope for life thereafter, it is necessary we unite as a team to achieve our purpose. God always blesses unity (Gen.11:6; Ps.133). A house that divides against itself shall fall (Mark 3: 25). United we stand, divided we fall. What you do to any member of the Church you do directly to Christ (Matt. 25:35-40; 1 Cor.12:27). Every time you abuse, disgrace, destroy or help and love a member of the Church, remember you are doing it unto Jesus Christ.

> **You need deep relationship with mankind as much as you need with God to live a fulfilled life.**

3. Focused Faith

Wherefore seeing we also are compassed about with so great a cloud of witnesses, let us lay aside every weight, and the sin which doth so easily beset us, and let us run with patience the race that is set before us, Looking unto Jesus the author and finisher of our faith; who for the joy that was set before him endured the cross, despising the shame, and is set down at the right hand of the throne of

*God. For consider him that endured such contradiction of sinners against himself, lest ye be wearied and faint in your minds. **(Hebrews 12:1-3)***

Brethren, I count not myself to have apprehended: but this one thing I do, forgetting those things which are behind, and reaching forth unto those things which are before, I press toward the mark for the prize of the high calling of God in Christ Jesus. Let us therefore, as many as be perfect, be thus minded. ***(Philippians 3:13-15)***

Only a finisher can reap the fruits of his labor.
We have been called to fight the good fight of faith which ends in a good report. We cannot afford to fail by giving up. Our duty is to continue to press on with all sense of endurance and perseverance.

4. Interdependence

And God hath set some in the Church, first apostles, secondarily prophets, thirdly teachers, after that miracles, then gifts of healings, helps, governments, diversities of tongues. ***(1 Corinthians 12:28)***

You are called not only to believe but also to belong to the body of Christ. As a kid born into a world family needs nurturing from a particular family, so does every Christian has a need for local fellowship. God has given the Church all spiritual gifts for the perfecting of all. Either you are a prophet, Church administrator or help; your gift is essential to the success of the body.
Use your gift and encourage others to use their own!
Imagine a man trying to learn about everything he needs to use in life. What a wasteful and useless life that would be. He will need to learn medicine, computer technology, aeronautic flying, car mechanics, bread-baking, dish making, farming, hunting etceteras.
The world is created to move on the wheel of interdependence.
Even if you have the ability and capability to learn everything well, you have no sufficient time in life to do it all. Like every other human system, the Church is built on the positive interrelationship among members. It is left for individuals to learn of personal strength and weakness and contribute his or her best to the good of all.

5. Co-operation

Till we all come in the unity of the faith, and of the knowledge of the Son of God, unto a perfect man, unto the measure of the stature of the fulness of Christ. ***(Ephesians 4:13)***

It takes everyone willing to share and use their talents for a team to win. It is our duty to support and backup each other to fulfill our duties. We are pursuing the same goal even in different roles so everyone needs to be his brother's keeper.

6. Communication

Brethren, by the name of our Lord Jesus Christ, that ye all speak the same thing, and that there be no divisions among you; but that ye be perfectly joined together in the same mind and in the same judgment. **(1 Corinthians 1:10)**

Imagine a body with its part not communicating together!
The body will not only be exhausted in confusion but will die a uselessness death. Every member should learn to give feedbacks, encouragement, correction. We must learn to offer supports unto the leadership and as many members that might need it.

7. Competence

Now he that planteth and he that watereth are one: and every man shall receive his own reward according to his own labor. For we are labourers together with God: ye are God's husbandry, ye are God's building. **(1 Cor. 3:8-9)**

We are all a total of everyone's ability, capability and proficiency. Though we may not be perfect, we have great potentials that can still be developed to improve our co-existence. Take personal responsibility to improve your knowledge and habits. For as much as you know, you might be the only Bible some people will ever read.
Your influence affects the performance of others. People generalize the performance of the entire body of Christ with your conduct.

8. Consistency

Nevertheless, whereto we have already attained, let us walk by the same rule, let us mind the same thing. **(Philippians 3:16)**

Please stop attending your Church only in the spirit. Make it also your duty to attend regularly in the body. How will you feel if you arrive in Church only to find out that your preacher and the choirs would be attending in spirit and will not be physically around that day? How will you like to be in a prayer meeting alone?
Your punctual and regular attendance is of great importance to God and is a great encouragement to other believers and your pastor than you can ever imagine. If you occupy any position of service in your congregation, do not allow your performance to fluctuate.

Be predictable. Be part of the team your Church can depend on to move forward.

9. Maintenance

As we have therefore opportunity, let us do good unto all men, especially unto them who are of the household of faith. ***(Galatians 6:10)***

Share responsibility in offering social provision for your gathering. Bring foods and refreshments. Take part in welcoming new comers.
Participate in Church service organization, Church upkeep (tithes, offerings, donations) etceteras. Let your presence be felt in the house of your heavenly father. We are all children of the Lord and have an equal right to ensure things are running well in the house of the Lord. Play your financial stewardship role regularly. No one wants to have belatedly money to pay monthly bills. How often do we put our Church leaders through avoidable anguish? Money is the vehicle of the gospel. The gospel is free but every medium it is preached through requires money. Your preacher needs money for livelihood like you. The Church building needs maintenance like your house.
The Church workers need a salary like you. Contributing material and physical efforts are the ways to build an effective body of Christ.

10. Team Spirit

For as the body is one, and hath many members, and all the members of that one body, being many, are one body: so also is Christ. For by one Spirit are we all baptized into one body, whether we be Jews or Gentiles, whether we be bond or free; and have been all made to drink into one Spirit. ***(1 Cor. 12:12-13)***

Every mature member of a Church should desire to share in the burden of leadership in any area of relevance your gifts and talents permit you to participate. Everyone should pray for the Church and its leadership as a matter of duty.
Attending Church midweek and Sunday service regularly turns your Church alive and encourages new members to settle down.
Everyone should work together for the kingdom of God to be established in our midst. Are you a relevant member of your Church? If so, you should be able to talk of , "my God, my church, my pastor and my plan" when you are discussing your congregation with others.

CHAPTER 6: ROLES AND RESPONSIBILITIES OF LEADERSHIP

Every leader has services to offer to the people.
It is such a role that serves as the basis of recognition and empowerment. When an incumbent fails in the performance of such expected duties, the official basis for its continuous existence is eroded and new leadership can seek such an opportunity to evolve into power.

While it is possible to repress and supress people to continue to accept an obsolete leadership, the only peaceful and legitimate means of staying in any position of authority is the ability to deliver results and fulfill expected responsibilities attributed formally or informally to such office.

Every system has a process of carrying out this exercise. While social and elected bodies can be voted, vetoed, impeached or pressurised out of office, appointed and commissioned officers who cannot be voted or forced out can still lose the loyalty of their people.

A bad Church leader for instance will once lose his congregation while an appointed chief may be subjected to rebellious revolt from his subjects. Which ever way one wants to see it, it is a fact that every leadership has a social responsibility to play to his or her people.

SOCIAL RESPONSIBILITIES OF LEADERSHIP

1. Repository of relevant professional skills

Every good leader in the house of the Lord, like in all areas of life, must have sound knowledge of the word of God in addition to cultivating an earnestly intimate relationship with God.

In addition to that, a good leader must try to learn about the politics and economic situation affecting his world.

Every leader is a learner. As a leader, you need to be a committed student who learns broadly in order to richly provide leadership for others. A blind man cannot lead a blind man. Official or unofficial training could offer a priceless opportunity for hand-on experience and anointing as well as for leadership development. It also affords potential leaders in the house of Lord practical training ground to acquire necessary human relation skills that are needed in dealing

with people on a day to day basis. Remember, while other organisation deals with human resources, which is basically temporal, only Church deals with human destiny which is eternal.
Church alone deals on issues of life and death!
You need both the wisdom to relate with a man and the spiritual maturity to connect with the power of God without which ministry will become a great misery for you.
The Church is about God and anything you do without His back up will be an exercise in futility. That is why in addition to being so deep in worldly skills and the word of God; you still need to secure an intimate relationship with the Holy Spirit, the resident God on earth. Only the Holy Spirit has the power to Comfort, teach and remind you of all things pertaining to life and godliness (John 14:26).
Only with Him can you effectively perform your responsibilities to the body of Christ.

2. Godly representative

Foremost, a good Church leader is a mouthpiece of God to God's people. Such leaders, who should have a deep personal relationship with God, must be well trained in the word of God so that they can speak boldly as God's oracle (1 Peter 4:11).
The higher your responsibility the closer you should be to God. Every high priest taken from among men is appointed for men in things pertaining to God (Heb.5:1-3). Any leader appointed in the Church needs to be properly appointed and consecrated to office.

> *Then thou spakest in vision to thy holy one, and saidst, I have laid help upon one that is mighty; I have exalted one chosen out of the people. I have found David my servant; with my holy oil have I anointed him: With whom my hand shall be established: mine arm also shall strengthen him.*
> ***(Psalm 89:19-21)***

This Psalm written under the anointing of Holy Spirit revealed that though it was Prophet Samuel that anointed David physically, it was God who actually anointed King David into office. When men are properly consecrated to office, they have the full backing of God behind their services (1 Thess.5:24). After Prophet Samuel anointed King Saul to office, the spirit of the Lord fell upon Saul and he became another person. We saw samething happening to King David. Elisha received a double portion of God's anointing upon Prophet Elijah through his intimate relationship with him. We saw the same situation between Moses and Aaron. Consecrating people into office is still relevant today especially in equipping leaders to become spiritual representatives of God.

Many impatient people have been misled into potholes of self-destruction by believing that they do not need to serve or seek to be anointed to an office by any man of God.

3. Repository of people skill

Different leadership method flourishes in a different situation. The type of leadership model that will be effective in your organisation will depend on the type of leader you are and the type of followers you have. The situation of your environment matters! The different organisation demands a different leadership style. Church organisation requires great people skill. While many other organisations have an official way of penalizing people when they misbehave, such is not the case with Church where most workers are working free and voluntarily.

4. Expert in human relationship

You need to be able to build and maintain a cordial relationship with everyone around you without any discrimination, partiality, contempt and favour. Everyone appreciates a person that affords everyone equal opportunity to distinguish self. How can you claim to be an ambassador of God who is a no respecter of persons if you cannot accept and deal with everyone equally?

How do you want to attract people when you are unapproachable? People can only confide in you when they trust you. People will trust you if they know that you will understand and respect their opinions even when they disagree and have a contrary opinion to yours. A leader well skilled in a human relationship will be able to live in peace with every normal member of his team. Let us see what this means.

- *Broad knowledge of peoples' mentality and needs.*
  Though a man of God is responsible to God for his service, yet he is accountable to the people he serves. Jesus Christ spent early stage of His life mingling with His people in order to tap into their mentality and social way of life without which He would have been unable to relate and make an impact in their lives. Until you know the needs and condition of your people, you cannot effectively serve and satisfy them.

- *A great leader is a good listener.* A good leader needs to be able to show sincere interest in peoples' situation and feeling. This way he can identify with them easily and ameliorate their pains.

- *Treat others respectfully.* Spiritual leaders should deal with their subordinates as co-heir in the kingdom rather than as underlings who take orders from a boss.

- *Provide a loving and brotherly atmosphere.* Create a good relationship among different individuals and groups making up the congregation. Do not take side with anyone, treat all as equals. Give everyone a chance to maximize their potentials.

- *Provide for a meritorious system of appreciation.* Provide for a system that recognizes and appreciates productivity and performance rather than hierarchy or position.
  Recognise people based on their productivity and contribution to Church success rather than on their position in the hierarchy. Why will you make a person who cannot sing or teach others a leader of your choir when you have talents that could set your praise and worship on fire for the glory of God?
  Find other means to compensate people for their long and faithful service. A losing team is one that keeps its scorer on the reserved seat while bad players are featured in the game.

5. Committed team player

Others will follow you to achieve a goal you are transparently passionate to achieve. Your passion is the driver that drives you and other passengers sharing your vision with you.
Passion can be contagious to others.
To get others committed to any project, be committed first.
People will only replicate and duplicate what they see.
Leading by example is the most effective way of leading.
Practice what you preach. Put your hand where your mouth is or you will become a mere charlatan. Let your personality manifest your mission if you want to motivate your members to full maturity!
Take peoples frustration around you as challenging.
Do not give up on them, rather help them to come over it. They will never forget and will be glad to stay beside you when you need them too.

6. Provide for participatory decision making

This encourages the involvement of those that carry out the bulk of the duties in an organisation. Participatory management offers, over autocratic management, the advantage of carrying along, subordinates in a decision they participated in making. It is easier for people to take responsibility for the decision they felt involved in.

7. Knowledge manager and co-ordinator

The duty here includes co-ordinating projects of several task-focused teams across the organization to ensure that all parts work together to achieve the central goal of the organization.

Leaders also need to promote learning in their organizations. Leaders will need to show commitment to continuous learning not only by encouraging workers to acquire new knowledge but also by serving as models themselves in the learning, sharing and application of knowledge. The role of knowledge co-ordinator includes repeatedly teaching people in order to enhance their values.

Repeat the organisation's vision as much as possible until everyone learnt it by heart. Provision should also be made to allow the use of acquired training within the organization.

An organization where the same few people run every aspect of the Church for fear of new people making mistakes or taking over is hardly conducive for innovative breakthroughs.

8. Mentor

A good leader plays the role of an instructor and coach while mentoring his followers to leadership status. Good leaders are mentors who train others to be self independent.

It is a sign of bad leadership when every person hangs on you. Leadership is about bringing out the leaders in others and not about suppressing it. It is a sign of failure if you have a Church where everyone depends on the pastor to pray for their headaches and tooth ache instead of going out to the world to heal and save others for the Lord. Ironically, such weak leaders always complain of being overweighed with loads of dependants. Do your work in making leaders out of your people and you will earn your rest.

Train people to be less dependent on you.

Your duty is to direct them to God not to yourself.

In the Church I pastor, everyone is encouraged to take up leadership responsibility corresponding to areas of skills and expertise.

Why will you be playing the role of an accountant in the Church when you have qualified accountants?

What has your anointing as a pastor got to do with your keeping the keys to Church storage and stores? Set yourself free.

The Church is a property of God not man. Relax so you do not die before your time. Let anyone who feels save for tampering with the things of the Lord try to outsmart God. Jesus Christ knew that Judas was a dishonest accountant but still left him to do his job.

It is every leader's duty to create an atmosphere that helps members to step into independence out of dependence and hone their leadership skill to offer productive services to their God.

9. Cheerleader

Establish an encouraging atmosphere to try new things in your organization. The experiment is the mother of invention.

Every failure is a step closer to success.

Do not let people bury themselves in self-despair each time they fail. Raise them up on their feet by filling them up with encouragement born out of genuine understanding and support. Let them know failure is a situation not a person and that you still believe in them. Only these ways are you sure to bring to light the leadership potentials in your subordinates. If you leave them in their failure, you have failed yourself and your people hence your calling!

Your duty is to build strong confidence that is able to withhold every storm of demoralization and frustration.

10. Referee

Maintain a commitment to official goals by focusing on all individual and group activities to the central goal. Be fast to align people to the goals of the organisation. Quite often, situations tip focus of the people away from the mission of the organization.

It is the role of the leadership to restore the focus of the team and inspire them to move forward. Quite often, we open doors for new people to join us in the Church leadership with the hope of getting on board fresh ideas and new passion but things don't always work out fine. Some people. as soon as they come on board, proceed to try to change everything to look like their old Church or personal vision. It is the duty of a leader in his referee role to redress such situation and create a friendly, co-operative and peaceful atmosphere to focus on and achieve organizational goals.

11. Facilitator

The leadership facilitation role entails carrying out activities that remove obstructions and ensures that the group can achieve its goals. As trouble-shooter, any obstructive situation is eliminated in order to have a motivating atmosphere conducive to productivity.

The leader must be able to focus all members to the main goals and objectives of the organization and maintain a correlation between their activities and the official tasks and outputs expected of them.

12. Exemplar of virtues

In addition to all the above skills, a good leader should also be a man of good attitude and character. A good attitude is a good business. Good name after all is better than silver and gold.

Nothing affects followership like leadership by example.

How often you see people ruined by excessive ambition leading to oppression of their subordinates and destruction of the superiors.

13. A good servant

A good leader's ambition should be tempered with submission. Only passion, with refined motivation can lead to promotion. A good leader should be bold but he must be humble at the same time. Have you seen a good waiter in a five star hotel before? A good waiter looks confident, sure and quite willing to help you out. That is a good picture of a good leader. A good leader is a person who can lead himself to serve others. A good leader should also know how to balance immediate need with future goals. Champions make a decision that creates the future they desire. Losers, on the other hand, make decisions that gratify their immediate needs.

UNDERSTANDING ROLES OF KINGDOM LEADERSHIP

Let the elders that rule well be counted worthy of double honour, especially they who labor in the word and doctrine. **(1 Timothy 5:17)**

Many in the house of the Lord have misinterpreted the service nature of Kingdom leadership to mean dishonour for leadership. Many have confused the fact that God is no respecter of persons (Act 10: 34) to mean everyone is the same in the Church and that anyone can handle the daily duties of spiritual and organizational leadership.

What a recipe for confusion and ultimate destruction. Such a stand couldn't be farther away from the stand of God of order.

A CASE FOR LEADERSHIP

Claiming no need for leadership in Church is stating that everyone from baby to parent, from visitor to member, from sinner to the faithful, from congregant to leaders can equally direct or decide the direction of worship and administration in a congregation.

There is no association or organization where such rubbish is tenable. Not even in playgroups. If everybody is not equal in calling and responsibility in our family, working place, business organization and other social groups, what makes anyone think it should happen in the house of the Lord? Claiming there is no need for leadership in any place under the pretence that everyone is a leader is a mere illusion.

While it is true that everyone can be a leader, it is a fact that not everyone will be. Not everyone will devote time to process their gifts to a skill. Because not all of us develop our potentials equally, we end up at a different level of development and status. Not all leaders are even developed at the same level and even if that is the case, there will always be a need to still appoint leaders among them.

For instance, when leaders of independent states meet in international organizations, they still select one of them to lead.

That is because no worthwhile progress can be made in any social association without a presiding authority. Every organization and institution as a matter of necessity and survival needs a leader.

More correctly, every organization needs an honourable leader if affairs shall be conducted in a civil, disciplined, logical and effective manner. When the Queen of England or President of the United States of America visits another country, they submit to the leadership of their host country. That is because God has instituted authority as a way of life to safeguard normal human conducts.

In fact what is common to all organizations everywhere in the world, both Christian and non- Christian is the institution of leadership.

When leaders of independent states meet in international organizations, they still select one of them to lead. That is because no worthwhile progress can be made in any social association without a presiding authority. Every organization and institution as a matter of necessity and survival needs a leader.

God is the Creator and the main Sustainer of every type of leadership. God gave different types of leaders to the people of Israel to administer their day-to-day activities. He did not only provided for offices of prophets, kings, parents and other forms of political, economic and social authorities, but the Bible is also filled with His various injunction to honour them.

> *Let every soul be subject unto the higher powers. For there is no power but of God: the powers that be are ordained of God. Whosoever therefore resisteth the power, resisteth the ordinance of God: and they that resist shall receive to themselves damnation.* **(Romans 13:1-2)**

God however requires humble and service oriented attitudes from such leaders. Kingdom leaders are expected to humble themselves following the example of Jesus Christ, the greatest leader that ever walked the face of the earth.

> *But Jesus called them to him, and saith unto them, Ye know that they which are accounted to rule over the Gentiles exercise lordship over them; and their great ones exercise authority upon them. But so shall it not be among you: but whosoever will be great among you, shall be your minister.* **(Mark 10:42-43)**

> *Let this mind be in you, which was also in Christ Jesus: Who, being in the form of God, thought it not robbery to be equal with God: But made himself of no reputation, and took upon him the form of a servant, and was made in the likeness of men: And being found in fashion as a man, he humbled himself.* **(Philippians 2:5-8)**

Thus, God that commanded that leaders be honoured also provided that such leaders should maintain their honour by humbly serving their people. Pride has no place in the kingdom of God. The distinguishing characteristic of kingdom leaders is humility.

The covenant relationship between leaders and followers

> *Render therefore to all their dues: tribute to whom tribute is due; custom to whom custom; fear to whom fear; honour to whom honour.* **(Romans 13:7)**

The house of the Lord is a house of honour and there are recommended steps to conduct relationship that edifies both the Lord and the body of His congregation.
Every conduct in the house of the Lord should show unreserved honour and adoration to the Creator of life. The entire body of Christ owes it a great duty to worship God together in love, unity and honour. They are also called to render onto each other befitting tributes in the course of their relationships. Once this condition is satisfied, the congregation can proceed to enter a covenant relationship.

Be ye followers of me, even as I also am of Christ. **(1 Corinthians 11:1)**

Any claim to leadership status in the house of Lord is based on complete submission to the instruction and lordship of the Trinity. Only a follower of Christ is scripturally qualified to be followed.
In essence, you have no business as a Christian to submit yourself under leadership that does not submit and operate wholly under the word of God and saviourship of Christ.

a) God is a judge and Rewarder who deals with everyone justly

Who leads and who is led should all operate under the same instruction of God. He is sure not a God that honours disobedience of the same authority He instituted. While He holds the exclusive authority to exercise mercy, He nonetheless expects people to obey His commandments according to which they will be justly judged.

b) Leaders are to render service to the body of Christ

Preach the word; be instant in season, out of season; reprove, rebuke, exhort with all longsuffering and doctrine. **(2 Timothy 4:2)**

The main purpose of a servant is to offer service.
A kingdom leader owes it as a duty to the congregation to teach, rebuke, encourage and lead the body to Jesus Christ. Every minister of God is a vessel through which God ministers His gifts, callings, blessings and instructions to His people. The various ways this can be achieved will be treated in details later in the book.

c) Congregations are to honour leaders for their service

Let the elders that rule well be counted worthy of **double honour***, especially they who labor in the word and doctrine. For the scripture saith,*

> *Thou shalt not muzzle the ox that treadeth out the corn. And, The labourer is worthy of his reward.* **(1 Timothy 5:17-18)**

Every Church has to strive to make sure that the congregation is purged clean of contemptuous relationship with its leadership. Dishonour of authority always results in the destruction of opportunities. Jesus couldn't perform any serious miracles in the congregation of His people for lack of recognition of His status as Son of God.

> *Is not this the carpenter, the son of Mary, the brother of James, and Joses, and of Juda, and Simon? and are not his sisters here with us? And they were offended at him. And he could there do no mighty work, save that he laid his hands upon a few sick folk, and healed them. And he marvelled because of their unbelief.* **(Mark 6:3, 5,6)**

Jesus' brethrens couldn't partake much in His miracles because they trivialized their relationship with Him. Because they ate with Him, grew up with Him, saw Him cried and witnessed some of His earthly frustrations, they lacked any expectation to fire up their faith to receive from Him. Familiarity always breeds contempt.

Every congregation mostly find it easier to appreciate visiting ministers and evangelists than local pastors that labor with them all year long. It takes maturity to appreciate efforts of those God places over you to labor for your spiritual nourishment and emancipation.

Many years ago, I was opportuned to preach in the pulpit of Pastor Sunday Adelaja, the visionary leader of a 30 thousand member Embassy of God Church in Ukraine. I was surprised by the way the congregation applauded and appreciated my message. I felt highly encouraged to minister with everything God laid in my spirit that day. Back home where I pastor just above a hundred people, I never felt such appreciation or encouragement. Now, mind you, I have one of the warmest and most loving people any pastor can ever pray to have but we are used to each other. We sort of digest what God sends us day after day coolly in a smooth and loving family atmosphere.

It however always takes the expectant atmosphere to push a man to go a bit further than the last time.

Jesus Christ experienced it and all pastors do.

Jesus Christ said unto them, "A prophet is not without honour, but in his own country!" To enjoy the anointing God has deposited upon

your pastor, you need to consciously cultivate the habit of appreciating Him.
Appreciation always brings the best out of people!

A call to honour

For this cause pay ye tribute also: for they are God's ministers, attending continually upon this very thing. Render therefore to all their dues: a tribute to whom tribute is due; custom to whom custom; fear to whom fear; honour to whom honour (**Romans 13:6-7).**

> *And we beseech you, brethren, to know them which labor among you, and are over you in the Lord, and admonish you; And to esteem them very highly in love for their work's sake. (**1 Thessalonians 5:12-13)***

Kingdom leadership requires more discipline and work than other earthly profession and God instructs His Church to accord people involved in His business more reverence and honour.
The impact of such people is not limited to our well-being in this world but will remain for eternity. God is their Rewarder; only He will judge and reward them according to their faithfulness.
All He expects from us is to honour them.
Every man of God holds sufficient authority and anointing from God to pass God's blessing to his congregation. It is left for every member to tap into such blessings through honourable services. You either resist disobediently and receive damnation to yourself (Rom 13: 2) or believe them and prosper (2 Chronicles 20: 20).
You see you can only attract what you appreciate. It is a fact of life that you do not receive from a person you do not appreciate.
That is why you need to attend a Church where you believe in the leadership. One of the most important decisions you can make as a Christian is to choose a godly congregation to worship with and the main basis of your choice should be the practice of the word of God. If you join a Church whose leadership is being led by personal opinions, the culture of the elders, the tradition of men rather than the pure word of God, then you are putting both your earthly and eternal life at great risk. Jim Jones, a self-acclaimed minister of God led his entire congregation to a forest and poisoned them. His personal squad of executioners shot to death those that will not take the poison willingly. Be a noble Christian, like the Church of Berea, that follows the preachers of the word of God alone (Acts 17:11). First make sure that the Church is committed to obeying the word of God. Then give your complete commitment to that body of Christ and you will be blessed of the Lord.

The blessing of honouring godly leaders

1) Prosperous living

Believe in the LORD your God, so shall ye be established; believe his prophets, so shall ye prosper. ***(2 Chronicles 20:20)***

2) Prophetic blessing

He that receiveth a prophet in the name of a prophet shall receive a prophet's reward; and he that receiveth a righteous man in the name of a righteous man shall receive a righteous man's reward. And whosoever shall give to drink unto one of these little ones a cup of cold water only in the name of a disciple, verily I say unto you, he shall in no wise lose his reward. ***(Matt. 10:41-42)***

3) Godly blessing

Now ye Philippians know also, that in the beginning of the gospel, when I departed from Macedonia, no Church communicated with me as concerning giving and But my God shall supply all your need according to his riches in glory by Christ Jesus. ***(Philippians 4:15-19)***

4) Open heaven

Bring ye all the tithes into the storehouse, that there may be meat in mine house, and prove me now herewith, saith the LORD of hosts, if I will not open you the windows of heaven, and pour you out a blessing, that there shall not be room enough to receive it. ***(Malachi 3:10)***

SPIRITUAL BASIS FOR KINGDOM LEADERSHIP

In addition to natural duties that an average leader in a human social organization takes, the leadership in the kingdom of God has additional responsibilities to play according to the will of God. These responsibilities not only make their services more demanding but also more sensitive since they serve as an intermediary between their people and the almighty God who is the main repository of every power in the world.

With critics both inside and outside the Church, it takes deep intimacy with God and strong sensitivity to the feelings of people to disperse the expected duties justifiably. There will however be always around such criticism no matter how sensitive, godly, loving and humble a man can be. Miriam, Aaron and the children of Korah among many others questioned the authority of Moses (Numbers 12 and 16). Even Jesus couldn't escape the sceptics of His time (Matt 21: 23-27). The challenge for every leader is to shun distraction that comes with the work and focus on the call of God in order to render expected service requested of such spiritual office with patience, humility and love. There are scriptural reasons for additional duties allocated to spiritual leaders.

1) God is a God of order

> *For God is not the author of confusion, but of peace, as in all Churches of the saints. Let all things be done decently and in order.* **(1 Cor. 14:33, 40)**

The Bible emphasises that all powers that be are ordained of God. All powers mean every form of authority that brings orderliness into God's world. That includes your Dad and Mum, police men and Presidents etceteras. God is not in control of things done without order. God will not take over a life run disorderly and disobediently until we clean up and hand over to Him. That is why you could decide to die in sin by choice and you will not be forced to be born again. That is why you can freely curse; fornicate and even refuse to pay tithe and God will not cause a thunderstorm to strike you down publicly. That is because He has left the kingdom of darkness and the people living under it under the control of Satan. God is only reigning where there is orderliness.

> *For God is not the **author of confusion**, but of peace, as in all Churches of the saints.* **(1 Corinthians 14:33)**

God in His infinite wisdom has created all systems; solar, body, breathing, nervous system, all of them. He expects everything to work together for good despite having a different specialised purpose.

2) God creates head over every thing

> *Behold, how good and how pleasant it is for brethren to dwell together in unity! It is like the precious ointment upon the head, that ran down upon the beard, even Aaron's beard: that went down to the skirts of his garments.* **(Psalm 133:1-2)**

God created over every organisation and creature a head to give it direction. Right from time immemorial, God has always led His chosen people through their leaders. Bible is filled with people like Moses, Joshua, David, Deborah, Peter and Paul, just name it! Though God can choose to communicate with individuals, yet He remains God of orderly and united people and not the Creator of Barbarians who speaks and act disorderly at the same time.

3) God guides and teaches us through our leaders

He saith unto him the third time, Simon, son of Jonas, lovest thou me? Peter was grieved because he said unto him the third time, Lovest thou me? And he said unto him, Lord, thou knowest all things; thou knowest that I love thee. Jesus saith unto him, Feed my sheep. **(John 21:17)**

Obey them that have the rule over you, and submit yourselves: for they watch for your souls, as they that must give account, that they may do it with joy, and not with grief: for that is unprofitable for you. **(Hebrews 13:17)**

God mostly lead His people through their heads.
As you observe the general leading of God and build a personal relationship with Him, you soon get to a position where you may receive instruction from Him.

4) God blesses us through our leaders

Believe in the LORD your God, so shall ye be established; believe his prophets, so shall ye prosper. **(2 Chronicles 20:20)**

Honour thy father and mother; (which is the first commandment with promise;) That it may be well with thee, and thou mayest live long on the earth. **(Ephesians 6:2-3)**

Honouring the leaders we see is a practical way to prove our obedience to the Lord we do not see. As we obey His words and instruction passed down to us, He Himself blesses our obedience.

5) Our leaders serve as a point of contact to God

He that receiveth a prophet in the name of a prophet shall receive a prophet's reward; and he that receiveth a righteous man in the name of a righteous man shall receive a righteous man's reward. **(Matthew 10:41)**

> *Let him that is taught in the word communicate unto him that teacheth in all good things. Be not deceived; God is not mocked: for whatsoever a man soweth, that shall he also reap.* ***(Galatians 6: 6-7)***

Many times, anointed leaders can be a direct point of contact with God's blessing or curses! Blessing a man of God is an indirect way of blessing God that sends such the same way offending men of God is an indirect way of offending God who sends them.

Miriam and Aaron got in to the wrath of God for dealing dishonourably with their younger brother Moses who God has made their leader. (Num. 12: 2-15). Ananias and Sapphira's lie to Peter cost them their lives (Acts 5: 1-10). King Saul's disrespect of the office of Prophet Samuel cost him his kingdom (1 Sam 15:23).

However when Prophet Eli blessed a barren Hannah, God opened her womb and blessed her with a son (1 Sam 1:17).

When Prophet Elijah blessed the widow of Zarephath, her cruse of oil sustained her throughout the famine in Israel (1 Kings 17: 12-15). When Elisha blessed the last pot of oil of the widow of a man of God, her lack came to an immediate end (2 Kings 4: 2-7). God's authority is behind every godly institution be it family, civil, social or vocational. The way we deal with such constituted authorities will determine the extent we are blessed or cursed (1 Tim. 2: 1-2; Ex. 20: 12, 25-26). Everyone is responsible for what s/he attracts upon self.

6) Our leaders serve as service channels from God

> *Woe be unto the pastors that destroy and scatter the sheep of my pasture! saith the LORD. Therefore thus saith the LORD God of Israel against the pastors that feed my people; Ye have scattered my flock, and driven them away, and have not visited them: behold, I will visit upon you the evil of your doings, saith the LORD.* ***(Jeremiah 23:1-2)***

> *How then shall they call on him in whom they have not believed? and how shall they believe in him of whom they have not heard? and how shall they hear without a preacher?* ***(Romans 10:14)***

God has chosen our leaders to lead us out of destruction into His presence by guiding, feeding, visiting and collecting God's people together to serve Him. Your pastor has a spiritual duty to watch over your soul! The least expected of you is to recognize that fact and co-operate with Him (Heb. 13:17). God uses our leaders to correct, heal, direct and serve us in various ways.

Now we exhort you, brethren, warn them that are unruly, comfort the feebleminded, support the weak, be patient toward all men. 15 See that none render evil for evil unto any man; but ever follow that which is good, both among yourselves, and to all men. **(1 Thessalonians 5:14-15)**

Is any sick among you? let him call for the elders of the Church; and let them pray over him, anointing him with oil in the name of the Lord: And the prayer of faith shall save the sick, and the Lord shall raise him up; and if he have committed sins, they shall be forgiven him. **(James 5:14-16)**

And he sat down, and called the twelve, and saith unto them, If any man desire to be first, the same shall be last of all, and servant of all. **(Mark 9:35-36)**

God had sent leaders to His people as shepherds who can protect them with ther lives and die for them as Jesus Christ - the great shephered did for us all when He died on the cross for the wellbeing of the entire mankind.

> **God created over every organisation and creature a head to give it direction. Right from time immemorial, God has always led His chosen people through their leaders.**

CHAPTER 7: KINGDOM MODEL OF LEADERSHIP

And he sat down, and called the twelve, and saith unto them, If any man desire to be first, the same shall be last of all, and servant of all. **(Mark 9:35)**

There was once a struggle amongst Jesus disciples concerning who should occupy a position of leadership around Him. The master took the opportunity to deliver a leadership seminar on the concept of kingdom leadership. One distinguishing factor of kingdom leadership is its emphasis on service.

It is about leading with the mentality of a servant.

It is the leadership of a service- minded person who has purposefully located his or her life purpose, refined it and is dedicated himself to adding values to the lives of other people.

The search for ideal human leadership which has taken the man through eras of autocracy, monarchy, oligarchy and democracy has finally returned us to a new leadership system sharing characteristics similar to priesthood era when leaders saw themselves as servants of God. While priesthood directly offered services to people around them, their main responsibility was to God.

God has created Everyman on earth with attributes to serve others! The fact that people not considered to have any special leadership trait have risen up in history to serve as transformational leaders' who achieved great feats for their people has supported the popular belief that everyone has a measure of leadership traits deposited in him or her. Yet not everyone will become a leader for not everyone can or will take up the responsibility to develop their leadership potentials.

And hast made us unto our God kings and priests: and we shall reign on the earth. **(Revelation 5:10)**

Kingdom leadership is about rendering valuable service efficiently and productively to your community. You are special and inbued with special values. Develop it and let it distinguish you in your area of service. Your talents and skills are God's way of establishing you as a leader in your area of service. Separate yourself from the crowd!

Revisiting the woes of the machine age

One of the woes of the industrialisation age was the breakdown of tasks to components that can be easily mastered by anyone trained for the job. The computer age has built on that development by translating human tasks into software programs that automatically run in robots and automated machines with great precision.

The standardization of duties has decreased special dependence on human skills and has ended up creating a class of faceless workers that can be changed at will by their employers like any spare parts. Works are broken down and trained so that the same knowledge can be re-used by any human mind or computer programs to re-process the same logic to produce the same outcomes. Because most works no more need subjective interpretation of information, anybody fitting job description could easily be trained to cope.

Industrialists then started to treat human beings as machine parts. Retrenching people from work then became as easy as changing machine parts. No wonder our civilisation at a point in time descended so low to the extent of using dehumanising terminologies like restructuring, re-engineering to handle human organisation.

The point I am making here is that you need to distinguish yourself from crowds of shadowy workers by rendering special values that cannot be easily replicated around you. You either distinguish yourself as a king of the earth or you will be lost in the shadow of the faceless armies of workers servicing our societies.

Great people are those whose values are irreplaceable for the people they serve. Kingdom leadership after all is not a pursuit of greatness or position but the pursuit of becoming a person of great value. Distinguish yourself from others around you!

Valuable people will easily attain greatness.

Imagine, two thousand years ago when there was no mass transportation, up to 5000 men regularly assembled themselves outside in the forest to listen to a 30 year old young preacher named Jesus Christ! That was because he made Himself greatly relevant in their lives. His service was unequalled that they chose to gather around Him. With only 12 disciples, Jesus Christ changed not only the people of His generation but the entire world until this very moment. No other leader ever recorded such an impact in the life of mankind. No contemporary leadership style could achieve this fit. Jesus' style of leadership thus deserved to be studied and emulated if one wants to truly reign on earth as ordained by God.

Can you catch it?
Jesus' life taught us a lot about good leadership.
Foremost, it taught us that true leadership is not measured by how many people serve you but how many people you serve!
Good leadership is not also measured by the salary you earn but by the value you add to the lives of your benefactors.
Yes, Jesus' life taught us that the sure way to kingdom leadership is true servitude. As you supply your gift to improve the lives of your generation, you will see no need to cheat, scheme or lobby to lead. Rather leadership will automatically locate you in your area of service.

WHAT IS SERVANT LEADERSHIP?

> *But Jesus called them unto him, and said, Ye know that the princes of the Gentiles exercise dominion over them, and they that are great exercise authority upon them. But it shall not be so among you: but whosoever will be great among you, let him be your minister; And whosoever will be chief among you, let him be your servant: Even as the Son of man came not to be ministered unto, but to minister, and to give his life a ransom for many.* **(Matthew 20:25-28)**

> *Let this mind be in you, which was also in Christ Jesus: Who, being in the form of God, thought it not robbery to be equal with God: But made himself of no reputation, and took upon him the form of a servant, and was made in the likeness of men: And being found in fashion as a man, he humbled himself, and became obedient unto death, even the death of the cross.* **(Phil. 2:5-9)**

Kingdom leadership (or servant leadership) has nothing to do with the ruling but with serving. Kingdom leaders see themselves as stewards using their God-given gifts in the service of the Giver of all gifts. They thus see their roles as having nothing to do about controlling people but rather about fulfilling the needs of such people. Every time you locate an area of great need and you put your skills and talents to work to provide a solution, your service will never fail to attract your benefactors to you.
This type of leadership, though the most influential is however the most unattractive by modern man.
That is because it mostly begins as a thankless service.
Yet, the people you do not serve cannot appreciate you.
Only faithful servants of today become graceful rulers of tomorrow.

Proud people have no true followers except for hordes of sycophants seeking a a source of livelihood at all cost. You can't be proud and pompous and call yourself a servant!

BECOMING A LEADER

> *And no man taketh this honour unto himself, but he that is called of God, as was Aaron* **(Hebrews 5:4)**

There are certain godly requirements needed to be fulfilled by anyone willing to ascend the leadership position in the house of the Lord.
How often you see a lot of impatient self-ordained ministers!
The fact that you appoint yourself into ministry is proof that you are not called.
No man takes this honour to himself but he that is called of God!
How is a man called to ministry? Like Aaron.
Aaron was called, trained, anointed and sent by a servant of God!

> *And take thou unto thee Aaron thy brother, and his sons with him, from among the children of Israel, that he may minister unto me in the priest's office, even Aaron, Nadab and Abihu, Eleazar and Ithamar, Aaron's sons.* **(Exodus 28:1)**

> *For I am the least of the apostles, that am not meet to be called an apostle, because I persecuted the Church of God. But by the grace of God I am what I am: and his grace which was bestowed upon me was not in vain; but I laboured more abundantly than they all: yet not I, but the grace of God which was with me.* **(1 Corinthians 15:9-10)**

Though Aaron's oratorical skill was noted the first time he was introduced in the Bible, he was not made a priest until he was trained and consecrated unto the Lord by a servant of God. Also Apostle Paul was well trained in a lot of fields but the office of leadership was bestowed upon him. He didn't usurp or encroach it!
That you attend Bible school prepares you for Church leadership and priesthood but does not make you one. You still needed to be ordained by a Church to minister. You can not confer honour on yourself in a normal social setting. That is ridiculous.
Doing that in the thing of God shows a lack of reverence for God. Such highly dishonourable conduct shows how indecent, irreverent and moraless some ambitious people have become in the work of

God. You do not call and confirm yourself into the 5 fold ministry except you are called by God. Don't let any blind leader of the blind lie to you that you can just wake up and declare yourself minister. Which great man of God in the Bible or in this generation came to ministry that way? Church leadership requires the backing of the Lord. Not everyone can be a Church leader.

> *But in a great house there are not only vessels of gold and of silver, but also of wood and of earth; and some to honour, and some to dishonour. If a man therefore purge himself from these, he shall be a vessel unto honour, sanctified, and meet for the master's use, and prepared unto every good work.*
> ***(2 Timothy 2:20-21)***

Many are called but few are chosen!
The chosen process is however determined by man. Many are failed by character deficiency, some by spiritual immaturity and some by simple impatience. To ascend the honourable leadership position among the people of the Lord, there are sailent attributes to possess.

ATTRIBUTES OF KINGDOM LEADERSHIP

There are certain attitudes and behaviours that are inherent to kingdom leadership. These are core values that cannot be separated from the personality of the minister of God.
I will now discuss certain qualities that anyone genuinely wants to serve God must have before he or she can consider self worthy and ready to serve God.

1) Godliness

> *Except the LORD build the house, they labor in vain that build it: except the LORD keep the city, the watchman waketh but in vain. It is vain for you to rise up early, to sit up late, to eat the bread of sorrows: for so he giveth his beloved sleep.* ***(Psalm 127:1-2)***

> *Wherefore, brethren, look ye out among you seven men of honest report, full of the Holy Ghost and wisdom, whom we may appoint over this business.*
> ***(Acts 6:3)***

God's presence and back up is all that we celebrate in ministry.
If God does not call you, whatever you end up building is in vain.

It will crumble down one day and all your labours and sleepness nights would all have been in vain. It takes complete trust in God to submit yourself under rigorous training to be qualified for His work. To be godly means that you have permitted Jesus Christ to be fully formed in you. In the early Church, it is required that people aspiring for leadership be filled with the Holy Spirit.
The proof that you are filled with the Holy Spirit will be demonstrated by the fruits of the spirit operating in your life.

> *But the fruit of the Spirit is love, joy, peace, longsuffering, gentleness, goodness, faith, Meekness, temperance: against such there is no law. And they that are Christ's have crucified the flesh with the affections and lusts.* **(Gal. 5:22-24)**

A godly leader needs to have unconditional love for God people however troublesome and difficult they might be. Such needs to be able to control anger and suffer long in a difficult situation.

2) Self- discipline

> *For this cause left I thee in Crete, that thou shouldest set in order the things that are wanting, and ordain elders in every city, as I had appointed thee: If any be blameless, the husband of one wife, having faithful children not accused of riot or unruly. For a bishop must be blameless, as the steward of God; not selfwilled, not soon angry, not given to wine, no striker, not given to filthy lucre; But a lover of hospitality, a lover of good men, sober, just, holy, temperate.* **(Titus 1:5-16)**

> *A bishop then must be blameless, the husband of one wife, vigilant, sober, of good behaviour, given to hospitality, apt to teach; Not given to wine, no striker, not greedy of filthy lucre; but patient, not a brawler, not covetous; One that ruleth well his own house, having his children in subjection with all gravity; (For if a man know not how to rule his own house, how shall he take care of the Church of God?) Not a novice, lest being lifted up with pride he fall into the condemnation of the devil. Moreover he must have a good report of them, which are without; lest he fall into reproach and the snare of the devil. Likewise must the deacons be grave, not doubletongued, not given to much wine, not greedy of filthy lucre.* **(1 Timothy 3:2-8)**

Discipline is a requirement for every disciple of Christ. The work of God is not for stubborn touts. It is not for irreverent roughians and social scoundrels who have no honour for God or servants of God. Until you show tangible proof that you can obey instructions, discipline yourself and lead your family, no one should submit themselves under your leadership. Kingdom Leadership begins with leading yourself in an exemplary way that is instructive to others. For your congregation to be law abiding, they need to be convinced of your ability and willingness not only to enforce rules but also to honour and obey them. Only committed servants become great leaders. Until you show proof of having served others profitably, no one should submit under your leadership. To be qualified to lead God's people, there must be some salient attributes in you that prepare and confirm you for the role.

While every Christian deserves additional pious living, such requirements are obligatory for those occupying position of leadership like Bishops, Pastors, Deacons and elders. In addition to observing some spiritual and moral standard, there are some peculiar characters and attitudes that a godly leader must possess in order to perform his duties objectively, honourable, effectively and perfectly.

- Blameless and orderly (Titus 1:5-6, 1 Tim. 3: 2, 12).
- Practice monogamy (Titus 1: 6, 1 Tim. 3:2) or remain single (1 Cor. 9: 5).
- Leads a disciplined home (Titus 1: 6; 1 Tim 3: 4 –6, 11).
- Self disciplined (Titus 1:7 , 1 Tim. 3:3).
- Non alcoholic lifestyle (Titus 1:7).
- Hospitable (Titus 1:8, 1 Tim. 3:2, 1 Pet 4: 9; Rom 12: 13).
- Sober and temperate. (Titus 1:8; Titus 2: 2;4- 5; 1 Tim. 3:2-3,11; 2 Tim. 1:7).
- Not covetous and corrupt (Titus 1:8; 1 Tim. 3:3; Heb. 13: 5; Luke 12:15).
- Indoctrinated (Titus 1:9-10, 13-14; 1 Tim. 3: 6, 10; 2 Tim. 2: 15; Titus 3: 9-11).
- Exemplary Trainer (1 Tim. 3:2; Rom. 1: 16; 2 Tim. 3: 16; 1 Pet. 1: 23, Titus 1: 7-9; 1 Tim. 2: 3-13).
- Honest. Just with a good report. (Titus 1: 12 ; 1 Tim. 3: 7, 13, 1 Tim. 5: 1-6,21).

3) Visionary

And the LORD answered me, and said, Write the vision, and make it plain upon tables, that he may run that readeth it. **(Habakkuk 2:2)**

Where there is no vision, the people perish **(Proverbs 29:18)**

Every leader must have a vision that drives his passion for the work of God and motivates others to follow him.
Leaders need to inspire and promote new ideas and knowledge that help to accomplish the joint purpose of the organization.
Nothing concentrates energy and focus priority as a clear vision.
From the onset, everyone in the organisation needs not only to know what to do and what not to do.
They should also know why they do what they do.
They should never be wasting their energy on frivolous things.

> *The labor of the foolish wearieth every one of them, because he knoweth not how to go to the city. Woe to thee, O land, when thy king is a child, and thy princes eat in the morning!* **(Ecclesiastes 10:15-16).**

> *This one thing I do, forgetting those things which are behind, and reaching forth unto those things which are before. I press toward the mark for the prize of the high calling of God in Christ Jesus.* **(Philippians 3:13-14)**

No matter how anointed you are, if you lack vision, you will be wearied down without any tangible result. Vision helps you to reach forward for your goals without losing focus to any diversions. Vision saves you from fruitlessness and guides you to the realm of productivity.
In the business realm, being efficient is differentiated from being effective. While being efficient is doing things right, being effective is doing the right thing. If I will give you my shirt to iron so that I can wear it to Church in thirty minutes and you decide to wash it first that by the time I return to wear it to my occasion you are still waiting for it to dry, you are not effective! Being effective has to do with achieving what you are instructed to do while being efficient simply means doing things well. Mind you, it is a great idea to wash a shirt considered dirty but it is a different ball game entirely from the original intention of the person giving instruction. Many Churches are buried in religious activity that has no bearing with God's expectation for the body of Christ. I was shocked to hear how many millions of dollars particular orthodox denomination reserves for the legal bill and public relations. Such money should have been spent on soul winning missions! Jesus main priority in life was to save sinners. Nowadays, you will be shocked by the irrelevance of many activities in the body of Christ. Some pastors even have time to baptise

animals. I am not against that service but I totally doubt if Church is the right place to do that. Many Churches nowadays never hold one outreach crusade in a year and they keep screaming for Holy Spirit. Holy Spirit is not meant for social enjoyment among Christians. It is the power of God to win souls for Christ. Clear vision always builds an atmosphere of unity and harmony around the purpose of an organisation.

Are you goal oriented?
Great leaders are recognized mostly for the main goal they chose to exchange their lives for. You too can learn to cultivate the habit of going out a day to dream purposeful dreams and write them down.
Then proceed to expand the dreams. Allow your life goals to be expandable as your life horizon widens.
Setting a goal is very easy to do.

- Set out a goal. Put it down on paper with a deadline.
- Set out a strategy and means of measuring milestones.
- Plan out your problems
- Build in reserve (mental, physical, financial, spiritual resources etcetera) to ensure the realisation of your dream.
- Relate to time frame. Time is an opportunity looking for a course. Wasting time is wasting your life.
- Create a master plan to get the plan done.
- Start acting now!

4) Passionate doer (actor)

For as the body without the spirit is dead, so faith without works is dead also. (James 2:26)

Talking without acting makes a charlatan of a man!
Leadership is action, not position. The only thing necessary for the triumph of evil is for good men to do nothing.
People may doubt what you say, but they will believe what you do.
By their fruits we shall know them. If you want your dreams to come true, don't over sleep. Wake up and work it out.
It is when you walk your talk that your habit carries its merit.

Are you hard working?

> *For a dream cometh through the multitude of business; and a fool's voice is known by multitude of words.* **(Ecclesiastes 5:3)**

> *Seest thou a man diligent in his business? he shall stand before kings; he shall not stand before mean men.* **(Proverbs 22:29)**

The only way to become what you want to become is to direct all your efforts at becoming it.
We have an equal opportunity to be unequal in distinction.
Your action and inaction determine your position and the level of your unction. You are not limited by your circumstances but by your diligence. Men decide their habits, their habits decide their future!
It takes various efforts to turn desire into reality. Labour is only a laboratory where a man's desire manifests into reality. God's blessing is available for His creatures but only laboures activate it.
For whatsoever he shall prosper (Psalms 1:3b).

5) Good Communicator

> *And the LORD answered me, and said, Write the vision, and make it plain upon tables, that he may run that readeth it.* **(Habakkuk 2:2)**

It is the leadership's duty to make vision available for others to read and run with. However, a vision not understood is as good as a non-existing vision. It is the duty of leadership to communicate clearly and effectively the vision (objectives) and missions (actions taken to fulfil the objectives) of the community as well as the role each member is expected to play to achieve that end. Good communication helps members to identify with the Church by giving the opportunity to contribute their opinions to the leadership. Communication is a two way process of sending and receiving clear information between the leaders and the people. It is a way of painting the picture in your mind into the mind of other people in order to bring them together with you in the same unity of purpose. A good leader doesn't just know what to do, he knows how to bring other people around to understand it and be committed to doing it. Every leader must make it his or her duty to communicate the truth of God's word to the congregation in words and in actions. Lack of sufficient teaching will make bad members out of your congregation.

The conscious program should be drawn to feed members richly with the word of God if the life of the congregation must reflect knowledge of Christ at work, at home and at play. Every avenue and opportunity must be used to teach the word of God. Jesus Christ was exemplary in the use of parables, pictures, stories and slogans in bringing his information across to his congregation. There is no more powerful way to drive home a point to people of the Lord than the word of God. Taking our examples from the Bible helps us to communicate our purpose clearly among the people of the Lord. It is clever to brighten up some of the allegories in the Bible with modern illustrations. Jesus used terms like shepherd and vine with his people who lived in agricultural age to clearly communicate His points. In the Church I pastor, we call ministry leaders "Ministers" for instance, not shepherds. Many members never saw a shepherd all their lives so they may not get the meaning you are communicating. Many new members find it offending too when you call them sheep! Think about it, that a person just joins your Church doesn't mean he is a baby in the Lord. Many serious Christians changing work and environment end up in another city for fellowship. The point I am making it, we can still modernise some of our expressions to communicate with the 21st century man without compromising the word of God. The Church should make use of modern communication tools to communicate information to both internal and external parties. Some of the avenues that can be utilised to disseminate relevant information include pulpit, notice board, newsletters, bulletin and Internet website.

6) Solution provider

> *And it shall come to pass in the last days, that the mountain of the LORD's house shall be established in the top of the mountains, and shall be exalted above the hills; and all nations shall flow unto it. And many people shall go and say, Come ye, and let us go up to the mountain of the LORD, to the house of the God of Jacob; and he will teach us of his ways, and we will walk in his paths: for out of Zion shall go forth the law.* **(Isaiah 2:2-3)**

Every leader is a solution provider. It is only those who can offer a solution to difficult matters that can become market leaders. To be the best in your profession will cost you many sleepless nights and restless days. Show me a leading company or personality and I will show you a person who has tirelessly invested resources in

researching and finding out things others have not been able to locate. You will have to burn a lot of midnight oil to remain relevant in your field. Ministry of Christ in this modern day especially is not a place for a lazy and non-creative leader. The internet made available to everyone the best preachers and events like never before and the people have high expectation from their Churches than before. You are pitted in conscious and unconscious comparism with more experienced and well established ministers so the least you can afford to give is your very best if you want to remain relevant for your people. Nobody comes to Church to help a Church grow or for sheer commitment, people come foremost to be blessed and inspired and if they are not fulfilled once, they know lots of other big and well established Churches where their nereds can be met. Thank God that every minister has something very special to serve. You just need to find what that thing is, as a leader, and serve it at its very best.
Only your difference can distinguish you in the contemporary service of the Lord. Literally, you will smell of midnight oil if you will attract the attention of your generation. To look like Tarzan, you will have to run like a cheetah (his companion pet)!
Your search for excellence will most often take you to places you will naturally have preferred not to go but that amounts to paying the price. What you do not pursue you do not become!

7) Disciplinarian

Smite a scorner, and the simple will beware: and reprove one that hath understanding, and he will understand knowledge. **(Proverbs 19:25)**

Cast out the scorner, and contention shall go out; yea, strife and reproach shall cease. **(Proverbs 22:10)**

It is important to maintain an atmosphere of discipline and honour in the house of the Lord.
There cannot be discipleship without discipline. A good leader must be able, ready and willing to take up every form of ungodly opposition and rebellion in the Church immediately. Indiscipline like rebellion can be contagious and the quicker you deal with it the better for everyone. It is not only good for the person you are correcting; it also serves as a teaching experience for other members of the congregation observing the situation. People hardly follow leaders they consider weak and easily intimidated. Act with strength and

dispatch to sanitise the house of the Lord. When you cast our scorner or douse strife, all forms of ungodly contention and strife shall seize! Every Church leader must be prepared to maintain sanity in the house of God of order, by readily confronting trouble makers, be they in the leadership or the congregation. The issue should be addressed and any form of errors and misconduct redressed.
The truth of the matter is that no problem disappears by ignoring it or sweeping it under the carpet.
There is only the danger that it will get worse and explosive.
Jesus Christ did not waste time in rebuking Peter after he took the liberty of his familiarity with his Master to abuse Him in the presence of other disciples. In fact Jesus Christ labelled his conduct as satanic.

And he spake that saying openly. And Peter took him, and began to rebuke him. But when he had turned about and looked on his disciples, he rebuked Peter, saying, Get thee behind me, Satan: for thou savourest not the things that be of God, but the things that be of men. (**Mark 8:32-33**)

Now I beseech you, brethren, mark them which cause divisions and offences contrary to the doctrine which ye have learned; and avoid them. For they that are such serve not our Lord Jesus Christ. (**Romans 16:17-18**)

Every act of disrespect and indiscipline directed against the institution of God should be promptly dealt with. You should be on the lookout for discontented members and appease their discomforts before it grows up to bitterness that can be misdirected in ways that can bring dishonour and discouragement into the service of God.

8) Role model

A bishop then must be blameless, the husband of one wife, vigilant, sober, of good behaviour, given to hospitality, apt to teach; Not given to wine, no striker, not greedy of filthy lucre; but patient, not a brawler, not covetous; One that ruleth well his own house, having his children in subjection with all gravity. (**1 Timothy 3:2-4**)

Any leader that will inspire and motivate others to follow him must be seen as transparently honest, sincere and loyal to the values of his organisation. It is by your fruit that you shall be known and related with. The characters of leaders are far more important than their looks, skills and abilities. People model after the personality of their leaders than after what they hear tsuch leaders say.

It is important that a leader should be apt to teach others, yet he must go a step ahead to demonstrate his instruction with his everyday action for people to get committed. If you preach on giving, you must be seen to have a giving lifestyle or your message will amount to nothing. A leader will always attract followers that fit his attitudes and conducts. Birds of the same feather will always flock together.

You need to show conviction and complete confident in your Church's vision before you can inspire others to trust in your leadership. It is easier to convince others of your ability only if you are convinced yourself. You need to be seen as ethical and morally sound, demonstrating your conviction practically by your lifestyle rather than words before you can hope to impress others.

While ethical values vary from organisation to another and from one country and race to another, godly virtues remain the same all over the world. The main source of values for every godly leader must remain the word of God. As you grow strong in godly virtues, you will be able to inspire confidence and love in your people who can then easily trust and rely on your integrity.

You need to inspire the congregation to grow up spiritually and take responsibility to raise others. If as a pastor you are still praying for members suffering from headache in your Church, when will the Church wake up to her God-given duty of saving the world?

9) Good delegator

> *And the LORD came down in a cloud, and spake unto him, and took of the spirit that was upon him, and gave it unto the seventy elders: and it came to pass, that, when the spirit rested upon them, they prophesied, and did not cease.* **(Numbers 11:25)**

One way God helped Moses to carry his leadership responsibility effectively is by passing the same anointing upon his life unto the seventy elders supporting him in the daily affirs of the people. You also can perform better by delegating less important diuties to your associates and subordinates while you focus on the most important duties. Better delegate your authority than relegate it.

You achieve more by giving part of your responsibilities to competent subordinates (to accomplish on your behalf great standard results rather by just pilling everything upon yourself.)

The less you delegate to others the less you permit them to grow up and accept leadership roles. Worse still, the more you lose concentration and sharp ability to be effectively productive.

10) Motivator

Be ye followers of me, even as I also am of Christ. (**1 Corinthians 11:1**)

A good leader should be able to motivate his followers to work with passion and commitment. Your lifestyle should be a living example from where others could copy virtuous living.
Your vision and doctrine should also be seen to be sound and consistent. Test your stand before you expose it for others consumption lest people stop to take your stand serious.
Either through your exemplary living or sound indoctrination and preaching of divine principles, you should be able to inspire and motivate your people to climb any obstacle coming to their ways in other to move to the other side where victory and breakthrough await them as rewards. Your passionate commitment to the achievement of group goal is a contagious means to commit others to participate. If it is worth all the strength of a trusted leader, it must worth it for the followers!

11) The epitome of positive personality traits

For a bishop must be blameless, as the steward of God; not selfwilled, not soon angry, not given to wine, no striker, not given to filthy lucre; But a lover of hospitality, a lover of good men, sober, just, holy, temperate; Holding fast the faithful word as he hath been taught, that he may be able by sound doctrine both to exhort and to convince the gainsayers. (**Titus 1:7-9**)

People learn more from what you do than what you say so it is important to cultivate positive attitudes that you expect your congregation to copy. Some of the attitudes a leader should exemplify includes the following:

a) Consistency
A leader must be predictably consistent in the pursuit of vision and goals. He needs to be bold enough to stick with the decision considered right even in the face of opposition. Church situation is no political arena where one allows self to be swayed by clever

argument or pressure. What God says on any situation is final and must be pursued uncompromisingly.

b) Persistence
Successful people in life never give up.
Great men always rise higher after their fall.
A crisis will always occur at the curve of change!
There can be no testimony without a test or a change of position without opposition. The greatest limitation of life is one placed on oneself. Beyond passion and action, it takes dedication and commitment to fulfil the will of God. David, Joseph and other powerful men of God had to triumph over their temptations with great determination to go all the way to the end in faith.

c) Honesty
The way to peoples' heart is honesty.
Let people know what you stand for and your life will be easier.
When people know that they can trust your words and conviction to deliver what you promise, they will show greater commitment to what they commit themselves to achieve with you. Dishonesty will deprive you of acceptance and co-operation of those who will make a difference in the fulfilment of your calling. Be honest to yourself by living a transparent life of honesty with others.

d) Accessible
Do not allow your status and position to remove you from the reach of people you have been sent to serve. Be genial, friendly, humble and approachable. How else can people confide in you when they do not feel free with you? I have met many leaders who look so serious that you could cry for them. Do not take yourself too seriously to the extent that you have no room for laughter. Be yourself.
Laugh when you feel like and cry when there is a need for it.
People trust leaders who demonstrate human feelings than the personality of steel. Jesus Christ laughed, moaned and cried.
Nothing is wrong with showing your emotion if you can control it in a way that it does not degenerate to excesses of indiscipline.
Be free to be yourself. Only then can people feel free to be with you.

e) Teachable
A leader is a natural learner. Scientists found out that the most ardent reader never uses up to 5% of the total intelligence capacity.

We all need to improve our latent capacity to learn new solutions to our problems. You have the ability for progressive improvement. You should never have a better yesterday!

f) Enduring

Jesus Christ endured the cross to ascend the throne of grace.
Godly endurance is your step to godly abundance.
Endurance is a measure of self-discipline. You know how to go the extra one mile to get your goal achieved. One of the watch words for an enduring man is, balance. To endure doesn't mean you need to run yourself mad till you break down. You need to master your strength and know when to stop and refresh your strength.
Many great leaders break down before learning to slow down!
Master your anger, do not blow up! Exploding quite often in anger or bitterness against those working with you could lower your self-esteem and destroy your health.

g) Relaxation

Taking a break saves you from breakdown.
Relaxation enhances your effectiveness.
Always find time to relax your body and soul from fatigue, exhaustion and anger. Lack of sufficient relaxation may lead to system breakdown. A well-maintained car for an additional small cost of service will no doubt outperformed one that is used without service. Repair mostly cost more than maintenance!
Why will you waste precious time recovering from exhaustion in the hospital when you could save more time by relaxing at the right time. Better be late in your project than become late.

h) Boldness

Be strong to carry out your conviction regardless of initial discouragement you may suffer from people disowning or distancing themselves from you. Every great man once suffered rejection. It is normal for people who do not see what you see to doubt you. You will be harming yourself if you distrust yourself. Let your action demonstrate your conviction and let posterity justify you. So long your goal is located correctly in the will of God and it is not intended to harm God's work, your neighbour or yourself, go on and prove your point. Those who never took risk never won victory. Until you follow your dream, you have no hope to see it fulfilled!

OTHER LEADERSHIP TRAITS

1. Committed to goals
2. Communicative
3. Conciliatory
4. Courageous (bold)
5. Discriminative
6. Effective
7. Focussed
8. Goal oriented
9. Good listener
10. Independent decision maker
11. Independent thinker
12. Innovative
13. Inspires confidence
14. Learn continuously
15. Loving
16. Motivative
17. Passionate
18. Relaxed when dissapointed
19. Result oriented
20. Self-confident
21. Self-disciplined
22. Selfless
23. Serving attitude
24. Social
25. Trustworthy

CHAPTER 8: A CALL TO SERVICE

And he sat down, and called the twelve, and saith unto them, If any man desire to be first, the same shall be last of all, and servant of all. (Mark 9:35)

*But Jesus called them to him, and saith unto them, Ye know that they which are accounted to rule over the Gentiles exercise lordship over them; and their great ones exercise authority upon them. 43 but so shall it not be among you: but whosoever will be great among you, shall be your minister: 44 and whosoever of you will be the chiefest shall be a **servant of all**. 45 For even the Son of man came not to be ministered unto, but to minister, and to give his life a ransom for many. (Mark 10:42-45)*

Leadership is a call to service!
That is why a good leader is a person that is able to lead himself to serve others. You must be committed to serving honestly your brethren to be qualified to lead them. Having a serving attitude is very important even more than the service you offer.
Leadership is a personal service rendered for the purpose of all.
Only selfless people who put other peoples' need above their personal needs merits been given a leadership position.
Leaders are not schemers or self-professed masters who scramble for positions and public recognition rather they are value-adding servants who habitually satisfy the needs of the people. Every organisation owes itself the duty of checking out people's past records to verify their commitment to working for public interest before committing their fates in to such people's hand. This way, who ever gets elected or appointed to the office will not go there to cheat, oppress or exploit his authority for personal enrichment.
Kingdom leadership is basically a servant leadership that thrives on serving mankind as uniquely exemplified in the sacrificial life of Jesus Christ and other great men of God like Apostle Paul.

A good leader is a person that is able to lead himself to serve others.

THE 8 P's OF SERVICE

For David, after he had served his own generation by the will of God, fell on sleep. **(Acts 13:36)**

Many people will like to remember King David as a great ruler who reigned over his subjects but Bible by divine inspiration referred to him as a servant. It is King David's service to his people that earned him greatness not his status and titles as Bible is dotted with many wicked kings who are remembered for nothing great!

Great people of God documented in various chapters of the Bible are exemplars of virtues in the way they rendered services to other people. Though their callings were different from each other, they all had a great balance of what I coined the "Seven P's of service". These are **Power, Purpose, Product, People, Plan, Place and Period** of services. All these seven variables are so much interelated that changing one will easily affect the performance of others.

1) POWER (With what authority do I serve?)

And God wrought special miracles by the hands of Paul: So that from his body were brought unto the sick handkerchiefs or aprons, and the diseases departed from them, and the evil spirits went out of them. **(Acts 19:11-12)**

God also bearing them witness, both with signs and wonders, and with divers miracles, and gifts of the Holy Ghost, according to his own will? **(Heb. 2:4)**

It is God that confirms His words with signs and wonders and diverse miracles! Every auction and virtues that any prophet or ministry leader lay claims to is from God. Not personal.

Nothing can be achieved without power. Knowing the authority that backs up your service helps determine the strength of your conviction and determination and the extent of your exploits.

Many anointed preachers will let you know that the most important thing that determines their entry in to ministry is the assurance of the calling of God in their lives. Ministry is no field you go because you feel you can quote scriptures profoundly or because you think you are a natural orator. Though Aaron was a natural orator, God called Moses, a stammerer to lead his people! Though David was the least good looking and muscular in his princely family, God instructed Prophet Samuel to anoint him as king.

What a shock for his father and brothers!
The same God who chose Moses to lead and appointed Aaron to serve as High Priest organized for both men to be ordained and consecrated for service. Only then did He released power upon them to back up their services.

> *For every high priest taken from among men is ordained for men in things pertaining to God, that he may offer both gifts and sacrifices for sins: And no man taketh this honour unto himself, but he that is called of God, as was Aaron.* **(Hebrews 5:1, 4)**

> *Faithful is he that calleth you, who also will do it.* **(1 Thess. 5:24)**

It is the power of God that is celebrated in any ministry!
So if you have not beeen called for any role, do not curse yourself by becoming an impostor. It is the calling of God that gives you great assurance and reassurance in your service years as you go through difficult and challenging situations that you cannot understand.
Joseph refused to commit adultery with Potiphar's wife because he did not want to sin against his God (Gen 39: 8-9). He saw the situation as a test of his devotion to God rather than human conduct of immorality against man. It is this view that put him in favour of God who lifted him above all his problems and installed him as a Prime Minister in a foreign land he entered as a slave. The three Hebrew men were able to face the threat of fire by their trust in God.

> *Shadrach, Meshach, and Abed-nego, answered and said to the king, O Nebuchadnezzar, we are not careful to answer thee in this matter. If it be so, our God whom we serve is able to deliver us from the burning fiery furnace, and he will deliver us out of thine hand, O king. But if not, be it known unto thee, O king, that we will not serve thy gods, nor worship the golden image which thou hast set up.* **(Daniel 3:16-18)**

Knowing the God you serve is the first step to making exploit in ministry! You can not make any difference in life until you recognise and acknowledge God in all areas of your life.

> *But the people that do know their God shall be strong, and do exploits.* **(Daniel 11:32)**

> *Abide in me, and I in you. As the branch cannot bear fruit of itself, except it abide in the vine; no more can ye, except ye abide in me. I am the vine, ye are*

> *the branches: He that abideth in me, and I in him, the same bringeth forth much fruit: for without me ye can do nothing.* ***(John 15:4-5)***

Yes, without God, you can do nothing.
However with Him, nothing will be impossible. So long you are where God places you, everything will work together for your own good as you daily operate according to His purpose (Rom. 8: 28).

2) PURPOSE (Why do I serve?)

> *He saith unto him the third time, Simon, son of Jonas, lovest thou me? Peter was grieved because he said unto him the third time, Lovest thou me? And he said unto him, Lord, thou knowest all things; thou knowest that I love thee. Jesus saith unto him, Feed my sheep.* ***(John 21:17)***

> *And he gave some, apostles; and some, prophets; and some, evangelists; and some, pastors and teachers; For the perfecting of the saints, for the work of the ministry, for the edifying of the body of Christ.* ***(Eph. 4:11-12)***

Meritorious service depends on the existence of clearly existing vision. Your vision not only focuses your energy on what to do but also reduces your loss by stating what not to do.
The clearer the purpose behind your service, the more concentrated and focussed you can direct your resources to reach your end.
This will make room for quality and distinguished service in any area of your assignment in life. For instance, it is not sufficient to pastor a Church; it must be done effectively to the glory of God!
You see. Any ass can preach!
The ass of Balaam didn't just preach; he went on to save its master's life (Num 22:28-30). It however remains the main intention of God that man should be the main messenger of His message to sons of men. In doing this, God expects His chosen messengers to minister with wisdom and grace. A man of God is expected to be well trained so that his ministration is devoid of folly smells and profane babbling that are hallmarks of mediocrity. The fact however remains that many Pastors have no Bible and Pastoral training, both formal and informal. They have no higher education and never took any course in leadership. It is no surprise that with poor knowledge of their duty and the psychology of their people, many men of God could not deliver. They depend on experience, advice and loyalty of people to remain in the office rather than focusing on God.

That is why it is essential for a man of God to be well indoctrinated in the biblical instructions and principles for optimal leadership of God people.

> **So long you are where God places you, everything will work together for your own good as you daily operate according to His purpose**

Service areas in Church

The Church in the pervading atmosphere of self freedom of the computer age needs godly men of impeccable characters to direct and instruct the body of Christ according to the will of God.

The Church needs adequate leadership in the following areas of Church activities on day to day basis.

a) **Doctrinal**

   All scripture is given by inspiration of God, and is profitable for doctrine, for reproof, for correction, for instruction in righteousness. **(2 Timothy 3:16)**

   Dead flies cause the ointment of the apothecary to send forth a stinking savour: so doth a little folly him that is in reputation for wisdom and honour. **(Ecclesiastes 10:1)**

   Of these things put them in remembrance, charging them before the Lord that they strive not about words to no profit, but to the subverting of the hearers. **(2 Timothy 2:14)**

b) **Fellowship**

   Thou shalt love the Lord thy God with all thy heart, and with all thy soul, and with all thy mind. This is the first and great commandment. And the second is like unto it, Thou shalt love thy neighbour as thyself. On these two commandments hang all the law and the prophets. **(Matthew 22:37-40)**

   Not forsaking the assembling of ourselves together, as the manner of some is; but exhorting one another: and so much the more, as ye see the day approaching. **(Hebrews 10:25)**

c) **Prayer**

   Praying always with all prayer and supplication in the Spirit, and watching thereunto with all perseverance and supplication for all saints. **(Eph. 6:18)**

   And he said unto them, This kind can come forth by nothing, but by prayer and fasting. **(Mark 9:29)**

d) **Evangelism**

   Go ye therefore, and teach all nations, baptizing them in the name of the Father, and of the Son, and of the Holy Ghost: Teaching them to observe all things whatsoever I have commanded you: and, lo, I am with you alway, even unto the end of the world. Amen. **(Matthew 28:19-20)**

e) **Divine ministration**

   That confirmeth the word of his servant, and performeth the counsel of his messengers. **(Isaiah 44:26)**

   Is any sick among you? let him call for the elders of the Church; and let them pray over him, anointing him with oil in the name of the Lord: And the prayer of faith shall save the sick, and the Lord shall raise him up; and if he have committed sins, they shall be forgiven him. **(James 5:14-16)**

f) **Spiritual impartation**

   For I long to see you, that I may impart unto you some spiritual gift, to the end ye may be established. **(Romans 1:11)**

   For this cause we also, since the day we heard it, do not cease to pray for you, and to desire that ye might be filled with the knowledge of his will in all wisdom and spiritual understanding. **(Collosians 1:9)**

g) **General Administration**

   And in those days, when the number of the disciples was multiplied, there arose a murmuring of the Grecians against the Hebrews, because their widows were neglected in the daily ministration. Then the twelve called the multitude of the disciples unto them, and said, It is not reason that we

> *should leave the word of God, and serve tables. Wherefore, brethren, look ye out among you seven men of honest report, full of the Holy Ghost and wisdom, whom we may appoint over this business. But we will give ourselves continually to prayer, and to the ministry of the word.* **(Acts 6:1-4)**

> *Now we exhort you, brethren, warn them that are unruly, comfort the feebleminded, support the weak, be patient toward all men. See that none render evil for evil unto any man; but ever follow that which is good, both among yourselves, and to all men.* **(1 Thessalonians 5:14-15)**

Church duty is both spiritual and physical.

That is because, though man is a spirit, he relates in the physical world with the responsibility to satisfy social requirements as much as the spiritual needs. The first sets of Christians faced this need right from the beginning of Christianity and every church will have to cope with the same reality. Church leaders are expected to offer leadership for all forms of association in the house of the Lord. They are to provide visions, shape goals and provide for the emotional and spiritual need of the people.

3) PRINCIPLE (How do I serve?)

> *The labour of the foolish wearieth every one of them, because he knoweth not how to go to the city. Woe to thee, O land, when thy king is a child, and thy princes eat in the morning!* **(Ecclesiastes 10:15-16)**.

A clear purpose and vision should lead to the formulation of operating principles to guide your organisation to the end you have in view. It is one thing to have a vision; it is another thing to have clear principles to make the achievement of the vision possible.

Principles are guiding rules for your behaviours and are applicable in all situations. It is a constant reaction expected in varying situations.

If your principle is to trust and praise God for all things, it wouldn't matter if you are in a bad or good situation, you will continue to trust and praise Him. When you see the story of Joseph in the Bible, he did not allow changes in his status and situation to halt the achievement of his dream because he was soundly principled. His disciplined lifestyle born out of his godly principles brought him recognition and promotion not only in Potiphar's house but also in the prison where he spent years for the offence he didn't commit. Remaining true to himself throughout his trials, his principles soon led him to become Prime Minister of a foreign country he entered as a slave. The same situation happened to Daniel who was too principled to stop his three timely prayer session to God even at the face of the threat from the King of the land and other ministers that conspired against him. Rather than being destroyed, his principle led to his promotion. Principle puts you on course regardless of emotional and situational distraction.

You see, the principle makes all the difference between a predictable man and an undependable and unpredictable one.

It helps to direct your attitudes towards an expected end.

Though a foolish man may have a good vision of going to the city, he nonetheless will grow weary as he wastes his resources everywhere if he lacks systematic rules on how to pursue his lofty goals.

A man with lofty goals and no principle is likened in this verse to a childish king or an indolent prince. It makes a great difference in life to have principles to hinge your life accomplishment on. That is why you can almost not find a reasonable organisation (be it Church, company, ministry or club) with no mission statement. Your mission statement should, at least, contain your vision (that is your intention, "what we want to do"), mission (that is your modus operandi) and action ("what we are doing") and principles (values upon which our intention and actions are based).

4) PRODUCT (What do I have to serve?)

And in those days, when the number of the disciples was multiplied, there arose a murmuring of the Grecians against the Hebrews, because their widows were neglected in the daily ministration. Then the twelve called the multitude of the disciples unto them, and said, It is not reason that we should leave the word of God, and serve tables. Wherefore, brethren, look ye out among you seven men of honest report, full of the Holy Ghost and wisdom, whom we may appoint over this business. But we will give ourselves continually to prayer, and to the ministry of the word. And the saying pleased the whole multitude.
(Acts 6:1-5)

In general, every man has his areas of weakness and strength.

Your area of advantages in life identifies the divine deposits you are created to serve. It is the ability to locate where your purpose is needed that makes you relevant and most valuable.

I. **Area of gifting**

The gifts and callings of a man are without repentant! What are the talents that distinguish you above average person? What do you do naturally well than other people? Everyone has talents given to him or her to occupy until God comes back (Matt 25: 14-30).

II. **Area of calling**

This has nothing to do with your natural abilities. It is God's ability working in you (1 Thes 5:24). Do you have any supernatural anointing to perform duties? When the Apostles faced the problem of satisfying the administrative needs of their people, they chose to remain focussed on their callings of serving the word rather than the table. Every thing and every man on earth is created for a purpose. No service is inferior only everyone has different roles to play.

If you are talented to be an usher, or a chorister, fine, do it!

III. **Area of experience**

Some people become policemen because of the problems of insecurity they faced as a youth. Sometimes your suffering prepares you to serve in a special way. If his parents had not maltreated him, David would not have graduated from the leadership school of wilderness to triumph over Goliath.

IV. **Area of passion**

What drives you and ingests you with strength? Bill gates' passion for softwares made him one of the richest man on earth.

V. **Area of profession**

Sometimes, what you do in life is simply your desire (Ps. 37:4).

God loves to grant your heart desires. If you do not locate any particular talents or calling in your life, then you can freely choose! What are you trained to do? Use your skill! Paul was a great scholar and God used him to write almost half of the New Testament of the Bible. That was what other illiterate Apostles couldn't have achieved.

Every one just needs to locate his or her area of calling and serve it.

Peter identified his weakness and strength when he saw the lame man at the gate of beautiful and then went on to serve his strength.

He simply limited himself to the area of his divine calling.

You may also locate your service through any of the avenues of; prophecy, presents (divine gifting), practice, passion and personal preference. Whichever way you locate it, you need to consciously improve your performance through training and enhance your confidence through practice.

Sometimes, what we serve changes as God promotes us in ministry or as we grow in skills and experience. David first served as a shepherd and later as a military man and still later as a king. The good thing is that as you carry along past knowledge and experience for your new calling, your service becomes richer even as you grow more specialised. As a primary school boy, I was in my Church choir. As an adult, I became a Sunday school teacher and bulletin publisher for my Church. I was soon called to start a ministry in the Church and after some other roles and indepth thelogical training, I was later sent out to start a new branch for the Church.

I have in the professional realm worked also as a political scientist, a magazine publisher, information technology system engineer and later as a business manager (MBA). I enjoyed my duties perfectly in all these positions and today as a pastor of a Church, I feel all the more accomplished and contended sice all my earlier careers seemecd to have prpered me for my present duties. Nothing in my past experiences both as a lay worker in the Church or as a trained professional is wasted but all work together perfectly to help me serve my calling better. I could do many things on my own without calling for any professional support.

Every training and experience you go through is valuable for your life's purpose. You will always find out that you are most equipped to serve a particular service more at a particular time.

There are different types of service that could be offered to an organisation and each of them is equally important. The Apostles' priority was to serve the word of God to the congregation. The need to satisfy the people's social need was also equally pressing and necessary that they had to make provisions to ordain other ministers to satisfy that aspect.

Leadership is simply finding a need and providing for it's fulfilment. That is how every service minded Christian should think. What a pity that many mistake Church to be a social club where they are served as a member or leader with special status. That is sheer carnality!

Leadership is about service not status!

David, for instance, served his own generation in different realms as shepherd, musician , warrior and King. Like David, you could be a top general and a king of a whole kingdom and still be a servant!

At every stage of development of David, he served the best skill he had to offer, using all the past knowledge and experience as additional strength to depend on. He served his way all the way up!
Never scheme your way into a position, serve to it and you will be well equipped and divinely backed up to offer distinguished service. Put your best into all you do, knowing you are doing it for the Lord, who in due time will promote you to serve in greater level!

> **You may also locate your service through any of the avenues of; prophecy, presents (divine gifting), practice, passion and personal preference. Whichever way you locate it, you need to consciously improve your performance through training and enhance your confidence through practice.**

5) PEOPLE (Who do I have to serve?)

For David, after he had served his own generation by the will of God, fell on sleep, and was laid unto his fathers, and saw corruption. **(Acts 13:36)**

Leaders are servants not rulers.
King David served his generation, so can you!
Your education, experience, training, relationship, status and passion, among many other things have prepared you to influence some particular group of people than others. As a doctor, the best people you can serve most are patients whose sickness falls within your speciality. As a traditional musician, the local folk and lovers of local music are the people who will mostly profit from your service. You need to analyse your talents and skills and search through webs of relationship you daily share with others to specifically identify the group you are most suited and best equipped to serve.
Man as a relational being, goes through routines of shared relationship with God and man every day. As you are reading my book, you are sharing a relationship of an "Author-reader" with me. In our lifetime webs of relationships, we affect some people and some people affect us. Due to your status and placement in people's

life, you are more disposed to offer profound service of great influence to some people than others.

The closer your association is to a person, the stronger your action can have an impact on their lives.

Distance or age need no more restrict such association, in this information age of the computer.

Many youths are affected by the lifestyle of their pop role models living a generation or a continent apart than that of their parents.

Who can I influence?

Your area of influence covers everyone within your area of leadership. Everyone under a family, civil authority, business and other vocational institution and Church organisations are directly under the influence and control of an authority.

As a parent, your children are under your major influence.

Your area of influence could be in depth or breadth.

You have depth influence for instance if you lead an organization that has several departments and missions (outreach ministry, music outreach, books and media outlets etc).

You have a breadth influence across your generation for instance if you play several leadership roles across different structures of authority in your society. You are not only recognised as a spiritual voice for your generation but also as a business leader, political authority, civil right activist, community leader etc. Joseph of Arimathaea who buried Jesus in his tomb was not just a disciple of Jesus Christ but also an influential political leader of his time. That was why Pilate could cave in to his request when other disciples out of fear have escaped out of the city.

Inboth cases, the size of your ministry and the wideness of its reach will determine the extent of your influence in your generation. Men of God like Dr. Yongi Cho of South Korea, Pastor Sunday Adelaja of Ukraine, Bishop David Oyedepo of Nigeria and Evangelists like Benny Hinn and Reynold Bonkie influence millions of souls all around the world through their highly broad and deeply populated ministry. As a Church leader, God has deposited lots of virtues in you for the profit of your congregation. However your congregation is not limited to the four walls of the Church. You can profit from internet technology and affect lives all over the world. You should use every available opportunity and technology to share knowledge and understanding of the word of God with your generation.

And I will give you pastors according to mine heart, which shall feed you with knowledge and understanding. (Jeremiah 3:15)

The way people honour their pastors and relate to them will determine what virtue that is released into their lives. When you hold any grudge against your spiritual father, you are only blocking your own breakthrough. It is important you reverence who impacts your life. Refuse to be offended by the people you learn from.

See time spent with them as quality time well invested. Only then could you tap into resources deposited in them for your own good.

Many people do not like their boss; no wonder their work places become a place of torture for them.

Many foreigners are filled with abusive language for their host nations. No wonder they are always unable to attract any blessing of the country to themselves. You only attract what you appreciate! That is why it is dangerous for parents to leave their children to the mercy of their ungodly idols. Both parents and children need to choose godly people as their role models in life if achieving God's purpose for their lives is their goal.

Spiritual duty of men of God includes guiding, and directing their congregation to achieve their needs within the purpose of God and the provisions of their Church. The leadership do not only formulate the goals and vision for their body, they also provide structures that will facilitate the achievement of such visions.

Such a structure should be clear in teaching and motivating members to achieve such values. In Christ international Church, our mandate is, "raising kingdom's ambassadors" and to do that , we observe our three foundational values, called the three L's are to:

1) Love the Lord with all your might
2) Love your neighbour like yourself
3) Lovingly lead people to Christ

The entire activities of the Church are built around the fulfilment of these visions and mandate. They determine what we do and what we do not do and how we do what we do!

Every leader is trained to show leadership by example by their commitment to the fulfilment of every policy of the house.

No decision is taken for the congregation without praying seriously and consulting God till divine direction is secured on the issue.

As a well-respected Priest, be careful that you exercise your influence with the fear of the Lord for your impact in the lives of your congregation could become a matter of death and life, here and in the eternity. The congregation also needs to be careful that their Pastor is in rightstanding with the Lord and that he has enough time to devote to providing them with spiritual nourishment. A Church where members are premature and their Pastors do all the unnecessary jobs and spend quality time campaigning for giving of tithes and offering will miss a great deal of growth in wasted time.

How do I have an enduring influence?

a) Focus your training and influence on faithful associates

And the things that thou hast heard of me among many witnesses, the same commit thou to faithful men, who shall be able to teach others also.
(2 Timothy 2:2)

Though Jesus came to save the whole world (John 3: 17), He concentrated His whole teaching effort on twelve disciples. This decision is not meant to limit the scope of His mission but rather to concentrate His focus and energy on effectively grooming abled Apostles within His three and a half years ministry. That strategy worked for over two thousand years after, His ministry continues to wax bigger, wider and stronger. Jesus only concentrated on committed disciples who were able to multiply and reproduce His service to others.

Now when they saw the boldness of Peter and John, and perceived that they were unlearned and ignorant men, they marvelled; and they took knowledge of them, that they had been with Jesus. (**Acts 4:13**)

Only very close associates that understand and are committed to the vision of your ministry can share with you the burden to reach others. While the large crowd around your ministry see only your anointing, the close associates alone will recognise your human weakness and needs. You need to make a difference between these associates who can extend your service further and the public who have come to enjoy the blessing of your service. To the crowd, Jesus ministered from far, healing them and changing their sinful life but the teaching of His principles He taught clearly to His disciples in private. To the multitude, he only taught in parables.

> And with many such parables spake he the word unto them, as they were able to hear it. But without a parable spake he not unto them: and when they were alone, he expounded all things to his disciples. **(Mark 4:33-3)**
>
> And as he sat upon the mount of Olives, the disciples came unto him privately, saying, Tell us, when shall these things be? **(Matthew 24:3).**

At the beginning of my ministry, I used to confide in all the people hanging around me but with experience, I have come to see that not all so called leaders are committed. Many are around you for personal reasons and motives. Some are only hanging around to pick sufficient experience to launch out to pursue their selfish goals outside the church. Nowadays, unless I notice complete commitment in a minister (we call our ministry leaders ministers), I do not invest my time bringing him or her up to date with the vision of the Church for the future he or she might no more be around to witness. Though Elijah only found Elisha at the tail end of his ministry, he was able to pour himself to this committed assistant that through deep commitment and endurance was able to secure double portion of the anointing on his master's life. Even when Elijah advised Elisha to leave him, he refused! Could you imagine how many undependable assistants would have galloped away to declare their new found freedom and brand new ministry! Only committed and faithful subordinates can secure double portion anointing. Only such dependable ones can spread your influence far. As the hand that stretches forwards the torch light of your message, they are the future of productive ministry and deserve your utmost attention.

b) Do not seek to influence those who limit your influence

> Give not that which is holy unto the dogs, neither cast ye your pearls before swine, lest they trample them under their feet, and turn again and rend you. **(Matthew 7:6)**
>
> But he answered and said, It is not meet to take the children's bread, and to cast it to dogs. **(Matthew 15:26)**

Jesus instructed us by His exemplary action to verify that we invest more energy on those able to multiply our missions and services. The energy of the leadership should be invested more in reproducing leaders who can increase the progress of the work of God more than in creating followership wanting only to be fed forever rather than feeding others. Yes, leaders should relate to the public but not on the same deep and intimate level like they do with the core members of the leadership who have proven their commitment to the Lord and their faithfulness to the ministry beyond any reasonable doubt. People change and so should your treatment of them. As soon as you find out the insincerety and lack of commitment of people you place in position of authority, re-evaluate their contribution and position in the organisation. Putting the wrong person in the wrong place communicated the wrong thing about the organisation and this can easily discourage and dismotivate others with passion and potentials. Accessment and allocation of leaders is an ever on-going process in every dynamic organisation. Until you increase the fire of accessment, some people's real identity and quality will never be revealed. There is a big difference between being good and being qualified. Try as much as possible to place qualified people in the right places as soon as possible. Water will always find its position anyway. The problem with leaving people in the position they are not qualified to lead for so long is that they end up becoming disgruntled and discouraged and they may easily begin to peddle wrong information about the organisation to maintain their position or to rationalize their imperfection.

Not everyone responds well to training. That is just how it is in life!

While Elisha was a successful successor to Elijah, Elisha was less fortunate with Gehazi, his own assistant. Gehazi, though a top-level authority in Elisha's ministry was not a faithful and teachable assistant. He was a man with his own private agenda. Despite the entire miracles accompanying his master's ministry, he believed he knew more than the man of God. He was many time disobedient and non-submissive contrary to the biblical injunction (Heb 13: 17).

At the end of the story, his greed did not only destroy him but also his entire household (2 Kings 5: 20-27). Elisha died without a successor to take over the staff of his prophetic ministry.

He went to his grave with all his anointing (2 Kings 13: 21).

Strict accessment of your close associates can save you future of regrets. Accept the reality that some of your hitherto faithful people may lose their commitment and ranks while some from the outside circle may grow in commitment to join the inside circle of leaders.

> *But in a great house there are not only vessels of gold and of silver, but also of wood and of earth; and some to honour, and some to dishonour. If a man*

therefore purge himself from these, he shall be a vessel unto honour, sanctified, and meet for the master's use, and prepared unto every good work.
(2 Timothy 2:20-21)

The selection process of those who partake in the intensive impartation is an ever-going process. Every one who purges himself can become a vessel of honour worthy of God's use!

Find the right location for your ministry

Except God spiritually guides you to choose a place, it is important that you choose a place closer to the people you want to serve.

The place should be convenient and public enough to attract people to benefit from your service. Locating your headquarters in a strategic location could save you lots of administrative costs in the future. Many times, when a ministry shift places too often, it always adds one problem or another to their programs.

Many variables may affect your location:

i) **Geographic segmentation**

If your ministry is benefiting mostly from a particular group for instance campus students, then it might be a good idea to locate into the campus or so close to them. If you focus on a particular racial group or community, you stand to make fast progress if you locate close to them.

ii) **Demographic segmentation**

Your ministry might attract people in particular age, educational standard or marital situation. You should secure relevant information from government body on areas where your ministry could offer the greatest help to the need of that particular segment of your focus.

iii) **Behavioural segmentation**

By observation, some particular programs at a particular time of the year attract crowds to your service. You should seek the face of God for confirmation in case those are pointers to a field God wants your ministry to major. In Christ International Church, we notice that far many people attend our services for new believers and we focus more resources there monthly to satisfy the growing needs. That need has led us to make some strategic decisions we would never have made earlier. We now have regular invitational service for this group and we change our service to cater for their needs, even showing cinemas with great Christian values as a starter to introduce them to life in the family of God.

iv) **Psychographic segmentation**

This depends on taking note of the taste, interests, opinions and lifestyles of the people in arranging your program. If people in your area like particular music, you may need to use it to communicate your gospel message to them. If they like coming to Church more on Saturday evening than Sunday morning, it might be a great idea to offer also an additional service on Saturdays. Like Paul, you need to use the lifestyle of people to minister to them (1 Cor.19:19-23).

c) **Invest time in cultivating links to relevant outsiders**

Every ministry needs powerful men in the society who can help to influence the government on behalf of the body of Christ.
Jesus Christ had His Nicodemus and Paul had his Zenas!

> *There was a man of the Pharisees, named Nicodemus, a ruler of the Jews: The same came to Jesus by night.* ***(John 3:1-2)***

> *Bring Zenas the lawyer and Apollos on their journey diligently, that nothing be wanting unto them.* ***(Titus 3:13)***

Jesus Christ made time to receive at night Nicodemus, a prominent Jewish ruler who could only afford to be seen with Jesus outside the scrutiny of the public. Jesus also had among His cherished company a rich politician called Joseph of Arimathaea. It was he who took the responsibility to give Jesus Christ an honoured burial after the disciples and other closed associates of Jesus Christ deserted Him and escaped for their lives. Joseph of Arimathaea, a powerful member of the council, was powerful and influential enough to confince Pilate to release for him the body of Christ.

> *When the even was come, there came a rich man of Arimathaea, named Joseph, who also himself was Jesus' disciple: He went to Pilate, and begged the body of Jesus. Then Pilate commanded the body to be delivered. And when Joseph had taken the body, he wrapped it in a clean linen cloth, And laid it in his own new tomb, which he had hewn out in the rock: and he rolled a great stone to the door of the sepulchre, and departed.* ***(Matt. 27:57-60)***

Jesus Christ had many rich and famous people in His ministry!
Not only Joseph Arimathaea was a disciple of Jesus. There was another affluent one who gave Him a brand new transporter (colt) to ride victoriously to Jerusalem. Another property owner offered Jesus

Christ and His disciples the top area of his house that Jesus used for the Last Supper. Often when Jesus travelled for ministration, His wealthy followers accompanied him in convoys of privately owned ships (Mark 4: 36).

The gospel of Christ can do better with rich accomplices!

Money is like the blood of gospel. It is a vehicle that transports gospel from one area to another. The gospel of Christ is free but the means of preaching it requires money. If Jesus needed such wealthy people around Him, we sure do too. The gospel of the kingdom of God will benefit greatly from the wealth of prominent people if men of God will disabuse their minds from the fear of being wrongly accused of courting and putting affluent people around them.

Ask great evangelists and international preachers the awful torture they go through always to gather sufficient fund to organise a most needed crusade. Many millions of souls are in danger of hell fire because the money needed to sponsor outreaches are not just available. Jesus didn't have such problem in His ministry. No wonder, with such men like Levi (the wealthy publican), Nicodemus (prominent Jewish ruler) and Arimathaea (influential politician) Jesus Christ never needed to make a never-ending fund raising.

How many people of influence you know in the seat of government, economic institutions, media outlets, and other relevant social institutions will determine how far your service would spread.

d) Target your public ministry to a broader audience

> *But ye shall receive power, after that the Holy Ghost is come upon you: and ye shall be witnesses unto me both in Jerusalem, and in all Judaea, and in Samaria, and unto the uttermost part of the earth.* **(Acts 1:8)**

The broad audience is the main benefactor of your service.

They are the people God has sent your way to minister to.

They have mostly come to take from you and not to give to you. They have come to receive benefits from you and not to assist you in accomplishing your mission. Yet they are as important as your close associates for without the multitude, you can not have a ministry. Every pastor knows without a congregation, there can not be a church. Jesus Christ understood these people. He tolerated some of them who attended His crusade to receive a solution to their needs. He also had to deal with some group that cam to trap and destroy Him. Jesus always used the evil plot of his critics as an opportunity to enlighten others through the display of divine wisdom. Such sidelines do not distract Jesus Christ from feeding the multitudes that came to Him spiritually and physically. He healed them, taught them, freed them of demons and converted them back to God.

He went through all odds to deliver His service to them.

That should be the ultimate vision of every minister. You do not have to submit to accusations, frustrations and every form of opposition from the enemy and his human messengers. Such will surely come your way to test your resolve to go on. They will come to obstruct you from offering your service to those God has sent you to. Beware that anything that will stop you from delivering your service to your audience will deny you of your reward in the Lord. Refuse to co-opearte with such an attack. You need to fight it, overcome it and climb it to reach a greater height in your ministry.

While you can only manage to impact the few closed people to you with a great vision of your ministry, the general message of your ministry should minister to a far-reaching audience.

In addition to having big Churches and many branches in every area possible, endeavour to use mass media to spread your message. You will reach more people trough television and radio broadcast, website, satelite stations and other means of mass communication. This age of information has many technologies that could help you reach the whole universe provided you have sufficient resources to acquire them. Every ministry should use such modern facilities to spread the gospel of Christ.

e) Do not waste your outreach efforts on sterile ground

And when ye come into an house, salute it. And if the house be worthy, let your peace come upon it: but if it be not worthy, let your peace return to you. And whosoever shall not receive you, nor hear your words, when ye depart out of that house or city, shake off the dust of your feet. **(Matthew 10:12-14)**

The biggest deception you can give yourself is to believe that your message is equally relevant to all people of the world because it is gospel. Something must be wrong with you if every body likes you.

Every one has a particular segment of people that responds to his service more than others. Even though technology could give you access to every region of the world, yet not everybody can flow with your ministry. If you notice a place where people are not responding to your message whatsoever you do, simply relocate to where people are responding positively. Every ministry is anointed to reach some particular type of people than another.

Even, some people did not receive the message of Jesus Christ.
The Pharisees and sadduccees refused His ministry (Matt 21: 23-27).
His own people disapproved of His personality and service.

> *Is not this the carpenter, the son of Mary, the brother of James, and Joses, and of Juda, and Simon? and are not his sisters here with us? And they were offended at him. But Jesus said unto them, A prophet is not without honour, but in his own country, and among his own kin, and in his own house. And he could there do no mighty work, save that he laid his hands upon a few sick folk, and healed them. And he marvelled because of their unbelief. And he went round about the villages, teaching.* **(Mark 6:3-6)**

Familiarity breeds contempt!
Jesus never fought this natural syndrome.
He simply ignored the doubting people and concentrated His focus on the highly expectant multitudes that followed Him everywhere.
Your anointing can not be greater than that of Jesus Christ.
Every body cannot and will not flow with you or approve of you!
It is important to find out the segment within the city, nation or world where your service is well received. Then move forward to find out the needs and taste of this segment in order to offer your service effectively to them. Every ministry has the duty of finding out where its message is most productive and concentrate on such areas to maximise the impact of its influence. Pastor Benny Hinn is a household name in Europe with his miracle service but in Africa, people only know the German evangelist, Reynold Bonkie.
The Lord's ministers' well known in America are not the ones favoured in Asia and Australia. Every minister needs to find out whom God has sent him or her to. That is the area your message will have a great impact and effect. Focus your energy there if having a hundred folds returns from your labour is your heart desire.

f) Master the art of advertising your services

> *The Lord gave the word: great was the company of those that published it.* **(Psalm 68:11)**

The Church needs value-expressive publicity and advertisement that are attractive and expressive of your service. Many people are refusing to listen to the gospel because many felt it is all to scare them with damnation and hell. The gospel is good news.

It is all about the love of God for a man not about the threat of damnation of hell. Church among all the institutions in this world has the greatest values to offer mankind. Everyone needs the assurance of a blessed and protected life now and thereafter.

Everyone needs love and God is love.

The Church should learn to attract people to herself with her great values and lovingly deliver the greatest news of salvation that no sane person will like to miss. Many Churches are falling to self-fulfilling prophecy trap of threat and condemnation through their outdated style of outreach and way of conducting service.

It is almost impossible to attract youth to a conservative church today without exerting one form of force or another.

Many churches have become a piece of antiques. They still dress as their great grand parents did centuries ago, continue to repeat the same old and boring songs, prefer to distribute leaflets regularly on the street as people jeered them and walked past etceteras.

Compare this to how ungodly information pops up on your screen each time you go on the Internet. Many churches are still travelling at snail speed in this computer age. Many churches seemed not to be aware of all the technological advancement going on every where. My son at the age of four was already talking about 50 and 100 thousand. He educated himself to be able to catch up with the Game Boy's rich offers of games. At his young age, I couldn't do many things that this young boy could do with computer devices and gadgets even when I attended university. Is it not a joke to want the same boy to be attracted to worship in the same way my forefather did?

We need to be careful not to lose all the next generation to the world. The Church needs to preach the pure word of the Lord but our approach and structures must be modernised if we do not want to lose the next generations to the ungodly lifestyle of the world.

I am sure that if Jesus will have to evangelize today, He will no more ride around on an ass but rather will be flying around in airplanes to have a far-reaching influence all around the world.

I also believe that His expressions would be more contemporary. Many conservative churches still prefer to use terms like "Shepherd" to refer to their leaders. Jesus used this familiar expression two thousand years ago to paint a picture for the people who lived in the agricultural era where that word was quite understood.

Some evangelists still believe in singing the same church music they used in Europe to win soul in Africa not realising or appreciating the cultural differences. No matter how talented you are, you need to subject yourself to the regular process of training and development that will make your skill more relevant. Whatever area of ministry God has called you, there is a need for you to polish your skills and talents and serve it in the most attractive, relevant and impactful way if you want your service to have the influence it merits.

g) Maximise your strength through rest

And on the seventh day God ended his work which he had made; and he rested on the seventh day from all his work which he had made. **(Gen. 2:2)**

To optimise your best, you need to maximise your rest!
If the all-powerful everlasting God rested on the seventh day, you need to rest too. Do not kill yourself untimely with a tight schedule. You do not need to do everything other ministries do if it has no direct impact on the way your service is delivered. When our Church started, we were involved in many activities. We have come to cut off many of such time and energy wasting activities. If it doesn't help to achieve any of the Church visions, we strike it out. If is not helping to achieve our goals then it is useless for it is weakening and depleting our strengths. An activity that is not building you up could only break you down. Your influence is more felt through the quality of your service than in its quantity.

6) PLAN (How do I have to serve?)

For which of you, intending to build a tower, sitteth not down first, and counteth the cost, whether he have sufficient to finish it? Lest haply, after he hath laid the foundation, and is not able to finish it, all that behold it begin to mock him. **(Luke 14:28-29)**

Those who fail to plan plan to fail!
Before you embark on your vision, count the cost.
Nothing goods come so easy, it will cost you precious resources.
It will take your time.
Only those who are prepared to pay the price can win the prize.
Do not make yourself a laughing stock for the anxiozus crowds of mockers waiting to celebrate your failure.
Set your goals and prioritize them. Set your strategy in order.
Set your milestones to help you measure your progress. Document every guideline you need for the crystallisation of desire into action

If you notice that your plan has become ineffective, change it and make room for the new demands. Plan, replan and expand your plans. Your achievement can not outsize your plan. The greatest plan to achieve your godly mission is to decide to have God in all your programs. It is not sufficient to choose to serve the Lord.
You need to fully decide to serve Him according to His will.
Many people are using their wills to do the work of the Lord.
That is dangerous. Nothing is as dangerous as serving with your self-righteousness as against the righteousness of God.

> *No man can serve two masters: for either he will hate the one, and love the other; or else he will hold to the one, and despise the other. Ye cannot serve God and mammon.* **(Matthew 6:24)**

> *Not every one that saith unto me, Lord, Lord, shall enter into the kingdom of heaven; but he that doeth the will of my Father which is in heaven.* **(Matthew 7:21)**

I have watched with pain how young people in ministry, honestly on fire for the Lord misfire their enthusiasm in the wrong direction.
The Bible is very clear on the way we should serve in order to please our heavenly Master.

a) Serve your heavenly Master with all your might

> *And thou shalt love the LORD thy God with all thine heart, and with all thy soul, and with all thy might.* **(Deuteronomy 6:5)**

> *Whatsoever thy hand findeth to do, do it with thy might; for there is no work, nor device, nor knowledge, nor wisdom, in the grave, whither thou goest.* **(Ecclesiastes 9:10)**

Remember always that you are whom you are by the grace of God (Eph 2: 8) and because of that, you can do all things through Christ which strengthened you (Phil 4:13). There is nothing you have that you are not given. You are simply a caretaker of whatever gifts, relationship or resources that are in your procession. The sole owner of all things is the Lord. Learn to serve Him with all your being.

b) Serve under human authority

> *Let every soul be subject unto the higher powers. For there is no power but of God: the powers that be are ordained of God. Whosoever therefore resisteth the power, resisteth the ordinance of God: and they that resist shall receive to themselves damnation. For rulers are not a terror to good works, but to the evil. Wilt thou then not be afraid of the power? do that which is good, and thou shalt have praise of the same: Render therefore to all their dues: tribute to whom tribute is due; custom to whom custom; fear to whom fear; honour to whom honour.* **(Romans 13:1-3, 7)**

All human authority is not perfect yet we must serve under them in obedience to God's instruction. Finally, all genuine authority is of the Lord. Even when some governors are self serving, all government (as agents of orderliness) are of the Lord. God is the God of order not the author of confusion. The powers that be are ordained of God!

c) Serve others with love

> *If a man say, I love God, and hateth his brother, he is a liar: for he that loveth not his brother whom he hath seen, how can he love God whom he hath not seen.* **(1 John 4:20-21)**

> *For, brethren, ye have been called unto liberty; only use not liberty for an occasion to the flesh, but by love serve one another.* **(Galatians 5:13)**

If you do not love and respect others, you can not serve them. Until people become respectable and valuable to you, you can not appreciate them or serve them either they lead or serve you. You need to learn how to respect and love others. You can not love yourself alone. You can not work for God alone. You can not serve yourself alone. If you only sing to yourself alone, probably you are a bad singer. If you preach alone to yourself, you have wasted God's talent however anointed you may be. Your impact can be felt in relations with others, even if they are imperfect. One of our major duties in life is to learn to be like God. Until you love others you can not know God for God is love (1 John 4: 8).

The power of God is the power of love.

> *Let love be without dissimulation. Abhor that which is evil; cleave to that which is good. Be kindly affectioned one to another with brotherly love; in honour preferring one another.* **(Romans 12:9-10)**

Love is a platform where everything works together for good.

Even our faith works only by love (Gal.5:6).
Don't just serve, serve in love!

d) Serve with other members with the unity of purpose

And let us consider one another to provoke unto love and to good works: Not forsaking the assembling of ourselves together, as the manner of some is; but exhorting one another: and so much the more, as ye see the day approaching. **(Hebrews 10:24-25)** *Also Romans 12: 4-11*

Every person and ministry is valuable even when not visible.
Despite our different duties, we remain interdependent and not independent of each other (1 Corinthians 12: 18-22).
Every one's talent is important and interdependent.
Only together are we complete. The same way the body parts differ in duty but make up a whole together, same way are we designed to work together with unity of purpose and mind as the body of Christ.

e) Serve fearlessly with a winning heart

That he would grant unto us, that we being delivered out of the hand of our enemies might serve him without fear. **(Luke 1:74)**

Because it is written, Be ye holy; for I am holy. And if ye call on the Father, who without respect of persons judgeth according to every man's work, pass the time of your sojourning here in fear. **(1 Peter 1:16-17)**

The fear of the Lord is the beginning of wisdom.
A good understanding begins with obeying the commandments of the awesome God (Ps 111:10-11).
As you do things with the awareness that He sees you and will judge you once, every area of your life will be baptised with holiness.
You stand to gain every protection, divine provision and blessed assurance of God being in your life always.
That is why Job insisted that the fear of the Lord is not the beginning of wisdom but the end product itself (Job 28:28)!

f) Serve with sincerity

Servants, be obedient to them that are your masters according to the flesh, with fear and trembling, in singleness of your heart, as unto Christ; Not with eyeservice, as menpleasers; but as the servants of Christ, doing the will of God from the heart; With good will doing service, as to the Lord, and not to men: Knowing that whatsoever good thing any man doeth, the same shall he receive of the Lord, whether he be bond or free. ***(Ephesians 6:5-8)***

We are expected to serve not with eye service but as a genuine bondservant of Christ. You do not need to be timid, nor be a sycophant or hypocrite.
Express your views, discomfort and suggestions to the leadership with genuine love and desire to see improvement and solution in your organisation. You need to serve honestly from deep in your heart with great conviction.

g) Serve with honour

If any man speak, let him speak as the oracles of God; if any man minister, let him do it as of the ability which God giveth: that God in all things may be glorified through Jesus Christ, to whom be praise and dominion for ever and ever. Amen. ***(1 Peter 4:11)***

Now when they saw the boldness of Peter and John, and perceived that they were unlearned and ignorant men, they marvelled; and they took knowledge of them, that they had been with Jesus. ***(Acts 4:13)***

After the ascension of Jesus Christ, His disciples ministered with so much power and authority that people took special notice of them. People need to notice that He that is in you is greater than he that is in the world (1 John 4:4). God is great and every service rendered on His behalf should reflect His attributes. God expects us to offer our services gracefully. You need to give your best energy and ability to the work of God so that people can appreciate the magnitude of His power and authority and end up giving praise and glory to Him.

7) PLACE (Where do I have to serve?)

These twelve Jesus sent forth, and commanded them, saying, Go not into the way of the Gentiles, and into any city of the Samaritans enter ye not: But go rather to the lost sheep of the house of Israel. ***(Matthew 10:5-6)***

*And we know that all things work together for good to them that love God, to them who are the called according to his purpose. (**Romans 8:28**)*

Every one has a definite purpose for being in life.
It is when you operate within His divine purpose that you can bear greatest fruits. The physical location of your service sometimes can affect greatly its success. Much importance should be placed on seeking the guidance of God concerning the place you locate your organisation. It is very important to abide where God placed you.
If your ministry is focussing on reaching out to the Europeans, then locating yourself in Asia will be highly unprofitable since the spread of your influence will be extremely hindered by distance.
Mother Theresa, feeling she was called to reach poor people of Asia left her country and relocated in Calcutta at the heart of the congregation she served till she died.
Locating yourself also in the area where your skill is most appreciated and demanded will also make your service quite valuable.
Everybody has an area of passioin life where he or she can greatly influence the outcome and result of the situations. That is where your service has a greater impact on peoples' lives than that of many others around you. As you devote your time and efforts to acquire more knowledge and increase your skill in the best area you can offer effective service, your range of influence and appreciation will grow.
For maximum impact, you should locate yourself where:

a) You believe God has sent you. It is Him who orders the steps of the righteous. Consult Him and let Him influence the choice of your location. That will be a place God will prosper you.

b) The people your ministry focuses on could be reached more with limited efforts. Follow your passion and compassion for only that could keep you moving when everything else fails.

c) You provide the greatest impact on your target group. You must know the conditions that aid you to produce the best service. We are not all the same and can not produce in the same environment.

d) Your previous training and experience have prepared you to bear the most fruit. Jesus Christ for instance started His ministry among Jews who were conscious of God's promises concerning the coming Messiah. He would have needed far more years to teach other nations about God's dealing with the forefathers of Israelites.

e) You are received and needed (Mark 6: 11). It is productive to serve where your talents and efforts are needed and appreciated.

f) You are highly motivated to give your best. Do not work where you are forced to complain against others or where others are forced to regularly complain against you. Many people live their lives in hell, choosing to live in countries, companies and with people that torment their lives with fear and hatred. If you can, chose to stay with people that can encourage you and love you rather than those that will harm and destroy you. Better is a simple location where there is peace of mind than a great place with confusion and frustration (Eccl. 4:6; Prov. 15:17; Prov. 16:8).

g) You can feel deep fulfilment. This intrinsic motivation is beyond financial compensation and incentives. In this type of environment, either you are paid salary or not, you are simply happy to serve.

8) PERIOD (When do I have to serve?)

To every thing there is a season, and a time to every purpose under the heaven. **(Ecclesiastes 3:1)**

Doing the right thing at the right time is the right recept to get the right result. Though David was anointed to become King, he didn't step into that office until later ages when the occupant died.

Having passion and compassion to become an evangelist is not enough to hit the road and start preaching. You first need to submit yourself under formal or informal training to get prepared for the duties ahead. It is shocking to see many school drop-outs branding themselves everywhere as honorary doctors, bishop, prophets, evangelists and preachers because they felt they were called by God. It is only an organisation like the Church that people dabble to without previous training, knowledge and experience.

> **Doing the right thing at the right time is the right recept to get right result. Though David was anointed to become King, he didn't step into that office until later ages when the occupant died.**

What an unfortunate situation. What a dangerous experiment!
Ministry of God is the only calling that has to do with people's destiny. An issue of life and death. Yet people toy with it anyhow.
No medical student is allowed to practice after completing medical training until he completes housemanship, which is a practical hand-on training to supplement the theoretical knowledge.
No wonder we have so many sects with baby preachers everywhere. They do not have any profound knowledge of the word of God nor the people they are trying to serve. No wonder we have lots of holy – bath prophets who go around knocking doors and looking for who will pay them to bath with holy soap and water.
What a mischievous misconduct!
I was in informal pastoral training for many years before I was given the responsibility to lead a ministry in Church. I had many years in intensive training before I was sent to lead a Church branch.
Some people attend formal Bible school for theology training for a few years before finding a ministry to practice and be ordained.
That is also equally good.
The point is, every worthwhile service requires adeguate preparation.
When Apostle Paul was commissioned by Jesus Christ to preach the gospel, he first went to study and prepare himself for three years (Gal. 1: 17-18). Then he went to meet Peter for two weeks before he proceded to serve. When God ordained David, he didn't organise a coup d'etat to oust Saul. He waited for his time.
There is a right time to serve. It is better you serve when you have completed your training and preparation or when you receive the permission, unction or authority to serve.

1) You serve after completing training and preparation
To every profession there is a time to train and time to practice.

If you rush in to do what you are not prepared to do, you will be rushed out of your destiny.

Have you ever seen any student practising before completing the training? They call such people dropout!

Until you receive what to serve with, you lack the blessing to serve.

If you are under any formal and informal training, falling off to practice before your graduation or ordination will do more harm to you than right. You will also be laying bad precedence for bands of impatient dropouts like you who will mess up your field of influence.

The least expected of us is to be orderly as children of the Lord.

2) You serve when authorised by the authority that trains you

In some places, people are appointed, selected or elected to serve according to the decision of the leadership. In any situation, the blessing of such leaders carries the anointing and blessing of heaven. Though David was a man after God's heart yet he did not receive the anointing to serve until Prophet Samuel anointed him (1 Sam 16:13). It was only as the Prophet anointed him that the Spirit of the Lord came upon Him!

As soon as some people receive recognition or notice some talents manifesting in their lives, they become so proud and rebellious, that they hardly can stay under any authority.

I have painfully observed talented young people in ministry messing up their chances in the Lord, moving around scripturally unsound people that deceive them by exaggerating their importance.

Watch out that you do not put the wrong people around you. The wrong and premature advice you will receive will only take you out of your place and pull you down to the level of such wrong advisers. Make sure the person you turn to for advice has an accomplishment you wish to measure up to. If you are asking incompetent people for advice, what can you expect?

Stewardship in the kingdom of God

> *The earth is the LORD's, and the fulness thereof; the world, and they that dwell therein.* **(Psalm 24:1)**

And he called him, and said unto him, How is it that I hear this of thee? give an account of thy stewardship; for thou mayest be no longer steward.
(Luke 16:2)

God is the ultimate Head of mankind.
Every man is a servant employed in His service.
God created the earth and everything within it.
Regardless of who we are and what we do for a profession, we are all in the business of the Lord and only He, the Rewarder and the Judge of all, will determine your reward as His steward.

> **There is a right time to serve. It is better you serve when you have completed your training and preparation or when you receive the permission, unction or authority to serve.**

CHAPTER 9: WHICH TYPE OF SERVANT ARE YOU?

And the lord said unto the servant, Go out into the highways and hedges, and compel them to come in, that my house may be filled. **(Luke 14:23)**

The platform for understanding service to mankind is the knowledge of God as the Creator of heaven and the earth - the ultimate Master to whom all His creatures will offer the report of their service on earth when their tenures on earth come to an end. Most of Jesus' proverbs (Matt. 18; Matt. 25; Luke 19 etceteras) support this stewardship view of our existence on earth.

Everything in this world has its own purpose and timing.

The all-purposeful God couldn't have created any man without a purpose. That is why rather than complaining about your background, experience and situation; you need to focus on the final product such situations have made out of you. This is important for God has predestined us all to offer particular service to our community and generation within an allocated period of time.

Your family, race, language and situation are set up to make you serve well your calling. When you locate your personal purpose, all things shall work together for your good.

The renowned people are those who have found out what their lives are about and have dipped themselves passionately to fulfilling it. You can join such a purposeful team today. Our saviour, Jesus Christ and other men of God confessed their convictions on being in the world to serve the purpose of the Lord. Though they offered themselves completely to providing for people in different areas of need, they nonetheless knew their ultimate service was to God.

Paul, a servant of Jesus Christ, called to be an apostle, separated unto the gospel of God. **(Romans 1:1)**

James, a servant of God and of the Lord Jesus Christ, to the twelve tribes which are scattered abroad, greeting. **(James 1:1)**

> *Simon Peter, a servant and an apostle of Jesus Christ, to them that have obtained like precious faith with us through the righteousness of God and our Saviour Jesus Christ.* **(2 Peter 1:1)**

> *Jude, the servant of Jesus Christ, and brother of James, to them that are sanctified by God the Father, and preserved in Jesus Christ, and called.* **(Jude 1:1)**

> *And they sing the song of Moses the servant of God, and the song of the Lamb, saying, Great and marvellous are thy works, Lord God Almighty; just and true are thy ways, thou King of saints.* **(Revelation 15:3)**

You can say the same of yourself today that you have been called and sent to your world to make a worthy change for the Lord.
Moses, John the Baptist, Paul, James, Peter and other great servants of God we read about in the Bible have completed their missions on earth and have returned home. It is the turn of the living saints to preach the living word of God to our dying word. Stop looking down at yourself, look up unto the Lord and focus on His promise to be with you in accomplishing your mission on earth. God sees you as greater even than John the Baptist if you are in His kingdom.

> *Verily I say unto you, Among them that are born of women there hath not risen a greater than John the Baptist: notwithstanding he that is least in the kingdom of heaven is greater than he.* **(Matthew 11:11)**

Refresh your mind with a "Greater than" mentality to accomplish your personal mission and God's general purpose for all mankind on earth. You are greater than John the Baptist because the Jesus Christ in you is greater than he that is in the world. You and I are here and we have the divine commission to win our world for the Lord.

> *Verily, verily, I say unto you, He that believeth on me, the works that I do shall he do also; and greater works than these shall he do; because I go unto my Father.* **(John 14:12)**

> *Then said Jesus to them again, Peace be unto you: as my Father hath sent me, even so send I you.* **(John 20:21)**

> *And these signs shall follow them that believe; In my name shall they cast out devils; they shall speak with new tongues; They shall take up serpents; and if they drink any deadly thing, it shall not hurt them; they shall lay hands on the sick, and they shall recover.* ***(Mark 16:17-18)***

May your generation rise up to praise the Lord for your life.
May your impact on others make them better people.
May you become true salt and light to our world as you convert your talents and existence to the service of the Lord.

Characteristics of a good servant

> *But he that is greatest among you shall be your servant. And whosoever shall exalt himself shall be abased; and he that shall humble himself shall be exalted.* ***(Matthew 23:11-12)***

A servant (meaning the same thing as a steward) is an employee in the service of his master to whom he is accountable at all time.

His duty is mainly to carry out the instruction of his master and represent his interest to his very best. Understanding your stewardship status will help you not to displease your master.

It helps you rather prepare to give an account of how you use the grace of Jesus Christ and your divine talents to impact your world and the lives of people that are sent your way.

1) Every servant is subject to the leadership of a master

The acknowledgement of the master is the beginning of stewardship. Until you see yourself accountable to a person of higher status, you can not truly serve your skill as a service. A servant is someone that knows his power is being exercised on behalf of another person in order to carry out duties he has been instructed to do. Until you see yourself as a servant of God, you can not achieve exploit in life.

Until you see your service to man as an extension of your service to God, you will misuse and abuse your relationship with the people God has put either above or under you.

a) Master – focused

> *The disciple is not above his master, nor the servant above his lord.* ***Matt. 10:24***

> *Jesus saith unto them, My meat is to do the will of him that sent me, and to finish his work.* ***John 4:34***

The parable of the steward in Luke 16 teaches us that the fate of the servant depends on the judgment of his master. As God's servants, God the Master decides on what becomes of our lives and resources. He expects us to use all our resources for the accomplishment of His assignment to His own glory. Jesus lived to do only the will of God. He acknowledged the fact that He had been sent!

> **Many men of God are failing to make good impact on their congregation because they are lifting themselves up instead of God. It is only a God-fearing congregation that can devote self to doing the will of God. A God focussed preacher will never lack the blessing of God and honour of men.**

Jesus was aware that He was using the authority of God so He fully focused and depended on Him .
Everytime you are world focussed, you lose the focus of God!

> *Ye adulterers and adulteresses, know ye not that the friendship of the world is enmity with God? whosoever therefore will be a friend of the world is the enemy of God. Do ye think that the scripture saith in vain, The spirit that dwelleth in us lusteth to envy?* **(James 4:4-5)**

Sometimes, such people even convert the Master's business into their private use.

> *Then said he to another, And how much owest thou? And he said, An hundred measures of wheat. And he said unto him, Take thy bill, and write fourscore. And the lord commended the unjust steward, because he had done wisely: for the children of this world are in their generation wiser than the children of light.* **(Luke 16:7-8)**

A bad servant always thinks what belongs to his master is his own.
A bad servant thinks of cheating the Master for his own enrichment.
It is bad enough as a believer to use part of God's resources left in our cares for personal gains. It is however sheer abuse to use all our master's resources invested in us for the service of His enemy. Will you expect such master to reward the action of such unworthy

servants with blessing? Unfortunately, hell is the destination of every unbeliever who has chosen to rob God to pay Satan by devoting their lives to mislead themselves and others away from Jesus; the way, the truth and the life.

b) Master – dependence

And he said, Therefore said I unto you, that no man can come unto me, except it were given unto him of my Father. ***(John 6:65)***

Then said Jesus unto them, When ye have lifted up the Son of man, then shall ye know that I am he, and that I do nothing of myself; but as my Father hath taught me, I speak these things. ***(John 8:28)***

Every servant depends on the authority of his or her Master.
Your master determines your mandate!
Jesus Christ knew and depended on God, His heavenly Father and Master throughout His ministry on earth.
He did nothing without previous consultation of God.
Even the people He ministered to He permitted only God to determine. He was God yet preferred not to do things by His personal opinion. Compare that to many Christians doing work of God with their personal will today. What an expressway to hell.
That road leads no where close to the kingdom of God (Matt. 7: 21). Only the purpose located in the will of God is assured of divine backup. We only need to feed our faith strong and starve our unbelief lean to walk through every limitation to become whom the word of God says we are. Nothing can stop us if we are lead by the Lord.

What shall we then say to these things? If God be for us, who can be against us? ***(Romans 8:31)***

I can do all things through Christ which strengtheneth me. ***(Phil. 4:13)***

You can do all things! That is the truth.
So long you can depend faithfully on God, nothing can stand against you. Christ's strength in you will enable you to do all things!

c) Servants use service to promote the image of their master

He must increase, but I must decrease. ***(John 3:30)***

Have you ever seen a state minister representing his Prime Minister or President praising himself instead of the leader? Never!

Everytime, radio and television broadcasters remind you of the name of their institution more than they mention their names. That is because the more important your master is, the more importance and authority you carry. Your honour and respect come from the status of your master. Many men of God are failing to make a good impact on their congregation because they are lifting themselves up instead of God. It is only a God-fearing congregation that can devote self to doing the will of God. A God focussed preacher will never lack the blessing of God and the honour of men.

The same thing applies to our conducts with a fellow human being.
An assistant that honors his seniors or leaders will not only be honored by those above him but also by those below him. Elevating your superior is a godly way of lifting up your status.

d) Servants are accountable to their master

For promotion cometh neither from the east, nor from the west, nor from the south. But God is the judge: he putteth down one, and setteth up another. **(Psalm 75:6-7)**

Blessed is that servant, whom his lord when he cometh shall find so doing. Verily I say unto you, That he shall make him ruler over all his goods.
But and if that evil servant shall say in his heart, My lord delayeth his coming; And shall begin to smite his fellowservants, and to eat and drink with the drunken; The lord of that servant shall come in a day when he looketh not for him, and in an hour that he is not aware of, And shall cut him asunder, and appoint him his portion with the hypocrites: there shall be weeping and gnashing of teeth. **(Matthew. 24: 46)**

A good servant sees all his skills and talents as resources given to him by his master to carry out his duties. He doesn't brag with such talents but rather convert it to doing profitable service for the business of his master. He sees himself as a mere caretaker of the talents he has and the office he is located. He is not the owner of the business nor the equipment used in rendering the service. When you know that your promotion comes from God, you will have no time to play pranks that menpleasers spend their time perfecting.

A good servant sees all his skills and talents as resources given to him by his master to carry out his duties.

2) Every good servant is service oriented

And the King shall answer and say unto them, Verily I say unto you, Inasmuch as ye have done it unto one of the least of these my brethren, ye have done it unto me. ***(Matthew 25:40)***

Service of the Lord covers the entire world and every area of human endeavour. Every one should serve according to his or her talents and callings. Naturally, not all services are acceptable to God.
There are ways however that we can make our services totally acceptable to Him.

a) Offers service humbly to people

Let this mind be in you, which was also in Christ Jesus: Who, being in the form of God, thought it not robbery to be equal with God: But made himself of no reputation, and took upon him the form of a servant, and was made in the likeness of men: And being found in fashion as a man, he humbled himself, and became obedient unto death, even the death of the cross. ***(Philippians 2:5-8)***

Servants are people who humbly render their services to others without expecting special appreciation. A good servant only looks towards his master for compensation. Others appreciation is additional and secondary.

A good servant is wholeheartedly commited to the peole God has sent him to serve. He loves men like he loves God their maker (1 John 4:20-21). We are all servants of God and we need to acknowledge this in anything and everything we do. Regardless of where we do what we do, we must see ourselves doing it for the Lord. Only He is the ultimate rewarder of all services rendered on earth. As a child of God, wait for no title to offer the service you know you can best offer. A child doesn't think of a title. A child only thinks of pleasing his or her parents.

b) Self initiative

For though I be free from all men, yet have I made myself servant unto all, that I might gain the more. And unto the Jews I became as a Jew, that I might gain the Jews; to them that are under the law, as under the law, that I might gain them that are under the law; To them that are without law, as without law, (being not without law to God, but under the law to Christ,) that I might gain them that are without law. **(1 Corinthians 9:19-21)**

Jesus washed the feet of His disciples!
He simply took the initiative of rendering such unprecedented service by leaders of His calibre by His personal will. A bad servant will never try to do more than he is given. Such a person has no excitement to initiate new ideas and suggestions. They are always waiting for someone to do it. You too do not need to wait for people to seek your service before you render it. You only need to locate a need ahead of demands and go on to seek and offer a solution.

As a genuine servant of the Lord, look around the needy world and offer your service of love on behalf of your heavenly Master who is a sure Rewarder. It is your God given-duty to save sinners. It is your heavenly obligation to take care of your family (1 Tim 5: 8).

You become a leader the day you find something you passionately feel you must do for the world.

What do you know you must do before you die?

In a word, what will you like the world to remember you by?

c) Self motivating

To the weak became I as weak, that I might gain the weak: I am made all things to all men, that I might by all means save some. And this I do for the gospel's sake, that I might be partaker thereof with you. **(1 Cor. 9: 22-23)**

And this I do for the gospel's sake!
Paul knew why he did what he did so nothing can stop him.
You must convince yourself of the greatness of what you are doing. Knowing your end invigorates you and mostly stabilises your pursuit. Sometimes, you need to encourage yourself and motivate yourself by yourself in discouraging moments when nobody shows recognition or appreciation for your efforts.

Be willing to serve others at allcost even when you are obviously not appreciated. Godly appreciation outweighs anything a man can offer. Permit no one to deny you of your reward in your Master.

Sometimes, you need to encourage yourself and motivate yourself by yourself in discouraging moments when nobody shows recognition or appreciation for your efforts.

Servants are not appreciated!

> *But which of you, having a servant plowing or feeding cattle, will say unto him by and by, when he is come from the field, Go and sit down to meat?*
> *And will not rather say unto him, Make ready wherewith I may sup, and gird thyself, and serve me, till I have eaten and drunken; and afterward thou shalt eat and drink? Doth he thank that servant because he did the things that were commanded him? I trow not. So likewise ye, when ye shall have done all those things which are commanded you, say, We are unprofitable servants: we have done that which was our duty to do.* **(Luke 17:7-10)**

Though servants are expected to be hard working, nobody specially considers them specially worthy of appreciattion. You need to learn to encourage and motivate yourself to give your best service to ungrateful people. Imagine a restaurant steward losing his anger on a bad customer that the Master considers good enough to die for. Wouldn't that servant lose his favour with the master immediately?

It takes special grace to continue to work with joy and dedication in challenging condition and that is what makes servants great leaders. Despite great miracles performed by Jesus Christ while on earth, His people rose up against Him and demanded that He be crucified.

They prefered to release a convicted armed robber than their Saviour. The fact is, people can be unappreciative. This is the first fact every servant of God should settle with before going into the service of God. Only God can appreciate and pay you for your efforts.

No human salary or appreciation can compesate your effort.

d) Non forceful

> *And there was also a strife among them, which of them should be accounted the greatest. And he said unto them, The kings of the Gentiles exercise lordship over them; and they that exercise authority upon them are called benefactors. But ye shall not be so: but he that is greatest among you, let him be as the younger; and he that is chief, as he that doth serve.* **(Lk. 22:24-26)**

Leaders do not own their members nor have authority to lord it over them. You are given dominion over animals and not over people. Stop misleading people! Stop coercing, manipulating and misusing people. Your authority is finding the area God has given you to operate. What are you authorised to do? Dominion means to master something. When you master a thing, people will seek you out. You should exercise your authority over your gift.

4) Hard working

> *Who then is a faithful and wise servant, whom his lord hath made ruler over his household, to give them meat in due season?* ***(Matthew 24:45- 51)***
>
> *But Jesus answered them, My Father worketh hitherto, and I work.* ***(John 5:17)***

A servant is a fervent worker. She or he simply seeks the opportunity to serve his or her talents. To be a good leader according to the standard of Jesus Christ, we need to know what a good servant is. Some basic characteristics of a good servant include the following;
A good servant is a solution provider.
A hardworking leader will always have more values to add to the service of his people. Such people are usually prosperous by providing services with greater quality than offered by other people around them. When you help a man to get what he wants, you will always get what you need.
A leader is constantly giving out himself even when not appreciated or compensated. That is why you can not retire from true leadership. Bible says every member of the body of Christ has been given a gift to bless the body of Christ. Leadership is found in effectively serving your gifts to the world. We are all Kings meant to serve our people.
While the non-believers believe in forcing their ways to lead, Kingdom leaders serve their way to the top. Jesus Christ our saviour came to serve others to the extent of offering His life as a ransom. That is the heart of a true shepherd who will give up everything to defend his sheep from the attack of the enemy.

> *I am the good shepherd: the good shepherd giveth his life for the sheep. But he that is an hireling, and not the shepherd, whose own the sheep are not, seeth the wolf coming, and leaveth the sheep, and fleeth: and the wolf catcheth them, and scattereth the sheep. The hireling fleeth, because he is an hireling, and careth not for the sheep. I am the good shepherd, and know my sheep, and am known of mine.* ***(John 10:11-14)***

A true leader wholeheartedly cares for the wellbeing of his people and will do everything at personal expense to protect and defend his followers. A true leader knows the real need of his sheep and does provide for them to the best of his ability and at all cost.

3) Faithful

*Moreover it is required in stewards, that a man be found **faithful**.*
(1 Corinthians 4:2)

It is not sufficient to serve just anyhow.
Your service is only meaningful if it is done faithfully.
The world is filled with eye-service people. Such group extend across the long lists of sycophants, boot lickers and their likes to include shallow self-centred personalities whose main goal for involving in any thing is self-enrichment. As a kingdom leader, the least expected of you concerning your service is faithfulness to God and man.

a) Be Faithful to God

For who maketh thee to differ from another? and what hast thou that thou didst not receive? now if thou didst receive it, why dost thou glory, as if thou hadst not received it? ***(1 Corinthians 4:7)***

If you are not faithful to the visions God gave to and through others, He will not send one through you!
As you prove your leadership through service to others, God the lifter up of the humble (James 4: 10) will then lift you up.
Show me one powerful man of God who preaches from another book apart from the Bible. Bible documents visions given to others ahead and and as we live by it and fulfil general instruction inside it, God begins to relate in particular to each one of us.

b) Be faithful to others

He that is faithful in that which is least is faithful also in much: and he that is unjust in the least is unjust also in much. If therefore ye have not been faithful in the unrighteous mammon, who will commit to your trust the true riches? And if ye have not been faithful in that which is another man's, who shall give you that which is your own? No servant can serve two masters: for either he will hate the one, and love the other; or else he will hold to the one, and despise the other. Ye cannot serve God and mammon. **(Luke 16:10-13)**

Many people failed to support visions of God given to other men believing it makes them subjective to others. No! Nothing can be far from the truth than that. Being a visionary doesn't mean you are clever, better or favoured by God than another. It is a choice made by God for the best reason He alone knows. Such misconception has been buttressed by the misconduct of some ignorant leaders who abuse their flocks. Your congregation is not yours but Gods! Church congregants are members of the body of Christ so you can not send them to cater for your private needs as if they are your servants.

The basis of honour for every kingdom leader is the love for people of God. Not understanding that will make you misuse God's people as your personal staff. God works a different thing through different people. All of us are equally necessary for God's service.

> *I have planted, Apollos watered; but God gave the increase. So then neither is he that planteth any thing, neither he that watereth; but God that giveth the increase. 8 Now he that planteth and he that watereth are one: and every man shall receive his own reward according to his own labour. 9 For we are labourers together with God: ye are God's husbandry, ye are God's building.* **(1 Corinthians 3:6-9)**

God works a different thing through different people.
It was Moses that God called to lead Children of Israel from Egypt to the Promised Land but it was Joshua who took them into land!
Who was more important, Paul or Apollos? Moses or Joshua?
Everyone is equally important to ensure the fulfilment of the purpose of God. Also, everyone will receive rewards according to his efforts. It is when everyone plays his role well that the body of Christ can run perfectly.

c) Be faithful to yourself by giving your best to the Lord

> *For promotion cometh neither from the east, nor from the west, nor from the south. he judge: he putteth down one, and setteth up another.* **(Ps. 75:6-7)**

Anything that will take your focus away from God is a sure thing to rob you of your heavenly rewards.

Be resolute in giving your best to the Lord for only He promotes not your boss or your people. If He could make a Prime Minister out of a slave boy Joseph in a foreign Land, you have more hope in life. Serving God and man faithfully is the best way to serve yourself for God will cause you to reap everything you sowed. Whatever you do, put your best there and then leave the rest to Him.

4) Humble

> *Let this mind be in you, which was also in Christ Jesus: Who, being in the form of God, thought it not robbery to be equal with God: But made himself of no reputation, and took upon him the form of a servant, and was made in the likeness of men: And being found in fashion as a man, he **humbled himself**, and became obedient unto death, even the death of the cross. Wherefore God also hath highly exalted him, and given him a name which is above every name.* **(Philippians 2:5-9)**

It is not sufficient to desire to serve; how you serve also matters. Humility is the hallmark of leadership. When Moses choose to suffer affliction with the people of the Lord, above the princely life of the palace, God called him to lead his people out of bondage (Heb 11: 24,25). The passion to serve his people was more pressing in his mind than all the pleasures that the comfort of the palace can afford him. Humility is synonymous with meekness. A good servant leader is not proud but very humble in offering his service. He is strong and authoritative in preaching the word of God without any compromise but is gentle enough to correct people in love so that the word of God can take its full course in moulding people to perfection.

> *For we preach not ourselves, but Christ Jesus the Lord; and ourselves your servants for Jesus' sake.* **(2 Corinthians 4:5)**

Meekness is not what you do, it is who you are. It has nothing to do with your actions but your attitude. Humility refers to a natural disposition to be submissive, patient and long suffering at will.
It is having a calm temper of mind that can not easily be provoked.
It is not expected of a servant to be proud and pompous. A servant that gets angry easily often gets fired more than often.
Bible recommends meekness in human conduct for lots of reasons.

a) Meekness overcomes strife and malice

> *He that is of a proud heart stirreth up strife: but he that putteth his trust in the LORD shall be made fat.* **(Proverbs 28:25)**

Better is the end of a thing than the beginning thereof: and the patient in spirit is better than the proud in spirit. Be not hasty in thy spirit to be angry: for anger resteth in the bosom of fools. **(Ecclesiastes. 7:8-9)**

b) God loves the humble and distastes the proud

Whosoever therefore shall humble himself as this little child, the same is greatest in the kingdom of heaven. **(Matthew 18:4)**

If there is anything God totally disdain, it is pride.
Various biblical verses emphasised God's preference for humble people over proud ones. (Isa. 2: 12; Isa. 57: 15; Prov. 15: 25; Ps. 138: 6; Jer. 50: 31-32 , James 4: 6; Prov 16: 5,19; Prov. 29: 23 etceteras).

c) Humility attracts divine upliftment

And whosoever shall exalt himself shall be abased; and he that shall humble himself shall be exalted. **(Matthew 23:12)**

And one of the king of Israel's servants answered and said, Here is Elisha the son of Shaphat, which poured water on the hands of Elijah.
(2 Kings 3:11)

God waited 400 years till humble Moses came on the scene.
God prefered to use a stammering Moses than his senior brother, Aaron (a great orator who was neither humble nor God-fearing enough to respect God constituted authority). Though Elisha was an accomplished business man far older than Elijah, he called and served Elijah as a father. No wonder he ended up with the double anointing of the power of God in Elijah's ministry.When you humble yourself in the sight of the Lord, He shall lift you up by Himself.

d) Humility attracts peaceful rest

Take my yoke upon you, and learn of me; for I am meek and lowly in heart: and ye shall find rest unto your souls.30 For my yoke is easy, and my burden is light. **(Matthew 11:29-30)**

Anyone guided by almighty Lord can only have peace with God and all men. That is because when a man's way pleases the Lord, he makes even his enemies be at peace with him **(Proverbs 16: 7).**

e) Humility generates fruits of the spirit

But the fruit of the Spirit is love, joy, peace, longsuffering, gentleness, goodness, faith, Meekness, temperance: against such there is no law. **(Gal. 5:22-23)**

Blessed are the meek: for they shall inherit the earth. **(Matthew 5:5)**

Humble people by divine arrangement are meant to inherit the earth. Nothing promotes in life like humility. Everyone appreciates humble personalities. If you deserve promotion today, take forward a step of humility in anything you do. You need to humble yourself under the mighty hand of the Lord if you want your promotion to be complete, perfect and sure (1 Peter 5: 6).

5) Obedience

For whosoever shall keep the whole law, and yet offend in one point, he is guilty of all. For he that said, Do not commit adultery, said also, Do not kill. Now if thou commit no adultery, yet if thou kill, thou art become a transgressor of the law. **(James 2:10-11)**

As far as God is concerned, you can never grow beyond your level of obedience. God stops with you where you stopped obeying Him.
He is against all forms of selected obedience. Whoever defaults in any of His laws is considered to have defaulted in all. God gives us godly leaders and insists that we obey them! Every time we disobey genuinely constituted authority we disobey God who institutes them and attracts to our heads divine retribution.
Every institution that promotes orderliness is of God. The powers that be are ordained of the Lord. Saul lost his kingship for usurping Samuel's religious duty (1 Sam 13: 11-14). Aaron and Miriam were rebuked for contesting against Moses authority (Num. 12: 1-15).

Exhort servants to be obedient unto their own masters, and to please them well in all things; not answering again; Not purloining, but shewing all good fidelity; that they may adorn the doctrine of God our Saviour in all things. **(Titus 2:9-10)**

Therefore doth my Father love me, because I lay down my life, that I might take it again. No man taketh it from me, but I lay it down of myself. I have

> *power to lay it down, and I have power to take it again. This commandment have I received of my Father.* ***(John 10:17-18)***

Complete obedience is the hallmark of a good servant. Jesus Christ totally submitted Himself to the will and purpose of God even to the death on the cross! Learn not to judge people doing what God asks them to do lest you end up judging God who sends them.

6) Selflessness

> *Let nothing be done through strife or vainglory; but in lowliness of mind let each esteem other better than themselves. Look not every man on his own things, but every man also on the things of others. Let this mind be in you, which was also in Christ Jesus: Who, being in the form of God, thought it not robbery to be equal with God: But made himself of no reputation, and took upon him the form of a servant, and was made in the likeness of men.* ***(Philippians 2:3-7)***

The corruption, avariciousness, persecution and various vices of life are the direct product of man's selfish desires to sacrifice the good of others for his personal gain. We need to learn selfless practices of great men of God.

> *I have coveted no man's silver, or gold, or apparel. Yea, ye yourselves know, that these hands have ministered unto my necessities, and to them that were with me. I have shewed you all things, how that so labouring ye ought to support the weak, and to remember the words of the Lord Jesus, how he said, It is more blessed to give than to receive.* ***(Acts 20:33-35)***

It is time preachers learnt to support people, showing the caring and loving hand of God to people rather than misrepresenting God as a needy deity through their well cultivated life of begging and fundraising.

> *And every one that hath forsaken houses, or brethren, or sisters, or father, or mother, or wife, or children, or lands, for my name's sake, shall receive an hundredfold, and shall inherit everlasting life.* ***(Matthew 19:29)***

It is he that sows that will reap.
It is what you sow that you will reap (2 Cor 9: 6).
Every Christian is called to a selfless life of serving others.

The body of Christ needs selfless leaders who are conscious of their responsibility to give godly direction to their congregations. Selflessness is the opposite of selfishness.
Selflessness is putting needs of others above yours.

7) Honourable

Render therefore to all their dues: tribute to whom tribute is due; custom to whom custom; fear to whom fear; honour to whom honour. **(Romans 13:7)**

Honour thy father and mother; (which is the first commandment with promise;) That it may be well with thee, and thou mayest live long on the earth. **(Ephesians 6:2-3)**

The way you see your leader affects what you receive and how much you will be blessed! Don't let colour, education, age or your personal pride cuts you off from God's blessing. God knows why He chooses some people to lead you but if you are patient enough, you will find out later. Jesus was not accepted! For one, he was a carpenter (Mark 6: 1-5)! He was only 30 years old and He loved to eat with sinners. Nonetheless He was God on earth! Cultivating habit of honoring your leader places you in the right position to receive all the nutrition you require for growing in your Christian walk. Respect is however mutual. I have watched with shock how some Church leaders address elderly people disrespectfully while they expect everyone, both young and old to respect them dutifully. Such a double standard is not befitting in the house of the Lord. Bible doesn't teach believers not to honour elderly people be they in political, civil, vocational or social organisation. Nothing stops a leader from honoring his parents and other elderly members of his congregation but pride.

Render therefore to all their dues: tribute to whom tribute is due; custom to whom custom; fear to whom fear; honour to whom honour. **(Rom. 13:7)**

Watch out that you do not miuse or abuse your relationship with the Church people too. While it is not wrong to accept being blessed by people who willingly chose to bless you with their labours or substance, it is unscriptural and immoral to demand such assistance by force. There is a different between your personal staff and Church staff. Members of your congregation are not meant to wash your car, mow your lawn or drive your partner for shopping. We are all co-

labourers with Christ (1 Cor 3: 9) even when we are recruited at a different time for different purposes (Matt 20:2-6).
As a team working together for the glory of God, mutual respect is a requirement in our daily interactions. The basis of honour for every kingdom leader is the love of people for God. Leading body of Christ as a military battalion where one dictator screams orders down the throats of others has no scriptural basis.
In my early days in ministry, I have experienced many disrespectful acts of leadership that makes you wonder if such leaders are ever aware that congregations have come to worship God and not man.

I know what it means as a family man to be summoned up for an impromptu meeting on the first day of the New Year after just returning home same morning, completely exhausted , from the New Year eve's service. Even committed Christians deserve to be honoured. Respect is mutual.
God's people must be threated with honour and dignity at all time.
They are God's people following God not you. They are only connecting to God through God's gifts they located in you.
They come for God's gift in you so serve them with respect.
When you respect members of your congregation, they in turn will treat you respectfully. Misusing your people will only rob you of your deserved honour and breed unruly behaviour in the body of Christ.

8) Commitment

And the LORD God planted a garden eastward in Eden; and there he put the man whom he had formed. And the LORD God took the man, and put him into the garden of Eden to dress it and to keep it. ***(Genesis 2:8)***

Work is no curse. It existed before the fall of man.
God created the garden and commanded man to dress it and keep it.
God however provided rainfall and sunshine that guarantees increase.
Yours is to sow, He is to bless your effort!
Commitment is "hard work" and work has no substitute.
It is a commitment to your goal that makes your service outstanding and qualitative. A committed effort is required for your dream to come true. Hard work has productivity as its rewards (Prov. 6; Prov. 12: 24, Prov. 14: 23; 24: 27, 30).

Seest thou a man diligent in his business? he shall stand before kings; he shall not stand before mean men. **(Proverbs 22:29)**

Every Christian should see self as an asset rather than a parasite.
The earlier you cultivate a working habit, the better for you.
You should only feel comfortable in any association when you see your contribution is greater than your consumption.
The seat of a Church you have been attending for years without tithing should be pitching your bottom like a needle.

9) Sterling characteristics

For a bishop must be blameless, as the steward of God; not selfwilled, not soon angry, not given to wine, no striker, not given to filthy lucre; But a lover of hospitality, a lover of good men, sober, just, holy, temperate; Holding fast the faithful word as he hath been taught, that he may be able by sound doctrine both to exhort and to convince the gainsayers. **(Titus 1:7-9)**

And the servant of the Lord must not strive; but be gentle unto all men, apt to teach, patient, In meekness instructing those that oppose themselves; if God peradventure will give them repentance to the acknowledging of the truth; And that they may recover themselves out of the snare of the devil, who are taken captive by him at his will. **(2 Timothy 2:24-26)**

As an ambassador of Christ, sent to be the light and salt of the world, a servant of God is expected to demonstrate godly nature and attitudes. He is to serve as an exemplar of virtues for others to imitate. His family should be a good model and his lifestyle should be a talking example of righteous living among the body of Christ.
That is why though everybody can learn some verses by heart but not everyone can be a godly leader. By their fruits we shall know them!
Before you submit your life to serve in any ministry, study how dedicated the priest is to God and his duty of feeding the congregation before you jump on board.

11. Right relationship to authority

But Gehazi, the servant of Elisha the man of God, said, Behold, my master hath spared Naaman this Syrian, in not receiving at his hands that which he brought: but, as the LORD liveth, I will run after him, and take somewhat of him. **(2 Kings 5:20)**

A bad steward sees authority only as a means for attaining personal goals. If they are pastors, they pray for people and demand financial compensation immediately. They offer to fast together with members of their congregation with strings attached. They want you to pay some vows to commit God before they take you seriously.
If they are serving under another man, they treat every instruction on the basis of personal gratification.
If it is not good for her, it is not good for the whole ministry.
Bad servants contemptuously despise the authority of their master.
Gehazi believed he was wiser than his master, Elisha.
In worse cases, such bad leaders put themselves in shoes of God believing they knew better than God who puts them under a particular institution and authority. Such a servant is an authority to himself. Whatsoever instruction passed down is seen as a mere suggestion that can be overruled by personal discretion.
If such a person leads a department of the Church for instance, she might choose to be punctual but will see no need to follow Church teaching. Such a person selects the topics that fit her emotion and skip the rest. If any topic exposes her weakness, such topics will never be treated. Such a person passes down seperate instruction to surbodinates thereby cutting them off from overall instruction guiding the whole organisation. Watch out for such people for they could serve as destructive examples for others following. In the worse occasion such bad people will try to mislead the immediate subordinates by generalizing a personal problem.
"Are we not clever enough to reason and form our own notes?"
"Can't we teach too?" "Does God talk to our leaders alone?"

And Miriam and Aaron spake against Moses because of the Ethiopian woman whom he had married: for he had married an Ethiopian woman. And they said, Hath the LORD indeed spoken only by Moses? hath he not spoken also by us? And the LORD heard it. **(Numbers 12:1-2)**

Now Korah, the son of Izhar, the son of Kohath, the son of Levi, and Dathan and Abiram, the sons of Eliab, and On, the son of Peleth, sons of Reuben,

> *took men: And they rose up before Moses, with certain of the children of Israel, two hundred and fifty princes of the assembly, famous in the congregation, men of renown: And they gathered themselves together against Moses and against Aaron, and said unto them, Ye take too much upon you, seeing all the congregation are holy, every one of them, and the LORD is among them: wherefore then lift ye up yourselves above the congregation of the LORD?*
> *(Numbers 16:1-3)*

With experience in the ministry, it is easier to fish such dangerous people out and decode their seemingly unharmful statements that are ever loaded with pride. For instance, "Don't we have the power of Holy Spirit too?" and "Holy Spirit is my teacher" implies that I am not going to submit under any authority in this Church. I lead myself!

Beware of angels of light

> *But what I do, that I will do, that I may cut off occasion from them which desire occasion; that wherein they glory, they may be found even as we. For such are false apostles, deceitful workers, transforming themselves into the apostles of Christ. And no marvel; for Satan himself is transformed into an angel of light. Therefore it is no great thing if his ministers also be transformed as the ministers of righteousness; whose end shall be according to their works.*
> *(2 Corinthians 11:12-15)*

Beware of people newly joining your congregation who are always talking of what Holy Spirit told them every second. Most of the time, such are manipulative, self-opinionated and unsubmisive people, hiding under the name of Holy Spirit to pursue personal agenda. Verifying their background from their last Church may save your ministry avoidable pain. Every believer is expected to hear from the Holy Spirit everyday and when we come to Church, our intimacy with the Holy Spirit helps us to relate well together as a body of Christ. Intimacy with the Holy Spirit should help us to easily obey and co-operate with Church authority and not impose ourselves upon it. If every member of the Church only wants to do what they claim that Holy Spirit tells them, the Church will be in chaos all the time but God is a God of order and not the author of confusion.

No wonder, rebellious and prideful believers who can not settle down under any authority but go from one Church to another always sing the same baby tune, "Holy Spirit told me." If you hear so much from the Holy Spirit, why is it that you are not rooted in any Church till now? A couple like that attended the church I pastored some years ago. They started fighting the Choir leader the first week they joined Choir ministry. Though they were still under the "trial period"- that is a time for the leader to study their characters, gifts and fitting to the ministry before they are confirmed as a member- they already wanted the Choir leader to be removed.

They started phoning members of the Choir instigating them against their leader. When they were questioned, they claimed the Holy Spirit told them to do that. To cut a long story short, we had to tell them to find another Church to worship since their Holy Spirit is obviously different from the Holy Spirit that has been leading the church peacefully for many years without public fights and protest. You need to see how the couple manifested what was really in them.

They kicked the door, threw seats, cursed people and screamed down the house. Thank God that happened on a midweek meeting when choir members were practicing alone. These people operate under the flesh not spirit. They want democratic votes to gain attention and can not operate under a theocracy. They will like to equalize themselves with Church authorities even though they have no skill, experience or calling for the position.

They are fast to tell people to choose between the stand of the Church and what they say. Who are you to make yourself an authority inside an established organization with an established authority? Such frauds and impostors would have been penalized if accosted in the world but in the house of God, we tend to condone every indecent conduct in the name of tolerance.

Beware of these pretenders. They are deceitful workers.

They are the people Jesus Christ refered to as thief and robber who tried to climb into the sheepfold through other means than the door (John 10:1-10). If you do not discover and disconnect the wrong influence of these pretenders on time, their bad conducts may become like a little yeast that affects the whole dough (Gal.5:9).

Watch out for what such people are saying. I read an article on the internet recently on "seven last words or phrases of the Church" before it collapses written by James Emery White. It was so precise.

Every Church leader needs to understand the implications of bad statements uttered by uncommitted Church hoppers in order to protect their congregations from vicious attacks of such people.
I have taken the privilege to add and rearrange some words for easy understanding.

- *"There must be more" or "I need to be fed" means, "I am a spiritual infant that needs to be spoon-fed because I'm not mature enough to open up the Bible and dig into it for myself. I hold Church responsible to teach me in a short while everything my parents, schools and I have failed to teach me until now. I'm mad about something that didn't go my way. In case you ask me to die to myself or show more commitment, I will hide under a spiritual-sounding excuse that makes it seem like the Church is beneath my level of advanced maturity and move out to where I can be baby fed again."*

- *"I didn't get anything out of it" means "The worship service is all about me. I am the object of worship. Forget that this is idolatry at its worst; I mustn't be worried about such things. It also doesn't enter my mind that the important thing isn't what I get out of it, but what God gets out of it. I am a consumer, and my needs drive me and should drive the Church. And I'll keep Church hopping and shopping - and evaluating - until I find what does meet my personal tastes and current desires."*

- *"The music is too loud" means "I don't like the style of music. It's too "rock." Too contemporary. I came here liking a certain kind of music, and now you're changing it in the name of reaching the young and disaffected. So now I am going to be disaffected until you change it back. And don't offer me any of those blasted ear-plugs; I shouldn't have to wear earplugs in Church! I should just like what is being played and how it's being played. When you talked about dying to ourselves in order to reach the unChurched, you never mentioned music. I don't die to myself there."*

- *"You talk about money too much" means "I don't give, don't plan on giving, and certainly don't want to be challenged to give. And if you mention it even once a year I'm going to cry foul and pull this self-righteous phrase out as a way of making you the bad guy. My money is my god, it's not for God, which is why I'm hyper-sensitive about it. I have to find a spiritual-sounding reason for exiting out from the challenge so that it's about you and the evils of organized religion, and not me and my consumptive lifestyle."*

- *"Who's holding you accountable?" means "I'm into control and want to find a way to have it. But talking about "accountability" sounds more spiritual. What I'm really after is finding out about boards and committees, councils and business meetings, and then how to get on them. Let Church leaders lead? Let pastors pastor? Are you crazy? You don't send someone to seminary to learn how to lead the Church; you send them to seminary to come back and be led by those of us who like to talk about accountability as a euphemism for control. They are our chaplains, to care for us and do our bidding, not decision-makers or leaders. I, of course, can be trusted and don't need any vocational training whatsoever to lead, much less any ...accountability."*

- *"I don't know everybody anymore" means "The Church is growing, and I don't want it to grow. At least, not so fast it outgrows me. I don't find fast growth exhilarating, I find it threatening. My sense of security is tied to feeling like I know everything that's going on. I'm not even sure I know all the staff anymore! I even have to make an appointment to talk to the pastor, and even then, it might not be the senior pastor who sees me. That's where all this talk about reaching lost people and growing the Church really leads to. I want it to be "us four and no more," but they want to reach the whole world! Do you know what that would mean? Why, I would have to become less so it can become more! Where do ideas like that even come from?"*

- *"Let's disciple the ones we have" means "A Church can be about evangelism, or it can be about discipleship. Not both. We're obviously misinterpreting Jesus when He said that it could be. But more to the point, I'm a bit on the spiritually prideful side of things, which means I like to talk about discipleship to remind everyone how discipled I am compared to the rest of the Christian minions. You know, I'm on the meaty, mature, believer-oriented, expositional, go-deep, doctrinally sound side of things. Not the trendy, culturally-hip, Christianity 101, contemporary, Church for the unChurched, evangelistic side of things. And don't bother me with the idea that there is all of eternity to grow in faith and knowledge and worship, and only here and now to evangelize. Or that the first Church started with 3,000*

> *converts and no discipleship program except 11 overwhelmed followers of Jesus who had only moments before abandoned and even betrayed Him. That's Acts, and we all know Acts was written before anybody was, well, discipled.*

The most horrible thing about such childish believers is that though they hate to take instructions, they treasure giving instructions to subordinates. While such a person may not be able to concentrate on listening to any message for fifteen minutes, such a person can spend hours at every opportunity raining down instructions on others.

Take note that the same God who gives us spiritual companionship of Holy spirit gives us human instructors to help make us perfect for the work of the ministry (Eph.4:11-15). Such human vessels work hand in hand with the Holy Spirit to build up believers into perfection.

> *For I am a man under authority, having soldiers under me: and I say to this man, Go, and he goeth; and to another, Come, and he cometh; and to my servant, Do this, and he doeth it.* **(Matthew 8:9)**

Until you obediently take instruction from an authority above you, you have no duty instructing your subordinates. Each time we read the Bible, we are not only listening to God but are also referencing the vision God gave to faithful leaders ahead of us. A leader that does not listen to God and show commitment to visions God has given other men of God in the Bible has no duty leading anyone in the house of God.

11. Relationship to discipline

> *My son, despise not the chastening of the LORD; neither be weary of his correction: For whom the LORD loveth he correcteth; even as a father the son in whom he delighteth.* **(Proverbs 3:11-12)**

> *For rulers are not a terror to good works, but to the evil. Wilt thou then not be afraid of the power? do that which is good, and thou shalt have praise of the same: For he is the minister of God to thee for good. But if thou do that which is evil, be afraid; for he beareth not the sword in vain: for he is the minister of God, a revenger to execute wrath upon him that doeth evil.* **(Romans 13:3-4)**

Every mature servant of the Lord appreciates the need to be led according to the will of God however painful such correction could be. When King Hezekiah was corrected by God, he didn't justify himself but went on his knees to seek pardon (2 Kings 20: 1-3).
He knew that every correction of God is an act of love.

Better is a poor and a wise child than an old and foolish king, who will no more be admonished. ***(Ecclesiastes 4:13)***

A bad servant on the other hand is only interested in showing that his leader is wrong and unjust. He loses the opportunity to look inward and make the necessary adjustment to improve personal character and ability. Rather than concentrate on areas affecting him, he focuses on finding the wrong part of the leadership's observation. His attention is on proving that some parts of the correction are wrong rather than applying the required correction to improve his life. Years after you meet him, he is still retaining his limited views and still saying the same wrong thing.
He is too right and all knowing to the extent that every correction becomes personal persecution and victimization.
Everyone is wrong and only the bad servant is right. Always right!
The parents were unfair, the boss is wicked, the spouse is not wise, friends are undependable and the Church leaders are dishonest.
All corrections are acts of discrimination, oppression and suppression. Only the bad servants know the right way to do the right things. If such a person is a leader in the Church, every time he is corrected, he finds an opportunity to slight authority. If such a person leads a department, he finds verses in the Bible to quote to pollute the mind of innocent people.
Every avenue is used to justify personal stand in order to subvert whatsoever correction is coming from above. Watch out that you do not give such people undue advantage to mislead other subordinates by publicly discussing their misdeeds where necessary.
It is easier for people to escape the wrong instigation from a disgruntled person if they realize such is embittered.

CHAPTER 10: PRINCIPLES OF SERVICE

The earth is the LORD's, and the fulness thereof; the world, and they that dwell therein.
(Psalm 24:1)

The world and the entire beings in it belong to the Lord! Everything we do, we ultimately do for the Lord. It doesn't matter either people appreciate it or not! Anything good or bad you do to anyone you do it to God to whom there is no hidden intention or action (Heb. 4: 13). Do not allow people's attitude to alter your altitude. Take control of your life by doing what is right.

1) God is the source of all services

And the King shall answer and say unto them, Verily I say unto you, Inasmuch as ye have done it unto one of the least of these my brethren, ye have done it unto me. ***(Matthew 25:40)***

As you go to work or help a poor man on the street or save another sinner on the street, remember that you are doing everything for God. Do not just do it right, do it excitingly. Anywhere you find yourself, be determined to cheerfully offer your service to the Lord.

2) God is the provider of all powers that administer services

Let every soul be subject unto the higher powers. For there is no power but of God: the powers that be are ordained of God. Whosoever therefore resisteth the power, resisteth the ordinance of God: and they that resist shall receive to themselves damnation. ***(Romans 13:1-2)***

The scripture is very clear that God is the source of all the power that be. By inference all the services they offer are permitted by God. Even, the wicked King Pharaoh was permitted to oppress the children of God for a season and for a reason (Rom 9:17). Even when God is not behind a particular wicked governor, God is always behind the government as a means of orderly existence.

With this revelation, Christians need to fearfully submit to all the leaderships over them be they civil, family, vocational or spiritual.
In the Church circumstances, every believer is called to follow their leader so long their leaders follow God's instructions as documented in the Bible (1 Cor.11:1). Only ignorant believers will follow spiritual leaders like Jim Jones who committed mutiny over his ignorant followers. Like the Bereans, we are expected to be noble Christians.

> *These were more noble than those in Thessalonica, in that they received the word with all readiness of mind, and searched the scriptures daily, whether those things were so.* **(Acts 17:11)**

Our absolute obedience should always be to God, the source of all authority and services. Anytime instruction is contrary to the will of God, it is absolutely important to stick to that of God.
Disobedience to authority on the other hand translates to disregard for God. When we honour our leaders, God is able to turn them to work well on our behalfs (Prov. 21: 11).

> *Wherefore then were ye not afraid to speak against my servant Moses?* **(Numbers 12:8)**

> *Saying, Touch not mine anointed, and do my prophets no harm.* **(1 Chronicle 16:22)**

3) Every activity directed at securing orderliness is ordained and rewarded of the Lord

> *For God is not the author of confusion, but of peace, as in all Churches of the saints.* **(1 Corinthians 14:33)**

God is the author of all orderliness in the world.
That is why the Bible insists that we pray for, obey and honour all authorities (1Tim. 2: 1; Rom.13: 1-7). Any thing leading to disrespect, dishonour and disorderliness may easily distant you from the God of order and peace. In the other hand, every act that leads to orderliness and curbing of the destructive effect of evil both in the spiritual and in the physical is compensated by Him. Every person is as important as others so long you are solving problems with your skills and talents. Ultimately, it is God that will reward us all for our labours of love.

4) **The surest way to serve God is through your godly service to mankind**

When I was a child, I spake as a child, I understood as a child, I thought as a child: but when I became a man, I put away childish things.
(1 Corinthians 13:11)

I have heard a childish thing like, "I am only serving God, I can not serve any man!" from mouths of immature Christians. There is nothing far from gospel truth than that. You can worship God alone in the corner of your house but you cannot serve Him alone. It is simply impossible to serve God without serving the people He puts around you. Few of the ways Bible make this point crystal clear is discussed below.

a) **You cannot serve God without serving your household**

For if a man know not how to rule his own house, how shall he take care of the Church of God? **(1 Timothy 3:5)**

But if any provide not for his own, and specially for those of his own house, he hath denied the faith, and is worse than an infidel.
(1 Timothy 5:8)

God expects you to show faithfulness in the first social institution He created before you can proceed to genuinely worship Him.
Failure to honour that institution is tantamount to dishonoring divine instruction. Bible refers to such conduct as a denial of faith!
Your service to the Lord begins with your household!

b) **You cannot serve God correctly without serving mankind.**

For I was an hungred, and ye gave me meat: I was thirsty, and ye gave me drink: I was a stranger, and ye took me in: Naked, and ye clothed me: I was sick, and ye visited me: I was in prison, and ye came unto me. Then shall the righteous answer him, saying, Lord, when saw we thee an hungred, and fed thee? or thirsty, and gave thee drink? When saw we thee a stranger, and took thee in? or naked, and clothed thee? Or when saw we thee sick, or in prison, and came unto thee? And the King shall answer and say unto them, Verily I say unto you, Inasmuch as ye have done it unto one of the least of these my brethren, ye have done it unto me. **(Matthew 25:35-40)**

Service to the entire mankind is your dutiful service to God.

Every time you curse, insult, quarrel and disrespect people especially children of God, it is God you do it to. In the other hand if you are looking for a way to please God, you do not need to look further beyond the first pauper and needy you meet on the road. Inasmuch as you have done it to a creature of God, you have done it unto Him! There is nothing worse than treating fellow Christian bad. It pains me to witness one denomination quarrelling against another or one group in the same Church quarrelling against another. God is not devided. The body of Christ is united!

> *And let us not be weary in well doing: for in due season we shall reap, if we faint not. As we have therefore opportunity, let us do good unto all men, especially unto them who are of the household of faith.* **(Galatians 6:9-10)**

> *Let brotherly love continue. Be not forgetful to entertain strangers: for thereby some have entertained angels unawares. Remember them that are in bonds, as bound with them; and them which suffer adversity, as being yourselves also in the body.* **(Hebrews 13:1-31)**

The joy is as you serve strangers, you are sure to serve the Lord!

c) God anoints you for leadership through service to others

> *And the LORD said unto Samuel, How long wilt thou mourn for Saul, seeing I have rejected him from reigning over Israel? fill thine horn with oil, and go, I will send thee to Jesse the Bethlehemite: for I have provided me a king among his sons.* **Then Samuel took the horn of oil, and anointed him in the midst of his brethren: and the Spirit of the LORD came upon David** *from that day forward. So Samuel rose up, and went to Ramah.* **(1 Samuel 16:1, 13)**

When Prophet Samuel anointed David, the spirit of the Lord immediately came upon him!
Not only that, the scripture was written under the anointing of Holy Spirit revealed that, that action, though conducted by man, is a direct act of the Lord. It was God Himself that anointed David!

> *Then thou spakest in vision to thy holy one, and saidst, I have laid help upon one that is mighty; I have exalted one chosen out of the people.* **I have found David my servant; with my holy oil have I anointed**

him: With whom my hand shall be established: mine arm also shall strengthen him. **(Psalm 89:19-21)**

Many potential leaders are misled into potholes of self-destruction by believing that they do not need to acknowledge, serve or seek to be anointed into office by any man of God.

And no man taketh this honour unto himself, but he that is called of God, as was Aaron. **(Hebrews 5:4)**

Here is Elisha the son of Shaphat, which poured water on the hands of Elijah. **(2 Kings 3:11)**

Elisha received double anointing upon the life of Elijah through his humble service. Yes, God on special occasion may choose to come down and specially anoint a man for office but in most of the time, He does it through the human institution.

And Moses did as the LORD commanded him: and he took Joshua, and set him before Eleazar the priest, and before all the congregation: And he laid his hands upon him, and gave him a charge, as the LORD commanded by the hand of Moses. **(Numbers 27:22-23)**

And Joshua the son of Nun was full of the spirit of wisdom; for Moses had laid his hands upon him: and the children of Israel hearkened unto him, and did as the LORD commanded Moses. **(Deuteronomy 34:9)**

Prophet Samuel anointed Saul and David to the office the same way Elijah anointed Elisha. Many Old Testament leaders were ordained by God to the office through Moses. Jesus Christ didn't depart from this style when it was His time to assume office.

Then cometh Jesus from Galilee to Jordan unto John, to be baptized of him. But John forbad him, saying, I have need to be baptized of thee, and comest thou to me? And Jesus answering said unto him, Suffer it to be so now: for thus it becometh us to fulfil all righteousness. Then he suffered him. **(Matthew 3:13-15)**

God is still anointing His peopleto office today however only those humble enough to submit themselves under complete training and supervision of other men of God can enjoy that blessing of the Lord.

d)   You cannot claim to love God without loving people

> *If a man say, I love God, and hateth his brother, he is a liar: for he that loveth not his brother whom he hath seen, how can he love God whom he hath not seen? And this commandment have we from him, That he who loveth God love his brother also.* **(1 John 4:20-21)**

You cannot claim to love God when you distaste your brother!
He that doesn't love cannot know God for God is love (1 John 4:8). Love for God is shown through how we relate with the creatures of the Lord sorrounding us.
What are you doing to save myriads of unbelievers around you?
What are you doing to support the widows and fatherless?

> *Pure religion and undefiled before God and the Father is this, To visit the fatherless and widows in their affliction, and to keep himself unspotted from the world.* **(James 1:27)**

> *If ye oppress not the stranger, the fatherless, and the widow, and shed not innocent blood in this place, neither walk after other gods to your hurt: Then will I cause you to dwell in this place, in the land that I gave to your fathers, for ever and ever.* **(Jeremiah 7:6-7)**

God executes judgment on behalf of the fatherless, strangers and widow (Deut. 10: 17-19). Your faith only works with love (Gal. 5:6).

e) You can not be forgiven by God without forgiving man

> *And when ye stand praying, forgive, if ye have ought against any: that your Father also which is in heaven may forgive you your trespasses. But if ye do not forgive, neither will your Father which is in heaven forgive your trespasses.* **(Mark 11:25-26)**

> *So likewise shall my heavenly Father do also unto you, if ye from your hearts forgive not every one his brother their trespasses.* **(Matthew 18:35)**

Until you let people go off your hands, you cannot receive forgiveness from the Lord. You will need to cultivate Jesus' skill of making an excuse for your enemies (Luke 23:34) in order to be able to completely forgive them if you want to live to reap the blessing and divine provisions of God upon your life.

f) Disobedience to man is disobedience to God

Servants, be obedient to them that are your masters according to the flesh, with fear and trembling, in singleness of your heart, as unto Christ; Not with eyeservice, as menpleasers; but as the servants of Christ, doing the will of God from the heart; With good will doing service, as to the Lord, and not to men: Knowing that whatsoever good thing any man doeth, the same shall he receive of the Lord, whether he be bond or free. **(Ephesians 6:5-8)**

Let every soul be subject unto the higher powers. For there is no power but of God: the powers that be are ordained of God. Whosoever therefore resisteth the power, resisteth the ordinance of God: and they that resist shall receive to themselves damnation. For rulers are not a terror to good works, but to the evil. Wilt thou then not be afraid of the power? do that which is good, and thou shalt have praise of the same: For he is the minister of God to thee for good. But if thou do that which is evil, be afraid; for he beareth not the sword in vain: for he is the minister of God, a revenger to execute wrath upon him that doeth evil. Wherefore ye must needs be subject, not only for wrath, but also for conscience sake. For for this cause pay ye tribute also: for they are God's ministers, attending continually upon this very thing. **(Rom. 13:1-7)**

Saul was shocked to learn from Jesus that his persecution of Christ disciples is practical persecution of Jesus Christ Himself. Every time you lie against, attack or disobey people of the lord, have you ever wondered you might be doing that to God Himself?

But Peter said, Ananias, why hath Satan filled thine heart to lie to the Holy Ghost, and to keep back part of the price of the land? **(Acts 5:3)**

Many acts of disobedience to human vessels of the Lord could easily set us against the will of God and His awesome personality.

But Gehazi, the servant of Elisha the man of God, said, Behold, my master hath spared Naaman this Syrian, in not receiving at his hands that which he brought: but, as the LORD liveth, I will run after him, and take somewhat of him. So Gehazi followed after Naaman. And when Naaman saw him running after him, he lighted down from the chariot to meet him, and said, Is

> *all well? And he said, All is well. My master hath sent me, saying, Behold, even now there be come to me from mount Ephraim two young men of the sons of the prophets: give them, I pray thee, a talent of silver, and two changes of garments.* ***(2 Kings 5:20-22)***

> *But he went in, and stood before his master. And Elisha said unto him, Whence comest thou, Gehazi? And he said, Thy servant went no whither. And he said unto him, Went not mine heart with thee, when the man turned again from his chariot to meet thee? Is it a time to receive money, and to receive garments, and oliveyards, and vineyards, and sheep, and oxen, and menservants, and maidservants? The leprosy therefore of Naaman shall cleave unto thee, and unto thy seed for ever. And he went out from his presence a leper as white as snow. Render therefore to all their dues: tribute to whom tribute is due; custom to whom custom; fear to whom fear; honour to whom honour.* ***(2 Kings 5:25-27)***

Gehazi didn't see God in his boss. He saw a mere man who was not clever enough to make others pay for their services. By so doing, he did not just miss the chance to carry the mantle of Elisha but ended up inheriting his wrath and curse.

g) Sin to man is a sin to God.

> *There is none greater in this house than I; neither hath he kept back any thing from me but thee, because thou art his wife: how then can I do this great wickedness, and sin against God?* ***(Genesis 39:9)***

Joseph was clever to see that sin against godly authority over him was a sin against the Lord. This wisdom kept him from losing his greatness to sinful misconduct and retained God's favour upon him.

h) Forgiveness of man is forgiveness from God

> *And I will give unto thee the keys of the kingdom of heaven: and whatsoever thou shalt bind on earth shall be bound in heaven: and whatsoever thou shalt loose on earth shall be loosed in heaven.* ***(Matthew 16:19)***

> *Is any sick among you? let him call for the elders of the Church; and let them pray over him, anointing him with oil in the name of the Lord: And the prayer of faith shall save the sick, and the Lord shall raise him up; and if he have committed sins, they shall be forgiven him.* ***(James 5:14-15)***

> *To whom ye forgive any thing, I forgive also: for if I forgave any thing, to whom I forgave it, for your sakes forgave I it in the person of Christ; Lest Satan should get an advantage of us: for we are not ignorant of his devices.* **(2 Corinthians 2:10-11)**

God can forgive you through human institutions. While Jesus Christ was on earth as the son of God, He forgave many people their sins (Mark 2:6-12). Church of Christ retains that privilege today.

5) We win together by serving together

> *For though I be free from all men, yet have I made myself servant unto all, that I might gain the more. And unto the Jews I became as a Jew, that I might gain the Jews; to them that are under the law, as under the law, that I might gain them that are under the law; To them that are without law, as without law, (being not without law to God, but under the law to Christ,) that I might gain them that are without law. To the weak became I as weak, that I might gain the weak: I am made all things to all men, that I might by all means save some. And this I do for the gospel's sake, that I might be partaker thereof with you.* **(1 Corinthians 9:19-23)**

We are stronger together. By joining hands to work together for the Lord, we all partake in God's victory over the kingdom of darkness.

a) Leading together is serving together

> *So we, being many, are one body in Christ, and every one members one of another. Having then gifts differing according to the grace that is given to us, whether prophecy, let us prophesy according to the proportion of faith;*
> *Or ministry, let us wait on our ministering: or he that teacheth, on teaching; Or he that exhorteth, on exhortation: he that giveth, let him do it with simplicity; he that ruleth, with diligence; he that sheweth mercy, with cheerfulness.* **(Romans 12:5-8)**

In the Kingdom of God, everyone is created to be Kings and prophets (Rev. 1: 6; Rev. 5: 10). In essence everyone can be a leader. Every vessel that purges itself can become vessels of honour (2 Tim. 2: 20-21). As we lead together, we re simply serving together with the cause of the gospel so that all glory could be brought to the Lord.

b) We lose together by working against each other

> *But if ye bite and devour one another, take heed that ye be not consumed one of another.* **(Galatians 5:15)**

> *Recompense to no man evil for evil. Provide things honest in the sight of all men. If it be possible, as much as lieth in you, live peaceably with all men. Dearly beloved, avenge not yourselves, but rather give place unto wrath: for it is written, Vengeance is mine; I will repay, saith the Lord. Therefore if thine enemy hunger, feed him; if he thirst, give him drink: for in so doing thou shalt heap coals of fire on his head. Be not overcome of evil, but overcome evil with good.* **(Romans 12:17-21)**

The fact that you are wronged is no reason to do the wrong things. Two wrongs can not make a right. Remember that you step only on the feet of those who are so close to you. Bible expects us to forgive people so that we can restore them back to God. (James 5: 16-20)

c) We win forever by walking in truth and love together

> *For all the law is fulfilled in one word, even in this; Thou shalt love thy neighbour as thyself.* **(Galatians 5:14)**

> *We know that we have passed from death unto life, because we love the brethren. He that loveth not his brother abideth in death.* **(1 John 3:14)**

Church fellowship is meant to be an eternal relationship that outlasts life. A good understanding of this situation will make you realize why you need to invest every part of you being in building the Church together till death take us to our home where we shall part no more.

6) The influence of authority is pyramidal

> *The heaven, even the heavens, are the LORD's: but the earth hath he given to the children of men.* **(Psalm 115:16)**

Our Father who hath in heaven…
Thy will be done in earth, as it is in heaven (Matthew 6:10).
God's laws cover everywhere in heaven and on earth!
Man's dominion covers all services on earth. As far as you can see in the Bible is yours. Your service as an individual however only covers the area your service is located down wards.

7) Leadership is an act of service

> *I have coveted no man's silver, or gold, or apparel. Yea, ye yourselves know, that these hands have ministered unto my necessities, and to them that were with me. I have shewed you all things, how that so labouring ye ought to support the weak, and to remember the words of the Lord Jesus, how he said, It is more blessed to give than to receive.* **(Acts 20:33-35)**

Every man is created by the Lord to satisfy a particular need. The ability to locate such need and lead yourself to satisfy it purposefully with your talents and skills is an act of leadership. Leadership in Church is not just about leading as is in ministering. It is about serving some values you have been endowed with to enrich the life of other people. Paul is an exemplary leader who made a policy of not coveting possession of his people. He rather took the responsibility upon himself to cater to the need of his congregation.

Many preachers think selfishly in term of what they can gain from their congregation rather than selflessly thinking of a way to add values to them. Kingdom leaders are called not to milk the meek but to empower the weak to reach their peak. It is more blessed to give than to take. That gospel truth applies also to Church leaders.

It is God that has called you not the people so look up to Him for your compensation lest you turn gospel to burden for the same people you have been called to bless.

8) Honouring leaders avails you of the blessing in them

> *Honour thy father and mother; (which is the first commandment with promise;) That it may be well with thee, and thou mayest live long on the earth.* **(Ephesians 6:2-3)**

> *Believe in the LORD your God, so shall ye be established; believe his prophets, so shall ye prosper.* **(2 Chronicles 20:20)**

Though no God-fearing man should curse his people, be careful that you do not personally activate curses placed by God on disobedient people. The blessing of the Lord is withheld over you when you dishonour your parents!

> *And Samuel said, Hath the LORD as great delight in burnt offerings and sacrifices, as in obeying the voice of the LORD? Behold, to obey is better than sacrifice, and to hearken than the fat of rams.23 For rebellion is as the sin of witchcraft, and stubbornness is as iniquity and idolatry. Because thou hast rejected the word of the LORD, he hath also rejected thee from being king.*

(1 Samuel 15: 22-23)

But Peter said, Ananias, why hath Satan filled thine heart to lie to the Holy Ghost, and to keep back part of the price of the land? Whiles it remained, was it not thine own? and after it was sold, was it not in thine own power? why hast thou conceived this thing in thine heart? thou hast not lied unto men, but unto God. And Ananias hearing these words fell down, and gave up the ghost: and great fear came on all them that heard these things. And the young men arose, wound him up, and carried him out, and buried him.
(Acts 5:3-6)

Your prosperity is attached to your believing God's prophets.
In both incidences, though only men spoke, their words became a divine judgement. God is in the business of confirming the word of His servant and performing the counsel of his messengers (Isa 44:26).

9) Service is all about value not status

For David, after he had served his own generation by the will of God, fell on sleep. **(Acts 13:36a)**

Be motivated to add value to peoples' lives.
A man that truly lives is one whose achievement outlives him.
Stewardship is the faithful management of the resources within your care. Life is about raising your world higher rather than raping and reaping it off. Jesus Christ only lived for thirtythree years on earth but the impact he left behind is still talking and affecting lives today.
A true measure of a man's age is not chronological but in the service one renders to his generation. What value are you adding to your generation? What will people remember you for when you rest in the Lord? Today is the right time to begin to paint the picture you want to be remembered by. Position is about relevance not status.
A kingdom servant lives a live of relevance to his community, congregation, family and other accomplices.

10) Every relevant service is equally important

And he gave some, apostles; and some, prophets; and some, evangelists; and some, pastors and teachers; For the perfecting of the saints, for the work of the ministry, for the edifying of the body of Christ. **(Ephesians 4:11-12)**

No service is inferior to another. We are all called for different service but no service is inferior to other so long it is offered in great standard. Whatsoever you are called to do, do it to your very best. Serve according to your particular talents and calling.

11) Every service can be improved

If the iron be blunt, and he do not whet the edge, then must he put to more strength: but wisdom is profitable to direct. **(Ecclesiastes 10:10)**

Leadership is about finding your gift and serving is skillfull to others. It is the satisfaction of peoples needs with your deed. The process entails finding your gift, refining it and releasing it for the public good. Learning is lifetime and changes are forever recurring.
Every God given talent can be improved through training.
Wisdom is the key to victorious living. The quality of a service depends on the efforts put into it. God expects kingdom leaders to subject themselves to a lifetime of value added service to their congregation. Gospel is good news! Each time people reject it, it is because someone has wrongly presented the living word of God in a boring, scary and unexciting way. Only God is perfect.
Everyone else has sufficient room to improve on his service.

12) Your area of strength is the best area of your service

Then the twelve called the multitude of the disciples unto them, and said, It is not reason that we should leave the word of God, and serve tables.
(Acts 6:2)

Your best area of service is the area you are divinely equipped to outperform others. Your area of core advantages in life identifies the divine deposits you are created to serve.
Quite often in life, your area of service is the place the enemy will attack you. If you are called into a healing ministry, you may grow up as a sickler. If you are called to deliver prostitutes from the bondage of the enemy, you might start life as a prostitute yourself. Many great preachers I know were born as stammerers. Apostle Paul grew up to destroy the people whose life purpose was to protect. It took an encounter with Jesus Christ to turn his life around. Both the leper of Galilee and the mad man of Gadarenes that Jesus Christ healed

ended up as publishers of gospels. The enemy attacked their destinies knowing the great impacts they would have against his kingdom.

> *But he went out, and began to publish it much, and to blaze abroad the matter, insomuch that Jesus could no more openly enter into the city, but was without in desert places: and they came to him from every quarter.* **(Mark 1:45)**

> *And he departed, and began to publish in Decapolis how great things Jesus had done for him: and all men did marvel.* **(Mark 5:20)**

Jesus Christ warned Apostle Peter to encourage others after coming over the attack of depression that the enmy was about to unleash on him (Luke 22:31-32). So, your area of attack could be your area of calling. The best revenge against any attack of the enemy is to develop in your area of attack till it becomes your area of strength and influence where you deliver other victims from the molestation of the enemy. Other ways you can locate your area of strength are through impartation from prophecy, the discovery of divine gifts, personal experience and practice, passion, training or personal preference. Whichever way you locate your calling, you need to consciously develop and serve it.

13) Your area of service is related to areas of divine calling

> *Then the twelve called the multitude of the disciples unto them, and said, It is not reason that we should leave the word of God, and serve tables. Wherefore, brethren, look ye out among you seven men of honest report, full of the Holy Ghost and wisdom, whom we may appoint over this business. But we will give ourselves continually to prayer, and to the ministry of the word.* **(Acts 6:2-4)**

When the Church sporadically expanded and the challenges of administration emerged to compete with that to minister the word of God, the disciples of Jesus Christ chose what their calling prepared them for and left serving the tables to others.
As the body of Christ, our departments and talents are interelated and interdependent. None is independent of each other or complete without others. Together, we form a complete body with a complete blessing. Every one has a definite purpose for being alive.
It is when you operate within your divine purpose that you can bear fruits and add greatest values to people's lives.

14) Impact of every service is limited to its relevant area

And he said unto them, Render therefore unto Caesar the things which be Caesar's, and unto God the things which be God's. ***(Luke 20:25)***

The spiritual service of your Church though affects all areas of your life do not carry precedence over your duties in other institution. Church instruction is relevant to Church activities. Jesus did not deny the authority of Caesar over the political institution of His time.

As a leader of a fellowship in your Church, your authority is limited to those under you not even over those sharing the same status and authority as you. It is beyond your spiritual authority to bless your Pastor or try to instruct him. When Peter tried that with Jesus, he was rebuked as Satan for God is not the author of confusion, but of peace, as in all Churches of the saints (1 Cor 14:33). Your role as head of your family does not extend to your Church and your role as a leader in your Church do not extend to your local government.

Every office hasits own limited jurisdiction.

15) God is the source of all resources to accomplish the mission

God also bearing them witness, both with signs and wonders, and with divers miracles, and gifts of the Holy Ghost, according to his own will? ***(Heb. 2:4)***

But thou shalt remember the LORD thy God: for it is he that giveth thee power to get wealth, that he may establish his covenant which he sware unto thy fathers, as it is this day. ***(Deuteronomy 8:18)***

If you are sure of your source, your resource will always be sure!

Only he that has God as his shepherd could boldly say, "surely, goodness and mercy shall follow me all the days of my life (Ps 23:6)."

You however need to be careful not to mistake God's virtues in your life for your personal possession. It is His gift and virtues and must be used, with appreciation, for His glory.

a) The virtue that goes through you is His virtue

And God wrought special miracles by the hands of Paul: So that from his body were brought unto the sick handkerchiefs or aprons, and the diseases departed from them, and the evil spirits went out of them. ***(Acts 19:11-12)***

Faithful is he that calleth you, who also will do it. ***(1 Thess. 5:24)***

It is not your virtue that works a miracle. It is God!
Everything working fine in your ministry is worked by God.
You are only connecting into God's doing through your commitment and obedience. Without God, you can do nothing!

b) It is God that confirms His words with signs and wonder

That confirmeth the word of his servant, and performeth the counsel of his messengers. **(Isaiah 44:26)**

He is the Confirmer and Performer of your words and counsels.
He is the solution provider to your supplication, the Answer to your prayers. Prayer, at its best is an earthly demand tool for heavenly supply. God is the Supplier. Only God answers prayer. It is not the power of your priest that delivers but the mercy of God.

c) Your life and its achievement is by His grace

For by grace are ye saved through faith; and that not of yourselves: it is the gift of God: Not of works, lest any man should boast. **(Eph. 2:8-9)**

So then it is not of him that willeth, nor of him that runneth, but of God that sheweth mercy. **(Romans 9:16)**

The grace of Jesus Christ is undeserved favour offered through His sacrificial death long before you were born. Your work of faith only qualifies you to benefit from this available grace.
It is like passing an examination to benefit from free state education. Of course you need to pass your examination in order to benefit from the state's offer but your passing did not create the offer.
It only qualifies you to benefit from the offer.
Everytime a man accepts Jesus Christ into his life; he passes the test of faith, which qualifies him to enjoy the free grace of God. As long as you continue in this walk of faith, you can continue to enjoy the free grace same way your continuous enjoyment of the free education depends on your ability to continue to pass your examinations.

16) Everyone is created to serve a special purpose

And God blessed them, and God said unto them, Be fruitful, and multiply, and replenish the earth, and subdue it: and have dominion over the fish of the sea, and over the fowl of the air, and over every living thing that moveth upon the earth. **(Genesis 1:28)**

At Creation, all men are destined to have dominion in any area they chose to offer their services. Your service is not limited to believers alone. God is counting on the believers to restore the non-believers to Him. Regardless of your vocation in life, God expects you to locate it within His general purpose of reconciling mankind to Himself.

17) You never grow beyond the service you offered last

If therefore ye have not been faithful in the unrighteous mammon, who will commit to your trust the true riches? And if ye have not been faithful in that which is another man's, who shall give you that which is your own? No servant can serve two masters: for either he will hate the one, and love the other; or else he will hold to the one, and despise the other. Ye cannot serve God and mammon. **(Luke 16:11-13)**

You may have a calling upon your life to become a university professor but if you disobey your secondary school teacher and quit school, you may never rise to your destined height. Even if you manage through private lessons to progress further, you will spend a longer time. It is faster to drive over existing roads than to personally build new ones to your destination. To become a Professor, you need to expose yourself to the services of every small tutor that comes your way even if you will later become their professor. If God ordains you to be a bishop but you refuse to perform your initial duty of an usher well, you may never reach your intended end. That is because no man is indispensable in the kingdom of God. Wherever you locate yourself in the purpose of God, labor to make sure that the grace is not in vain. The recognition of this truth was the secret behind Paul's astounding success as Apostle. He laboured more abundantly than other apostles to make his calling sure.

18) Your godly service determines your greatness in life

But seek ye first the kingdom of God... **(Matthew 6:33)**

And cast ye the unprofitable servant into outer darkness: there shall be weeping and gnashing of teeth. **(Matthew 25:30)**

Disobedience to this simple instruction has cost both believers and non-believers alike easy access to prosperous living.

Your success in life is attached to your godly service.
Have you seen a man that is diligent in his business? He will stand before kings. He will not stand before low people (Prov.22:29).
Your gift will always make way for you into realms of greatness.
It is your godly service that determines your value to your generation.
The more you can not be replaced in terms of quality and quantity of efforts offered in service for the kingdom of God the more unique your impact and your greatness.
Businesses and individuals that are prosperous in the world are those serving their generations effectively. They are not selfish and self centered people but are rather selfless people devoted to the corporate wellbeing of the entire mankind. God honours always those who locate themselves in the purpose of the Maker for His corporate creatures. The best way to know how successful your service is, is to take a look at the people depending on your service. You are not successful until people around you are. A wise man in the company of fools is the king of fools, a full-blown buffoon.
Jesus commanded great followers because he was a great servant.
Until you serve your people you are not deserved to be served.

> *For whether is greater, he that sitteth at meat, or he that serveth? is not he that sitteth at meat? But I am among you as he that serveth.* **(Luke 22:27)**

Regardless of what you have, you are simply a caretaker going to give account once to your heavenly master. The best way to give a good account of your wealth is to use it to bless others.

Service to other begins with the death of self. Selfishness is the major disease that blinds one to the needs of others. Your destiny is tied to your service. Do not wait for people to show appreciation.

Do not wait till you are very rich before you begin to live a life of blessing. It is your faithfulness in little that will determine your future promotion. Focus on finding a kingdom need you are best equipped to satisfy and engage your talent to offer the required solution.

19) Your labour attracts God's favour upon your life

> *And ye shall serve the LORD your God, and he shall bless thy bread, and thy water; and I will take sickness away from the midst of thee. There shall nothing cast their young, nor be barren, in thy land: the number of thy days I will fulfil. I will send my fear before thee, and will destroy all the people to whom thou shalt come, and I will make all thine enemies turn their backs unto thee.* **(Exodus 23:25-27)**

Your labor is key to your blessing.
The reason God recruits people into His service is to bless them.
You shall serve and He shall bless you. That is a covenant!
However, God's reward is beyond human qualification. He gives us the priceless blessing that includes peace, joy, health, long life and eternal life. You can not serve God with gladness of heart and suffer from the enemy. He will fulfill your days and destroy your enemies.
Labour alone, however does not make rich or all labourers would be millionaires. So God knows and makes room for favour.
One time favour of God is worth more than a lifetime of labour.
One favour shot Joseph, an imprisoned slave into the office of a Prime Minister of a foreign country in less than 24 hours.
The same favour transferred the wealth of Egypt to Israelites within a day. Within less than 24 hours, they spoiled the Egyptians and made away with what they do not get for their slave labours of four hundred and thirty years. You should therefore not just labour anyhow for anything but should be wisely labouring for the favour of God. The key to a prosperous life is to labour for the blessing of God. It is the blessing of the Lord that maketh rich (Prov.10:22).
The Bible instructs us to seek foremost the kingdom of God and His righteousness promising that all other things shall be added unto us.

20) Righteous living connects human labour to God's favour

> *The righteous shall flourish like the palm tree: he shall grow like a cedar in Lebanon. Those that be planted in the house of the LORD shall flourish in the courts of our God. They shall still bring forth fruit in old age; they shall be fat and flourishing.* **(Psalm 92:12-14)**

God's blessing and favour are worth more than any human labor can ever deserve. It is therefore important for us to know and invest our lives in what qualifies a man's labour for the favour of God.
The first tip was given to us in God's order of human priorities.

> *But seek ye first the kingdom of God, and his righteousness; and all these things shall be added unto you.* **(Matthew 6:33)**

As simple as ABC, it takes commitment to God's kingdom and righteous existence to enjoy Gods' unlimited resources. Many simply put their hope in their sweat than in God's grace (favour).
It is the destiny of the righteous to flourish and be fruitful!
God's blessing is reserved for the righteous. Why you may say?

Because the Lord is righteous. His ways are righteous. His purposes are righteous. His plan remains to bless righteous people who can use His righteous blessings for His righteous purpose.
His plan is not to bless the wicked non-believer or greedy belivers who will confiscate divine blessing for personal use. Greediness in the kingdom of God is dangerous and deadly. It cost the rich fool his life because he misunderstood the purpose of prosperity.

And he spake a parable unto them, saying, The ground of a certain rich man brought forth plentifully: And he thought within himself, saying, What shall I do, because I have no room where to bestow my fruits? And he said, This will I do: I will pull down my barns, and build greater; and there will I bestow all my fruits and my goods. And I will say to my soul, Soul, thou hast much goods laid up for many years; take thine ease, eat, drink, and be merry. But God said unto him, Thou fool, this night thy soul shall be required of thee: then whose shall those things be, which thou hast provided? So is he that layeth up treasure for himself, and is not rich toward God. **(Luke 12:16-21)**

Favor is more than your labor deserves.
It is the supernatural act of God on behalf of the righteous.

For thou, LORD, wilt bless the righteous; with favour wilt thou compass him as with a shield. **(Psalm 5:12)**

Whatever you labour on that will cut you off from the favour of the Lord is a curse in disguise. Righteous God is a God of the righteous. What attracts God's favour to your labour is righteousness.
The Lord shall bless the righteous! With what? With favour!
Think about it, can God bless and favour what you are doing?
That is a multibillion dollar question of favour. Great people in the Bible are labourers of favour. Joseph, like Job refused to choose the path of sin even in their hours of trials and temptation. They chose not to do anything that will cut them off from God. They knew that only God could perfectly deliver man from problems.
Stop wasting your life labouring on temporal things that do not last.
Do not just labour for anything but for the favour of God.
One time God's favour is worth more than a lifetime of labour.

21) Your greatness in life determines your life legacy

> *Moreover whom he did predestinate, them he also called: and whom he called, them he also justified: and whom he justified, them he also glorified.* ***(Romans 8:30)***
>
> *And I heard a voice from heaven saying unto me, Write, Blessed are the dead which die in the Lord from henceforth: Yea, saith the Spirit, that they may rest from their labours; and their works do follow them.* ***(Rev. 14:13)***

What you take out of life is the legacy you leave behind.
Legacy refers to the eternal work you do that is sure to outlast your life. The day you die, would it have mattered that you ever lived? Invest life in things you are proud to associate your memory with.

a) Journey to greatness begins with the discovery of purpose.
If it doesn't worth dying for, it is worthless living for it. Doing the right thing makes the difference between living and existing. I might consider a shirt useful and successful in cleaning a table but its fulfillment and true glory are in being worn. Every product is judged by the producer upon its ability to solve the problem it is created to solve. Being busy, useful and successful is not enough if your life is focused on the wrong purpose. Until you discover your purpose, you are only existing not living.

b) The glory of man is to grow up and fulfill the purpose of his Maker. It is the glory of a bird to fly the same way it is the glory of a tree to bear fruits. Purpose makes all the difference between being busy and being productive.
Purpose gives focus, passion and motivation to life.
Purpose is the key to the fulfilment of a product (Rom. 8:28).

c) Glory is the fulfilment of purpose.
Your glory is attained at the completion of your purpose in life. Your greatness refers to your glory. Glorification is the ultimate destination for every man that fulfils His God-given purpose.
May you discover and fulfil your purpose in Jesus name. Amen.

d) Death is our common destiny. It is the logical conclusion to temporal existence and the Transition Bridge into eternity. Every product will expire one day. Will your life worth it at the expiration of your mortal body or would it have been better you were never born? Legacy is about living beyond your existence in the hearts of other people through your eternal service. What is your life dedicated to? Are you just acquiring material

things instead of building an eternal relationship with God and His people? Where is your treasure stored?
On temporal earth where moth corrupts and thieves steal or in eternal labor that can not be erased? Are you living the way you want to be remembered?

22) God is the final rewarder of all services

And cast ye the unprofitable servant into outer darkness: there shall be weeping and gnashing of teeth. ***(Matthew 25:30)***

Servants, be obedient to them that are your masters according to the flesh, with fear and trembling, in singleness of your heart, as unto Christ; Not with eyeservice, as menpleasers; but as the servants of Christ, doing the will of God from the heart; With good will doing service, as to the Lord, and not to men: Knowing that whatsoever good thing any man doeth, the same shall he receive of the Lord, whether he be bond or free. ***(Ephesians 6:5-8)***

Servants, obey in all things your masters according to the flesh; not with eyeservice, as menpleasers; but in singleness of heart, fearing God: And whatsoever ye do, do it heartily, as to the Lord, and not unto men; Knowing that of the Lord ye shall receive the reward of the inheritance: for ye serve the Lord Christ. But he that doeth wrong shall receive for the wrong which he hath done: and there is no respect of persons. ***(Colossians 3:22-25)***

Service is a heart matter. God honours our intentions to serve him, as a free moral agent than our perfection. That was the only reason Jesus Christ could rate the old lady who gave an offering of two mites from her lack higher than the rich ones who gave greater amounts from their surplus. The heart of the matter is that your walk of faith is a matter of the heart. Your heart matters!

For he that cometh to God must believe that he is, and that he is a rewarder of them that diligently seek him. ***(Hebrews 11:6)***

Sometimes in life we sow to fertile grounds and sometimes, those we bless are dry deserts, totally ungrateful and unappreciative but whatever you do, God will ultimately reward you. It doesn't matter who and when you do it, as far as your intention is good, Jesus Christ says that you have done it to Him (Matt. 25: 34-40).

> What you take out of life is the legacy you leave behind. Legacy refers to the eternal work you do that is sure to outlast your life. The day you die, would it have mattered that you ever lived?

CHAPTER 11: RENDERING SERVICE TO THE LORD

A son honoureth his father, and a servant his master: if then I be a father, where is mine honour? and if I be a master, where is my fear? (**Mal. 1:6**)

If any man serve me, let him follow me; and where I am, there shall also my servant be: if any man serve me, him will my Father honour. (**John 12:26**)

The ultimate perfect will of God for man is for us to be united with Him in purpose. He wants us to think of Him, meditate on His words, live to achieve His purpose and achieve all our breakthroughs in His presence. Surely if any man shall be able to completely rest his focus on God, the enemy will have no opportunity to tamper with his perfect destiny in the Lord. It is only when our focus is broken away from Him that we fall victim to the temptation of the enemy.

It is easy to see the level of a man's focus on God by observing how he lives, what he does and what he says. By a man's pursuit, you can easily tell whose servant he is, be it of God, Satan or himself. It is only when we use our existence and resources for the glory of God that we can be sure that we are truly His servant. I do not mean that you should give all your properties and resources to your Church. I only mean that you should put yourself in a position where you can richly give to the promotion of the work of God while alive.

That is the only way to store wealth in your eternal account.

Take note that giving is more than a financial obligation. You can give your time, skill, experience and work in worshipping God. You can worship God with every area of your life.

When you go to work, you should work in a way that honour God. Your conduct should attract people to God. When you suffer set backs, your conduct should prove your belief in God. Everything you do from morning till night could be in worship of God. Many Christians believe it is only when you serve as Church worker that you really serve God, no! You can be a great witness to the gospel of Christ through your way of life and relationship with other people.

Your blessing is attached to your service!

And ye shall serve the LORD your God, and he shall bless thy bread, and thy water; and I will take sickness away from the midst of thee. There shall nothing cast their young, nor be barren, in thy land: the number of thy days I will fulfil. I will send my fear before thee, and will destroy all the people to whom thou shalt come, and I will make all thine enemies turn their backs unto thee. **(Exodus 23:25-27)**

And they shall be mine, saith the LORD of hosts, in that day when I make up my jewels; and I will spare them, as a man spareth his own son that serveth him. Then shall ye return, and discern between the righteous and the wicked, between him that serveth God and him that serveth him not. **(Mal. 3:17-18)**

As much as God wants us to use all our beings to pursue His purpose on earth, He has great rewards for us in this world and the one thereafter. Let no one stop or discourage you from serving God. The only way the enemy can stop your harvest is to discourage you from sowing. God is a rewarder of those who seek and serve Him.

But as it is written, Eye hath not seen, nor ear heard, neither have entered into the heart of man, the things which God hath prepared for them that love him. **(1 Corinthians 2:9)**

There is nothing in this world that is worthy of denying you from claiming this promise. Live ready!

It is easy to see the level of a man's focus in God by observing how he lives, what he does and what he says. By a man's pursuit, you can easily tell whose servant he is, be it of God, Satan or himself.

RENDERING PURPOSEFUL SERVICE

But he that is greatest among you shall be your servant. ***(Matt. 23:11)***

Blessed is that servant, whom his lord when he cometh shall find so doing. Verily I say unto you, That he shall make him ruler over all his goods.
(Matthew 24:46-47)

A lot of people have been carried away with the discussion of who a servant or a son is in the kingdom. Unfortunately, such a discussion could take focus away from God's call of man to service in His kingdom if care is not taken. We must be careful not to lose the importance of the concept of service to semantics. In this book, I use the term "servant" like Jesus does many times to refer to Sons (that is son and daughters) of God using their will to pursue the will of God.

Are you a servant or a son?

And charged them that they should not make him known: That it might be fulfilled which was spoken by Esaias the prophet, saying. Behold my servant, whom I have chosen; my beloved, in whom my soul is well pleased: I will put my spirit upon him, and he shall shew judgment to the Gentiles.
(Matthew 12:16-18)

For whether is greater, he that sitteth at meat, or he that serveth? is not he that sitteth at meat? but I am among you as he that serveth. ***(Luke 22:27)***

Jesus Christ, the all-powerful God and Messiah made mentioned of Himself many times as the servant of the Lord and mankind.
He even washed the feet of His disciples (John 13:12).
Not only that, Jesus Christ made it crystal clear in His various parables that every child of God should see self as a steward of God. We are all in His world (Ps 24:1) trading the talents He has given us and we will all give an account of how we use the resources (life, time, money, people etceteras) to Him one day.

God's servants are sons in service

Who by the mouth of thy servant David hast said, Why did the heathen rage, and the people imagine vain things? ***(Acts 4:25)***

> *Paul, a servant of Jesus Christ, called to be an apostle, separated unto the gospel of God.* **(Romans 1:1)**

> *Moses the servant of God had commanded.* **(1 Chronicle 6:49)**

The Bible is filled with many incidences of men of God both in the Old and New Testament being referred to as servants of God. It is in this same context I am using the term in order to emphasis the need to use everything within us for the glorious service of our heavenly Master (Col. 4: 1). I hope it will appease those who will prefer to stick on with the title of sonship to know that the Bible uses the words Servant of God and Son of God many times to mean the same thing. In the context of this book however, I use the term servant and stewards to mean a son (child, daughter, man , woman etceteras) of God who uses his will, talent and skill to serve the purpose of God on earth.

> *Ye are my friends, if ye do whatsoever I command you. Henceforth I call you not servants; for the servant knoweth not what his lord doeth: but I have called you friends; for all things that I have heard of my Father I have made known unto you.* **(John 15:14-15)**

> *Wherefore thou art no more a servant, but a son; and if a son, then an heir of God through Christ.* **(Galatians 4:7)**

While servant in the world could mean a second class employee who enjoys fewer benefits under his human master, a servant in the kingdom of God refers to a child of God that uses his or her will to serve the will and purpose of God on earth.

> *And he called him, and said unto him, How is it that I hear this of thee? Give an account of thy stewardship; for thou mayest be no longer steward.* **(Luke 16:2)**

A kingdom servant is a Son of God that pursues the will of the Lord with everything within him. In the kingdom parlance therefore, a true servant is a Son of God!

HOW PROFITABLE ARE YOU SERVING?

So then every one of us shall give account of himself to God. **Rom. 14:12**

For the kingdom of heaven is as a man travelling into a far country, who called his own servants, and delivered unto them his goods. And unto one he gave five talents, to another two, and to another one; to every man according to his several ability; and straightway took his journey. His lord said unto him, Well done, thou good and faithful servant: thou hast been faithful over a few things, I will make thee ruler over many things: enter thou into the joy of thy lord. And cast ye the unprofitable servant into outer darkness: there shall be weeping and gnashing of teeth. **(Matthew 25:14-15, 21,30)**

Are you ready to give a good account of yourself to your master today? If Jesus Christ will come now or if you will join Him in heaven today, are you ready to give a good account of your sojourn on earth? God has created every man for a purpose and has given each person time and place to render his or her service. Wouldn't it be bad if on that day you meet your Maker, you are not able to prove that you spend most of the time He gives you to promote His kingdom?

And he called him, and said unto him, How is it that I hear this of thee? give an account of thy stewardship; for thou mayest be no longer steward. **(Luke 16:2)**

Bible makes it crystal clear that for everything we do, we will give account later. The type of service you render determines your accessment and reward!
It is how you serve that will determine the type of servant you are? Your action will judge you and Jesus, the way, the truth and life will only lead you to where your services prepare you to be.
God wants us to support the goal of His heavenly kingdom of God while we are still on earth. Since your destiny will be determined by your conduct, do not permit people's evil conduct to destroy your good intention and action. Let no man rob you of your rewards.
Be a profitable servant of the Lord.

A profitable servant:
- Sees himself as a caretaker, not the owner of the king's business (Luke 19:12-13; 2. Cor.5: 18-20)
- Converts none of the king's business into his private use (Jer. 23-24; 1Cor. 9-13)
- Understands his assignment and develops potentials to fulfill it. (1Cor.1:26-29)
- Is disciplined, hardworking and goal oriented (Prov. 28-18; Acts 20:22-24)
- Would be blessed and highly rewarded. (Matt. 25: 21,23)

An unprofitable servant:
- Remains wicked, lazy and unfaithful to his master. (Matt. 25: 26)
- Wastes and mismanages resources of his master (Matt. 25: 24-28)
- Speaks empty words and promises and is corrupt (2 Pet.2:10-19)
- Would be punished and rebuked by his master (Matt. 25: 26-28)

GOD AS A REWARDER

But without faith it is impossible to please him: for he that cometh to God must believe that he is, and that he is a rewarder of them that diligently seek him.
(Hebrews 11:6.)

Ye have said, It is vain to serve God: and what profit is it that we have kept his ordinance, and that we have walked mournfully before the LORD of hosts? And now we call the proud happy; yea, they that work wickedness are set up; yea, they that tempt God are even delivered. Then they that feared the LORD spake often one to another: and the LORD hearkened, and heard it, and a book of remembrance was written before him for them that feared the LORD, and that thought upon his name. And they shall be mine, saith the LORD of hosts, in that day when I make up my jewels; and I will spare them, as a man spareth his own son that serveth him. Then shall ye return, and discern between the righteous and the wicked, between him that serveth God and him that serveth him not.
(Malachi 3:14-18)

Contrary to what some people expect, the Bible describes God as a great rewarder of those who serve Him.
With Him no motive or action is hidden.
However since He is a timeless Lord, sometimes we mistake His operation within His timing as lateness or slowness.

There are some important points we need to learn about the rewarding act of God in order to develop a committed life of service.

i) **God honors all equally**

Knowing that whatsoever good thing any man doeth, the same shall he receive of the Lord, whether he be bond or free. ***(Ephesians 6:8)***

ii) **God requires from you according to what you are given**

But he that knew not, and did commit things worthy of stripes, shall be beaten with few stripes. For unto whomsoever much is given, of him shall be much required: and to whom men have committed much, of him they will ask the more. ***(Luke 12:48)***

iii) **God distastes laziness and unproductivity**

And about the eleventh hour he went out, and found others standing idle, and saith unto them, Why stand ye here all the day idle? They say unto him, Because no man hath hired us. He saith unto them, Go ye also into the vineyard; and whatsoever is right, that shall ye receive.
(Matthew 20:6-7)

His lord answered and said unto him, Thou wicked and slothful servant, thou knewest that I reap where I sowed not, and gather where I have not strawed: Thou oughtest therefore to have put my money to the exchangers, and then at my coming I should have received mine own with usury.
(Matthew 25:26-27)

The prodigal son lost the presence of the Lord after taking his resources away to waste in the kingdom of the enemy.
You say how do I know that he spent it on the kingdom of hell?
Because he took his journey into a far country (Luke 15:13-14), far away from God, His Father. The Bible also said that he wasted his substance with riotous living.
This lazy bone didn't invest but merely spent all his resources.
Many people are like this wasting all their God given resources on their personal lusts and things outside the kingdom of God forgetting that it is God that has blessed them with live and their resources. Though it is the will of the Lord that no one shall die and go to hell,

it remains also His will that everyone should reap the product of his decision and action.
The prodigal son's trauma was a product of his personal choice.
He was wasting away in foreign land eating with swine while his brother at home continued to serve under the blessing of the father. There is a blessing in serving. Sometimes, inexperienced Christians can cast envying eyes at prodigal sons wasting their future in the company of citizens of hell. There is nothing to envy from hell.
A blessing from hell is a curse from heaven!
The prodigal son's chaotic freedom in the foreign country however attractive it might have looked was a mere delusion from hell.
Stop being fooled that the greener pasture is outside home.
That is a deception of the enemy. We always have to rejoice for every lost soul that regains his senses and returns to God.

> *And he answering said to his father, Lo, these many years do **I serve thee**, neither transgressed I at any time thy commandment: and yet thou never gavest me a kid, that I might make merry with my friends: But as soon as this thy son was come, which hath devoured thy living with harlots, thou hast killed for him the fatted calf. And he said unto him, Son, thou art ever with me, and all that I have is thine. It was meet that we should make merry, and be glad: for **this thy brother was dead**, and is alive again; and was lost, and is found. **(Luke 15:29-32)**

Serving the Lord is your lifetime assurance to being blessed in this life and the one to come (**1 Timothy 4:8**).
Never underestimate the presence of the Lord! It not only offers you the fullness of joy but also pleasures forever more (Ps 16:11).

iv)   **God honors your faithfulness in service**

> *Moreover it is required in stewards, that a man be found faithful.* ***(1 Corinthians 4:2)***

> *He that is faithful in that which is least is faithful also in much: and he that is unjust in the least is unjust also in much. If therefore ye have not been faithful in the unrighteous mammon, who will commit to your trust the true riches? And if ye have not been faithful in that which is another man's, who shall give you that which is your own?* ***(Luke 16:10-12)***

God honors your faithfulness in service more than your talent.

He treasures your availability more than your ability.

Your talents are nothing in themselves but an instrument meant to help you become who He wants you to be. As we saw in the story of talents, you are either a faithful or a wicked steward (Matt. 25: 14-30). It is a choice one has to make to become a vessel of honour worthy of use for the Lord (Tim. 2: 20-26). All vessels are created to be used. If you are used and the extent that you are used is determined by your preparation. I encourage you to appraise your conducts and judge the type of servant you are to the Lord in order to be able to make adjustment where necessary.

v) God punishes all unfaithfulness

Then he which had received the one talent came and said, Lord, I knew thee that thou art an hard man, reaping where thou hast not sown, and gathering where thou hast not strawed: And I was afraid, and went and hid thy talent in the earth: lo, there thou hast that is thine. His lord answered and said unto him, Thou wicked and slothful servant, thou knewest that I reap where I sowed not, and gather where I have not strawed: And cast ye the unprofitable servant into outer darkness: there shall be weeping and gnashing of teeth. **(Matthew 25:24-26, 30)**

To God, every act of laziness is wickedness. God has blessed you with life, skills and other earthly resources for a purpose.

Many ignorant people claim that they can use their life the way they like. You can not be far away from truth than that. Suppose as a master, you employ a servant and equip him with resources, skills and time to serve you. How will you treat such a servant if he spends all the time and resources you give him to seek his own well-being rather than your assigned purpose? Wicked of course!

But last of all he sent unto them his son, saying, They will reverence my son. But when the husbandmen saw the son, they said among themselves, This is the heir; come, let us kill him, and let us seize on his inheritance. And they caught him, and cast him out of the vineyard, and slew him. When the lord therefore of the vineyard cometh, what will he do unto those husbandmen? They say unto him, He will miserably destroy those wicked men, and will let out his vineyard unto other husbandmen, which shall render him the fruits in their seasons. **(Matthew 21:37-41)**

Supposing that servant will go to the extent of using your resources to deny you, fight against your goal and destroy your other servants? Every act of unfruitfulness is sinful and wicked and deserves punishment. No wonder that God will also destroy wicked people
Your life and resources are not yours but that of God.
Every act of unfruitfulness therefore is sinful.
God considers you wicked everytime you refuse to use your talents productively for His kingdom or choose to use it against His glory.
The least form of appreciation expected of us is to use everything within us to give glory to God and win people to His kingdom.

vi) **God honors diligence**

He is a rewarder of them that diligently seek him. **(Hebrews 11:6)**

So likewise ye, when ye shall have done all those things which are commanded you, say, We are unprofitable servants: we have done that which was our duty to do. **(Luke 17:10)**

God wants us to justify our trust in Him as we repeat our act of faith over and over till we have rewards of our labor. Many people break tithing over and over proving their doubts about God's promise of abundance. It is only a seed that is left peacefully to die under the earth that bears fruit later.

vii) **God justifies your action according to your intention**

But this I say, He which soweth sparingly shall reap also sparingly; and he which soweth bountifully shall reap also bountifully. Every man according as he purposeth in his heart, so let him give; not grudgingly, or of necessity: for God loveth a cheerful giver. **(2 Corinthians 9:6-7)**

It is not only what you do that will determine your rewards from the Lord but also your motives.
Your heart justifies your act.
Remember that Jesus Christ declared the widow that gave the two mites offering to have given far more than other people in the

Church for she has given from her lack while others have given from their surplus.

viii) God rewards all according to mercy not our worth

And when they came that were hired about the eleventh hour, they received every man a penny. But when the first came, they supposed that they should have received more; and they likewise received every man a penny. And when they had received it, they murmured against the goodman of the house, Saying, These last have wrought but one hour, and thou hast made them equal unto us, which have borne the burden and heat of the day. But he answered one of them, and said, Friend, I do thee no wrong: didst not thou agree with me for a penny? Take that thine is, and go thy way: I will give unto this last, even as unto thee. Is it not lawful for me to do what I will with mine own? Is thine eye evil, because I am good? So the last shall be first, and the first last: for many be called, but few chosen. **(Matthew 20:9-16)**

In the parable above, Jesus Christ rewarded the workers recruited early in the morning, third hour, the sixth hour, ninth hour and eleventh hour equally. Many believers that come to God in their old age have often wondered if they have wasted their chances in the Lord. God does not reward as man does.

And he answering said to his father, Lo, these many years do I serve thee, neither transgressed I at any time thy commandment: and yet thou never gavest me a kid, that I might make merry with my friends: But as soon as this thy son was come, which hath devoured thy living with harlots, thou hast killed for him the fatted calf. And he said unto him, Son, thou art ever with me, and all that I have is thine. It was meet that we should make merry, and be glad: for this thy brother was dead, and is alive again; and was lost, and is found. **(Luke 15:29-32)**

In the story of the Loving Father (some call it "Prodigal Son") above, the senior brother of the prodigal son was surprised with how the father graciously received the lost but found son.
God is a good and gracious Lord. He honors our efforts and faithfulness according to His goodness and not our weakness.

CHAPTER 12: PRINCIPLES OF LEADERSHIP

Let this mind be in you, which was also in Christ Jesus: Who, being in the form of God, thought it not robbery to be equal with God: But made himself of no reputation, and took upon him the form of a servant, and was made in the likeness of men: And being found in fashion as a man, he humbled himself, and became obedient unto death, even the death of the cross. Wherefore God also hath highly exalted him, and given him a name which is above every name. **(Philippians 2:5-9)**

Jesus was the greatest leader that ever walked the face of the earth. Two thousand years after His departure from the earth; He had still over two billion followers on the face of the earth.

He achieved this great fit without waging any war or exercising any pressure on any body. His life is worthy of emulation to every genuine leader. There are timeless principles we could learn from His conducts.

1) Recognition of God as the source of all callings

And no man taketh this honour unto himself, but he that is called of God, as was Aaron **(Hebrews 5:4)**

The Church is an institution of God.
The calling to head the institution as a priest is a divine responsibility. You do not choose to become a priest because you can quote lots of verses or because you like to talk. You yield to the vocation only because you hear the call and feel the tangible leading of God to do so. The priesthood is one privilege no man takes unto himself lest he dishonours God and suffers the consequence greatly.
Also no one should ever enter the ministry or start a Church unless He hears clearly from God to do so.
It is the backing of God that is celebrated in Church.
If you lack it, you will be a giantic failure and a masterpiece example of frustration. That is why preaching is not a profession but a calling. You need to have a calling of God to make a great impact out of it.

Sometimes, you notice the calling on your life and sometimes other men of God see it, but which ever way it comes, it is important you subject yourself to relevant training to prepare yourself for productive service. Every leadership position in the house of the Lord requires appropriate and sufficient training!

While you might confirm your calling to any area of Church leadership through avenues of prophecy, presents (gifts of the Lord), practice, passion and preference, you need sufficient training and coaching by experienced ministers in that field to make great marks in your position.

Both gifts and calling of the Lord are equally productive!

They all signify divine empowerment that has been deposited in us to fulfill a specific purpose in life. Your level of training and preparation will have a direct influence on your level of excellence.

God calls you to preach or you choose another area of leadership fitting your gifts, you need to manifest some salient traits expected of kingdom leadership.

2) Accountability is to the Lord

So then every one of us shall give account of himself to God. (**Rom. 14:12**)

And he called him, and said unto him, How is it that I hear this of thee? give an account of thy stewardship; for thou mayest be no longer steward. (**Luke 16:2**)

We all have to give an account of our stewardship not only to leaders God has placed over us but also to God Himself, one day!

Every man is created to solve some problems.

Every man has the duty to reign in his areas of relevance as a problem shooter or solution provider. However, regardless of your profession, you should find time to prepare and focus on your calling to save the lost and serve as an ambassador of the Kingdom of God.

As a billionaire, you should still be able and willing to serve as an usher or choir member in your Church. I pray that God will grant you the same revelation He granted King David who despite being a king saw the importance of serving God more than the glory of his palace. Can you also see yourself as a gate keeper in your Church?

I had rather be a doorkeeper in the house of my God, than to dwell in the tents of wickedness. For the LORD God is a sun and shield: the LORD will give *grace and glory: no good thing will he withhold from them that walk uprightly. O LORD of hosts, blessed is the man that trusteth in thee. (**Ps. 84:10-12**)*

It is when you stop trusting in your status and accomplishment and you begin to trust in the Lord that placed you in your position that the Lord's blessing upon your life can be completely insured.

3) Responsibility of leadership is to the people

He saith unto him the third time, Simon, son of Jonas, lovest thou me? Peter was grieved because he said unto him the third time, Lovest thou me? And he said unto him, Lord, thou knowest all things; thou knowest that I love thee. Jesus saith unto him, Feed my sheep. (**John 21:17**)

As a kingdom leader, your responsibility is to serve and take care of the people of the Lord. You are not to oppress them but rather to build them up and challenge them to rise up and reign in their areas of calling. It is a save thing to always have around you people you can be accountable to. People that can correct and discipline you.
Moses subjected himself to the control of the elder of his people. That is what makes your leadership service to others and not just a duty to yourself. Only by having "accountability mentality" can you ensure the well-being of your congregation without oppressing and dominating them. Only in an atmosphere of accountability can the priest and king in your congregation be encouraged to rise up in order for them to make a significant contribution to Church success.

a) God Himself created the institution of leadership

And the LORD God took the man, and put him into the garden of Eden to dress it and to keep it. (**Genesis 2:15**)

It has always been God's purpose to rule and dominate the earth indirectly through mankind (Gen 1: 27-28). He created the first man to dress and keep the garden and when a man lost his leadership role to Satan God sent Adam and Eve out of the garden. The Church of God is filled with cunning people whose ungodly acts are as potent as that of the serpent. Many of such disobedient and rebellious people who easily thrives where there is no strong leadership normally seek to attack and discredit leadership structures so as to trivialize Church vision and attack ignorant people.

Having a form of godliness, but denying the power thereof: from such turn away. For of this sort are they which creep into houses, and lead captive silly women laden with sins, led away with divers lusts, Ever learning, and never able to come to the knowledge of the truth. **(2 Timothy 3:5-7)**

Watch out for such pretenders in your congregation.
By their fruits, you shall know them.
They are mostly not committed to any Church yet they position themselves above every Church organization, pretending to know everything by attacking every structure of your congregation. Such people are too independent. They attend any service they want and select the occasion they want to participate in. They mostly do not tithe or belong to any ministry or leadership group. They are too proud to surrender under any authority and are fast to complain about every great pastor in town. They might even attack your visions and try to impose their own upon the Church. They will do anything to discredit your leaderships, visions or programs in other to claim credibility for themselves. Never tolerate such thieves of people's hearts. Take them for what Jesus revealed them to be, thieves!

Verily, verily, I say unto you, He that entereth not by the door into the sheepfold, but climbeth up some other way, the same is a thief and a robber. But he that entereth in by the door is the shepherd of the sheep.
(John 10:1-2)

Reveal such pretenders immediately and teach your congregation not to be beguiled by them. I once had such a group in my congregation who tried to turn the backs of some leaders against me. They lavished praises at the unsuspecting leaders and challenged them to take a strong stand for God without any regard for the Church leadership. What an ungodly counsel!
First, you must be a great fool to serve under a Church leadership not serving God. Every Christian must first prove his or her Church before joining. Once that is done, you need to completely surrender and support leadership. Honoring God and worshipping Him wholeheartedly is not incompatible with honoring your leaders!
In fact, you can hardly separate both. Bible insists on both!

Let the elders that rule well be counted worthy of double honour, especially they who labor in the word and doctrine. **(1 Timothy 5:17)**

Bible not only provides for leadership, it demands double honour for it! Take it or leave it, if you can not accept or honour leaders God has set over His institutions to give it direction, drop out of the congregation and go to the nearby bush where you can worship and exercise all your freedoms alone.

b) We are not all equally talented or placed by God

And unto one he gave five talents, to another two, and to another one; to every man according to his several ability; and straightway took his journey ***(Matthew 25:15)***

And God hath set some in the Church, first apostles, secondarily prophets, thirdly teachers, after that miracles, then gifts of healings, helps, governments, diversities of tongues. ***(1 Corinthians 12:28) Also Rom 12:4-5***

God has deposited different talents in His body. The duty of leadership is to create an orderly and godly environment where all the people can bring their talents together to bless the entire body.

c) Everyone is created to lead in an area of gifting and calling

And God blessed them, and God said unto them, Be fruitful, and multiply, and replenish the earth, and subdue it: and have dominion over the fish of the sea, and over the fowl of the air, and over every living thing that moveth upon the earth. ***(Genesis 1:28)***

And hast made us unto our God kings and priests: and we shall reign on the earth. ***(Revelation 5:10)***

To think that some few people own leadership characteristics that convey on them the right to lord it over others is not biblically supported. Many of the chosen leaders in the Bible in fact received anointing to rule only after they were chosen and anointed by God.

And it was so, that when he had turned his back to go from Samuel, God gave him another heart: and all those signs came to pass that day. ***(1 Samuel 10:9)***

Then Samuel took the horn of oil, and anointed him in the midst of his brethren: and the Spirit of the LORD came upon David from that day forward. **(1 Samuel 16:13)**

The Bible in fact refers to every man as potential priest and ruler to buttress the fact the everyone has leadership traits to reign in his sphere of calling. God gave every man (both male and female) the capability and the mandate to have dominion over His creation.
By implication, everyone can lead but not all will. In reality, only those who endeavour to pay the price of leadership will become one.

d) Only prepared vessels will rise to lead

But in a great house there are not only vessels of gold and of silver, but also of wood and of earth; and some to honour, and some to dishonour. If a man therefore purge himself from these, he shall be a vessel unto honour, sanctified, and meet for the master's use, and prepared unto every good work. **(2 Timothy 2:20-21)**

And he gave some, apostles; and some, prophets; and some, evangelists; and some, pastors and teachers; For the perfecting of the saints, for the work of the ministry, for the edifying of the body of Christ. **(Ephesians 4:11-12)**

Though everyone is created equally to rule within his or her sphere of service, only those who locate and prepare themselves for effective service shall rule. There are different ways you are equipped to reign.

- **Specialist**. Acquisition of relevant skill, knowledge and experience can crown you for leadership in your chosen field.

- **Status**. Some people will lay claim to their authority as a result of their official position and status. This group of people includes Kings and Queens, inheritor and heirs of family business etceteras.

- **Charisma**. Transformational leaders are natural leaders born of different need and situation. People like Mother Teresa and Martin Luther King Jnr. ascended leadership stage by virtue of their charisma and virtue of integrity. People out of respect for their visions and commitments naturally submit under their leadership and serve them loyally.

- **Reward**. Some people use their wealth and powerful position to establish themselves over others. Based on denial or distribution of rewards (praise, money), others are forced to acknowledge and accept their leadership.
- **Force**. Many tyrants and dictators ascend office and continue to rule only through force and reign by threat and fear.

e) Leadership is about attitude not status

For David, after he had served his own generation by the will of God, fell on sleep, and was laid unto his fathers, and saw corruption. **(Acts 13:36)**

After several decades of theories and practice, the human civilization is arriving at Biblical notion of leadership as contemporary business schools begin to define leadership as an attitude of service that a person exhibits in a position of authority.

Bible, since time immemorial, has always emphasized that the attitude of a leader is of paramount importance than the office of a leader. Leadership is in what you do and not in your status and title!

In the Bible, we see how people receive leadership either through God's special anointing or indirectly through hands-on training by another leader. In any case, leadership is not about status or personality but about offering services to co-heirs in the kingdom of God. Biblically speaking, leadership is about leading yourself to serve others regardless of your status.

King David, though a king, was a servant of his people. He served! Despite your status, you can serve your people too!

f) Leadership is a recognised relationship between the leader and the led

For the Lamb which is in the midst of the throne shall feed them, and shall lead them unto living fountains of waters: and God shall wipe away all tears from their eyes. **(Revelation 7:17)**

For you to be an effective leader, you need to be accepted and recognised by your people. People like Absalom in the Bible were killed as pretenders to the throne while trying to force themselves on their people. In another hand, you need to accept yourself as a leader too to be able to serve your people well.

Moses and Gideon had to first accept themselves as leaders before they could later evolve as good leaders over their people.

You need to recognise and accept the leadership duty as much as you are recognised and accepted for the role before you can truly function well.

What we see in some parts of the world where dictators and autocrats forced themselves over others through military coups, social revolutions and other illegal and non-peaceful means are aberrations to true leadership. No wonder that such oppressive leadership never bears good fruits for both the leaders and their followers.

Godly leadership will always have the recognition of God, the acceptance of people and the willingness of the leader himself to serve. That is because whomever God chose to lead is meant to be a vessel through which God can lead His people.

CHAPTER 13: CASE STUDY OF KINGDOM LEADERSHIP

And God blessed them, and God said unto them, Be fruitful, and multiply, and replenish the earth, and subdue it: and have dominion over the fish of the sea, and over the fowl of the air, and over every living thing that moveth upon the earth. And God saw every thing that he had made, and, behold, it was very good. And the evening and the morning were the sixth day. **(Genesis 1:28, 31)**

And hast made us unto our God kings and priests: and we shall reign on the earth. **(Revelation 5:10)**

From these scriptures, it becomes obvious that:
a) Every thing created by the Lord is made perfect.
b) God has given man the dominion to reign on earth without unwarranted intervention and interference by a heavenly being.
c) Everyone has a deposit of priestly and political power
d) Every body has God's given potential to reign.
e) Where and how one reigns is better co-ordinated with God.
f) God has created human institutions and has given man the instruction with which to peacefully and perfectly govern them.

Though many institutions are of the Lord (family, marriage, governance etceteras), man has become the sole determinant of what becomes of them. Man has been given by God the sole dominion over everything on earth and he is now responsible for his situation.

The following case studies are meant to expose us to God's standard instruction on ensuring perfect results in our institutions. We will see how people succeeded or failed by working with or against divine principles. This study will help you not to put the blame for human errors on their Creator but will rather help us to take responsibility for good leadership by running the institution of God the godly way.

CASE STUDY ON KINGDOM LEADERSHIP STYLES

There have been different types of governance right from the time God appointed leaders for the people of Israel.

He first instituted prophets as leaders until the people, wanting to be like their neighbors, demanded for a King to rule over them.

God then in honour of their demands instructed Prophet Samuel to institute Saul as the first king of Israel.

That began a long march into the history of different monarchs; there were the ruthless and the gentle, the good, the bad and the ugly. While God was behind the governing institution of Israelis, many times, He was completely against the governors and leaders.

Some leaders simply imposed themselves on the people without being called by God or appointed by the people. Some, though called and anointed by God lost their focus and orientation on God and wrecked evil on their own people. Though God's plan remains good for all generation, such plans often got misrepresented by the nature of the people occupying leadership position over God's people.

Therefore, the character of each leader is very important since it plays a decicive role in the total performance of such a leader as we shall see from our various case studies.

PART A: SAUL THE RULER

Now there was a man of Benjamin, whose name was Kish, the son of Abiel, the son of Zeror, the son of Bechorath, the son of Aphiah, a Benjamite, a mighty man of power. And he had a son, whose name was Saul, a choice young man, and a goodly: and there was not among the children of Israel a goodlier person than he: from his shoulders and upward he was higher than any of the people. **(1 Samuel 9:1-2)**

Saul was the first king of Israel.

He was the choice of his people with the approval of God (1 Sam 9:17; 10:24; 2 Sam 21:6). King Saul was a handsome, and impressive man of great stature, taller than the people by head and shoulders.

1) Professional and service history

And the asses of Kish Saul's father were lost. And Kish said to Saul his son, Take now one of the servants with thee, and arise, go seek the asses.
(1 Samuel 9:3)

Then came the messengers to Gibeah of Saul, and told the tidings in the ears of the people: and all the people lifted up their voices, and wept. And, behold, Saul came after the herd out of the field; and Saul said, What aileth the people that they weep? And they told him the tidings of the men of Jabesh.
(1 Samuel 11:4-5)

Though much is not written in the bible concerning Saul's professional background, the fact that his father could send him and a servant to search for a lost donkey for as long as three days showed him to be a dependable worker in his father's business. Also after becoming king, Saul still found time to watch over his flocks in the field. It is relevant to emphasise that God mostly used people with a shepherd heart. I guess that is because it would be easier for those who have lived defending animals with their lives to become a great defender of humans' life.

2) Rise to leadership

a) Leadership Background

To morrow about this time I will send thee a man out of the land of Benjamin, and thou shalt anoint him to be captain over my people Israel, that he may save my people out of the hand of the Philistines: for I have looked upon my people, because their cry is come unto me. **(1 Samuel 9:16)**

And it was so, that when he had turned his back to go from Samuel, God gave him another heart: and all those signs came to pass that day. **(1 Samuel 10:9)**

God had not only watched the cry of His people but have also watched for the right man to lead them in the institution of kingship. The fact that Saul was very humble in his relationship with Samuel (1 Sam. 9:21) was proof that he was perhaps quite different at the beginning of his reign as King. Anyway, he was the people's choice and the most befitting personality for the throne then.

b) The calling

Then Samuel took a vial of oil, and poured it upon his head, and kissed him, and said, Is it not because the LORD hath anointed thee to be captain over his inheritance? **(1 Samuel 10:1)**

And they ran and fetched him thence: and when he stood among the people, he was higher than any of the people from his shoulders and upward. **(1 Samuel 10:23)**

Samuel anointed Saul and prophesized future incidences that will happen to him to convince him of his Godly choice to be king over His people. First in the plain of Tabor, three men going to make offerings to God in Bethel gave him two of three loaves, in recognition of his kingship. After that, some prophets met him, and suddenly the Spirit of God came upon him and he prophesied among them.

c) Paying the price for leadership

Saul was despised!

> *But the children of Belial said, How shall this man save us? And they despised him, and brought him no presents. But he held his peace.*
> **(1 Samuel 10:27)**

> *And all the people went to Gilgal; and there they made Saul king before the LORD in Gilgal; and there they sacrificed sacrifices of peace offerings before the LORD; and there Saul and all the men of Israel rejoiced greatly.*
> **(1 Samuel 11:15)**

The children of Belial despised the newly appointed King Saul.
He proved his leadership trait however by neglecting them, choosing to hold his peace.
Leadership is not forced but earned. It was interesting to note that after leading a war to defeat the challenge of Nahash the Ammonite against the people of Jabesh gilead, the whole of the people of Israel later came together to give their total recognition of Saul's kingship.

3) Leadership career

a) *Human qualities*

i. *Humble*

> *And Saul answered and said, Am not I a Benjamite, of the smallest of the tribes of Israel? and my family the least of all the families of the tribe of Benjamin? wherefore then speakest thou so to me?* **(1 Samuel 9:21)**

ii. *Forgiven*

> *And the people said unto Samuel, Who is he that said, Shall Saul reign over us? bring the men, that we may put them to death. And Saul said, There*

> *shall not a man be put to death this day: for to day the LORD hath wrought salvation in Israel.* **(1 Samuel 11:12-13)**

After protecting the people of Jabesh-Gilead against the attack of Ammonites, people of Israel wanted Saul to avenge those who did not accept him earlier as King but he demonstrated leading ability to unite by choosing to forgive his despisers.

b) Leadership achievements

i) Saul was the first king of Israel.
ii) Saul was a great warrior that brought many victories to his people.
iii) Saul began the unification process of the twelve tribes of Israel under the same monarchy.

c) Shortcomings

> *And Samuel said to Saul, Thou hast done foolishly: thou hast not kept the commandment of the LORD thy God, which he commanded thee: for now would the LORD have established thy kingdom upon Israel for ever. But now thy kingdom shall not continue: the LORD hath sought him a man after his own heart, and the LORD hath commanded him to be captain over his people, because thou hast not kept that which the LORD commanded thee.* **(1 Samuel 13:13-14)**

i) **Disobedience**

Saul was a disobedient man both to God and man in a position of authority. Many times he failed to carry out the commandments of God and instructions of Prophet Samuel preferring to react to situations according to his feelings and needs.

Saul never genuinely repented of any of his mistakes and this proved destructive to him. After Samuel condemned him for sacrificing to God in his stead, he only found an excuse for committing the mistake. For him, the voice of the people is of paramount importance than the voice of God. Instead of seeking full repentant in God, he only sought to make Samuel return and bless him among his people. It was this hunger for man's honour than God's acceptance that cost him and his family the kingdom of Israel.

Saul's final disobedience of sparing Agag, the king of Amalekite (1 Sam 15) and all that was good in the country was a blanket rejection of God's instruction which the prophet translated to mean God's rejection of Saul himself as king over his people (1 Chron 10:13). Thus Saul lost his calling to his lifestyle of disobedience.

ii) **Impatience**

Saul once offered sacrifice out of impatience. He could not wait for Prophet Samuel to arrive so he usurped the prophet's duty.
At the tale end of his leadership, he sought service of mediums contrary to the commandment of God.

iii) Jealous

Saul was a jealous man. Just because of the way women praised David for defeating Goliath (1 Sam 17; 18:7), Saul hated the man who protected his kingdom from defeat from Palestine and began to plot his death.

d) *Lessons from King Saul's lifestyles*

The fear of man bringeth a snare: but whoso putteth his trust in the LORD shall be safe. (**Proverbs 29:25**)

Thou shalt not follow a multitude to do evil; neither shalt thou speak in a cause to decline after many to wrest judgment. (**Exodus 23:2**)

a) Saul's life of disobedience to the instruction of God cut him off from his God given kingdom. As his disobedience robbed him off the presence of God, he began to be tormented regularly by an evil spirit, which led him to maltreat the same people God has sent him to watch over. He began to rule and ruin his people forgetting that he had been called to serve them.

b) Saul was self conscious rather than God conscious in playing his God given roles. He refused to follow God's commandments as would be expected. In fact, he broke God's commandment many times to satisfy his ego needs. He was self willed and disobedient to God, preferring to follow his own way than God's instruction. When he considered it necessary, he sought the service of mediums whom he had earlier banned in order to seek counsel from dead Samuel (1 Samuel 14:18).

c) Saul was a usurper. He took over the role of the prophet of God thereby disrespecting and violating the prophetic office of Samuel. When chastised, he gave the excuse of trying to appease people rather than accepting his faults.

d) Saul was overridden by the fear of his people more than the honour for God. Saul was misled to miss the grace of God upon his life. Every man of God should learn to stay focused on God for leadership. While it is good to care for the people, such care should not take your attention from the Master who gave you the duty. Only the fear of the Lord is wisdom (Job 28: 28), the fear of man is a trap!

e) Service without integrity

> *For a bishop must be blameless, as the steward of God; not selfwilled, not soon angry, not given to wine, no striker, not given to filthy lucre.*
(Titus 1:7)

Saul lost his dignity as a leader by losing his anger easily.
He too easily condemned people of unfounded offences.
Saul for no justifiable reason cast javelin both at David and his own son Jonathan (1 Sam 20:28-33). He accused his servants without reasons of conspiring with David (1 Sam. 8:14, 1 Sam. 22).
Once he slew his own priests.

PART B: DAVID THE SERVANT

> *And Samuel said unto Jesse, Are here all thy children? And he said, There remaineth yet the youngest, and, behold, he keepeth the sheep. And Samuel said unto Jesse, Send and fetch him: for we will not sit down till he come hither.* **(1 Samuel 16:11)**

David, according to Bible historians was a man of moderate stature.
He was not just the youngest of the eight sons of Jesse of Bethlehem, he was also the last son of His mother who earlier had two older daughters for Nahash before marrying Jesse (1 Chron 2:13-17; 2 Sam 17:25). Because he was of the same age as the children of his half sisters, he could relate more with them than his own brothers.

It is understandable that he was always in the servant role compared to his siblings, giving his last position in the family.

1) Professional and service history

> *And David came to Saul, and stood before him: and he loved him greatly; and he became his armourbearer.* **(1 Samuel 16:21)**

a) Professional history

Naturally, the servant duty of taking care of the sheep for the entire family fell on David's shoulder. He faithfully took care of his father's flocks even when the unappreciative father was not watching.
At the risk of losing his life, he fought against lions and bears in the protection of his father's sheep. He depended on God for his daily survival and provision from such early age, composing most of his psalms while serving his father. God, a respecter of no one, who rewards all according to their intention and action, saw the service heart of David and selected him as a leader over His people.

b) Service orientation to others

David lived a life of service to his family as the last born.
It was not strange to any member of the family that his name was missing in the princely list his Father presented to Prophet Samuel.
Anytime, he was mentioned in the Bible, he was always offering one service or the other.

2) Rise to leadership

a) The calling

> *Then Samuel took the horn of oil, and anointed him in the midst of his brethren: and the Spirit of the LORD came upon David from that day forward.* **(1 Samuel 16:13)**

David was located by God has a potential king while still watching over the sheep of his father. Instead of complaining and serving his father half-heatedly, he accepted his duty and spent his time growing in intimacy with God.

b) Leadership background

David spent his shepherd years in solitude.
He was often alone not by choice but by nature of his work.
He however converted the situation to his own advantage by using the time to meditate words of God and grow in intimacy with God.
This habit is common to many leaders in the Bible.
Moses was known to spend about 40 years in solitude in Midian before taking over his leadership role over Israel.
In addition to his 30 years preparation for ministry, Jesus Christ (following His public anointing by Holy Spirit) spent an additional forty days and nights in the wilderness seeking the face of the Lord.
Apostle Paul (converted from Saul) spent 3 years in solitude in Arabian (Gal 1:17) before embarking on his ministry.
David, following like other great men of God spent time alone especially in worship and prayerful meditations. It was in that period he could compose most of his psalms.

David as a bold warrior

David overcame Goliath with the same trust in God and sheer boldness that he has exercised many times while taking care of his father's flocks. Though He was aware all the while that he has been anointed to become king instead of Saul, he did not force nor scheme his way to power. Every promotion he was given by the king was in appreciation of his hard-work and unequal service.
All his promotions located him in the midst of his service!

David as anointed musician and armour-bearer

Following David's public anointment as King, he never ceased tending to his father's flock. Many people would have stopped that work the moment they were anointed but not humble David.
David remained a servant at heart.
His first official duty was to sing for Saul and deliver him from the attack of an evil spirit. It was the harp playing skill he secured from the shepherd years that made way for him into the king's palace!
He continued to serve even when the arrow of Saul almost killed him as Saul's musician and armour-bearer (1 Sam 16:20-21).

c) Paying the price for leadership

i. Rejection

> *And Samuel said unto Jesse, Are here all thy children? And he said, There remaineth yet the youngest, and, behold, he keepeth the sheep.*
> ***(1 Samuel 16:11)***

David suffered rejection at home to the extent that nobody noticed he was not around during Samuel's visit until the man of God himself made an enquiry! Yet, he didn't allow such rejection to turn to frustration capable of denying him of God's acceptance.

ii. Jealousy

> *And Saul was very wroth, and the saying displeased him; and he said, They have ascribed unto David ten thousands, and to me they have ascribed but thousands: and what can he have more but the kingdom? And Saul eyed David from that day and forward.* ***(1 Samuel 18:8-9)***

iii. Persecution

> *And the evil spirit from the LORD was upon Saul, as he sat in his house with his javelin in his hand: and David played with his hand. And Saul sought to smite David even to the wall with the javelin; but he slipped away out of Saul's presence, and he smote the javelin into the wall: and David fled, and escaped that night. Saul also sent messengers unto David's house, to watch him, and to slay him in the morning: and Michal David's wife told him, saying, If thou save not thy life to night, to morrow thou shalt be slain.*
> ***(1 Samuel 19:9-11)***

The persecution of David didn't stop there. Saul at various times with thousands of his armies hunted David to kill him just to make sure that he will not ascend the throne after him. David never sought to avenge himself even when Saul fell into his hands defenseless in the wilderness of Engedi (1 Samuel 24: 1-20) and wilderness of Ziph (1 Samuel 26: 1-25).

3) Leadership career

> *David was thirty years old when he began to reign, and he reigned forty years. In Hebron he reigned over Judah seven years and six months: and in Jerusalem he reigned thirty and three years over all Israel and Judah.* ***(2 Sam. 5:4-5)***

David began to reign when he was 30 years of age. First over Judah and then over all Israel (1 Kings 2:11; 1 Chron. 29:27).

a) Human qualities

i. *Fear of the Lord*

> *Then said Abishai to David, God hath delivered thine enemy into thine hand this day: now therefore let me smite him, I pray thee, with the spear even to the earth at once, and I will not smite him the second time. And David said to Abishai, Destroy him not: for who can stretch forth his hand against the LORD's anointed, and be guiltless?* **(1 Samuel 26: 8- 9)**

David served his generation by the will of God!
He was a leader who reigned with the fear of God in his heart.
At the peak of his persecution by Saul, he refused to seize the opportunity to take the life of his sworn enemy.
In each occasion, he left the right to judge in the hand of God (1 Sam 24:1-20; 1 Sam 26:6-25).
He will have nothing to do with harming the anointed man of God!
How many believers will show resistance today in condemning, criticising or fighting men of God placed over them? Many Church members have their pastors for dinners at home, mouth-lashing the chosen vessel of God without fear for God who has chosen them. David ordered the man that claimed to kill King Saul to be killed immediately for having no fear to lay hands on God's anointed.

> *So I stood upon him, and slew him, because I was sure that he could not live after that he was fallen: and I took the crown that was upon his head, and the bracelet that was on his arm, and have brought them hither unto my lord.*
> *Then David took hold on his clothes, and rent them; and likewise all the men that were with him: And David said unto the young man that told him, Whence art thou? And he answered, I am the son of a stranger, an Amalekite. And David said unto him, How wast thou not afraid to stretch forth thine hand to destroy the LORD's anointed? And David called one of the young men, and said, Go near, and fall upon him. And he smote him that he died. And David said unto him, Thy blood be upon thy head; for thy mouth hath testified against thee, saying, I have slain the LORD's anointed.*
> **(2 Samuel 1:10-11, 13-16)**

Do not forget that the fear of the Lord is the beginning of wisdom.
A wise person is one who exercises cautions in the things of the Lord. Choose to be wise in dealing with God and his agents.

i)   Great servant heart

> *And the three mighty men brake through the host of the Philistines, and drew water out of the well of Bethlehem, that was by the gate, and took it, and brought it to David: nevertheless he would not drink thereof, but poured it out unto the LORD. And he said, Be it far from me, O LORD, that I should do this: is not this the blood of the men that went in jeopardy of their lives? therefore he would not drink it. These things did these three mighty men.* **(2 Samuel 23:16-17)**

One of the reasons God must have promoted David over the head of King Saul was the meekness and kindness of his heart.
When three strongmen of his army risked their lives to fetch him water from Bethlehem, his heart prevented him from drinking it.
He remained servant at heart through out his reign.

ii)   Great worshipper

> *And they set the ark of God upon a new cart, and brought it out of the house of Abinadab that was in Gibeah: and Uzzah and Ahio, the sons of Abinadab, drave the new cart. And they brought it out of the house of Abinadab which was at Gibeah, accompanying the ark of God: and Ahio went before the ark. And David and all the house of Israel played before the LORD on all manner of instruments made of fir wood, even on harps, and on psalteries, and on timbrels, and on cornets, and on cymbals.* **(2 Samuel 6:3-5)**

> *And David built there an altar unto the LORD, and offered burnt offerings and peace offerings. So the LORD was intreated for the land, and the plague was stayed from Israel.* **(2 Samuel 24:25)**

David was a great worshipper of God.
It was a common happening in his days to celebrate God in all situations. Once he danced with his whole being to the shocking awe of Michal his wife (daughter of Saul) who considered the act too disrespectful for a king (2 Sam 6:14-23).

> *Wherefore David blessed the LORD before all the congregation: and David said, Blessed be thou, LORD God of Israel our father, for ever and ever.*
>
> *Thine, O LORD, is the greatness, and the power, and the glory, and the victory, and the majesty: for all that is in the heaven and in the earth is thine; thine is the kingdom, O LORD, and thou art exalted as head above all. Both riches and honour come of thee, and thou reignest over all; and in thine hand is power and might; and in thine hand it is to make great, and to give strength unto all. Now therefore, our God, we thank thee, and praise thy glorious name. But who am I, and what is my people, that we should be able to offer so willingly after this sort? for all things come of thee, and of thine own have we given thee.* **(1 Chronicle 29:10-14)**

iii) Humble

> *And Saul said to him, Whose son art thou, thou young man? And David answered, I am the son of thy servant Jesse the Bethlehemite.*
> **(1 Samuel 17:58)**

> *And David said unto Saul, Who am I? and what is my life, or my father's family in Israel, that I should be son in law to the king?* **(1 Sam. 18:18)**

David was never carried away by the fact that he has earlier been anointed to become king. He saw himself always as the shepherd boy. After defeating Goliath at war, he returned back to taking care of sheep. Being anointed as the next king could not stop him from serving his father.

a) Non revengeful

> *And David said, What have I to do with you, ye sons of Zeruiah, that ye should this day be adversaries unto me? shall there any man be put to death this day in Israel? for do not I know that I am this day king over Israel? Therefore the king said unto Shimei, Thou shalt not die. And the king sware unto him.* **(2 Samuel 19:22-23)**

David made it a policy not to revenge his enemies. He always left them in the hand of God. Despite Saul's attempt to kill him, he refused to take advantage of Saul (1 Sam 24: 12-21 ; 1 Sam 26: 7-29). Though it was clear Holy Spirit abided by him while evil spirit tormented Saul, he left God with the responsibility to decide what to do with Saul and when to do it.

b) Confident in the Lord

> *Thy servant slew both the lion and the bear: and this uncircumcised Philistine shall be as one of them, seeing he hath defied the armies of the living God. David said moreover, The LORD that delivered me out of the paw of the lion, and out of the paw of the bear, he will deliver me out of the hand of this Philistine. And Saul said unto David, Go, and the LORD be with thee.*
> **(1 Samuel 17:36-37)**

David had great confidence in God, based on his deep revelation of Him as an all-powerful and awesome God, capable of delivering man from every circumstance of life. He new God was all powerful.
So instead of focusing on his weakness compared to the giant, he focussed on God's mightiness compared to the frailty of the giant. He knew his small stone couldn't miss the big giant who has dared to defy the armies of the living God.

b) Leadership achievements of King David

i) Strong leader

He was able to rule over the entire twelve tribes of Israel setting the precedence for the United Kingdom of Israel. It was as a result of his strong leadership that he was able to lay precedence of throne ascendance by inheritance under the kingship of Solomon his son.

ii) Man of impeccable devoutness

> *And David behaved himself wisely in all his ways; and the LORD was with him. Wherefore when Saul saw that he behaved himself very wisely, he was afraid of him. But all Israel and Judah loved David, because he went out and came in before them.* **(1 Samuel 18:14-16)**

> *Then the princes of the Philistines went forth: and it came to pass, after they went forth, that David behaved himself more wisely than all the servants of Saul; so that his name was much set by.* **(1 Samuel 18:30)**

David was just in his conducts to God and man from his childhood to the adult stage of leadership. He was faithful in keeping his father's sheep. David faithfully fought Goliath, the same way he fought lions attacking his father's flocks. He was also faithful in all Saul sent him.

iii) *Honourable*

> *Then David took hold on his clothes, and rent them; and likewise all the men that were with him: And they mourned, and wept, and fasted until even, for Saul, and for Jonathan his son, and for the people of the LORD, and for the house of Israel; because they were fallen by the sword.* **(2 Sam. 1:11-12)**

David still mourned Saul and Jonathan despite the fact that Saul spent all his time attempting to kill him.

iv) *A just leader*

> *And David reigned over all Israel; and David executed judgment and justice unto all his people.* **(2 Samuel 8:15)**

> *The God of Israel said, the Rock of Israel spake to me, He that ruleth over men must be just, ruling in the fear of God.* **(2 Samuel 23:3)**

v) *Merciful*

> *And David said to Abishai, and to all his servants, Behold, my son, which came forth of my bowels, seeketh my life: how much more now may this Benjamite do it? let him alone, and let him curse; for the LORD hath bidden him. It may be that the LORD will look on mine affliction, and that the LORD will requite me good for his cursing this day.* **2 Sam. 16:11-12**

c) **Reaction to shortcomings**

i) *Weak father*

> *Howbeit he would not hearken unto her voice: but, being stronger than she, forced her, and lay with her. Then Amnon hated her exceedingly; so that the hatred wherewith he hated her was greater than the love wherewith he had loved her. And Amnon said unto her, Arise, be gone. And she said unto him, There is no cause: this evil in sending me away is greater than the other that thou didst unto me. But he would not hearken unto her.*

(2 Samuel 13:14-16)

And the king said, Let him turn to his own house, and let him not see my face. So Absalom returned to his own house, and saw not the king's face.
(2 Samuel 14:24)

After Amnon raped his sister (2 Sam 13:14-16), King David was not strong enough to punish him. In fact, the situation was left unattended until Absalom had to revenge for her sister. As if that was not enough, David forgave Absalom's murder years afterwards without penalizing him for it. It was that situation that gave Absalom sufficient chance and boldness to organize a revolt against David.

ii) Honest to self

And David said unto Nathan, I have sinned against the LORD. And Nathan said unto David, The LORD also hath put away thy sin; thou shalt not die. **(2 Samuel 12:13)**

While King David was not a perfect man, he was a perfect servant of God. When he committed adultery and murder as regards to Uriah, he fully repented of his sins. When God sent Prophet Nathan to condemn David for causing reproach to God by taking Uriah's life and wife, David fully repented and went to seek the face of the Lord.

4) Lessons from King David's lifestyles

For David, after he had served his own generation by the will of God, fell on sleep, and was laid unto his fathers, and saw corruption.
(Acts 13:36)

And he died in a good old age, full of days, riches, and honour: and Solomon his son reigned in his stead. **(1 Chronicle 29:28)**

a) David served as a servant in his different roles as shepherd, musician, war general and king. Unlike Saul, his heart never got elevated to the extent of forgetting his humble past. While Saul also came from a humble past but got carried away by his new status, David served with servant's heart all his days.

b) David served according to the will of God. He did not rule according to his interest or the culture of his people. No wonder

that he was so much successful that Jesus Christ had to come from his lineage (Matthew 7: 21; Luke 6: 46-49).
c) David, though a great leader, was a weak father. That weakness caused the death of Absalom and Amnon.
d) David served his way from lower level to kingship level. Every skill he acquired in a lower stage he used to enrich his service in a higher stage. Take note that every progressive growth starts from
e) God always takes good care of those who live a life that honors Him. King David died in a good old age-a blessed man!

CHAPTER 14: CASE STUDY ON KINGDOM SUCCESSION

And Jehu the son of Nimshi shalt thou anoint to be king over Israel: and Elisha the son of Shaphat of Abel-meholah shalt thou anoint to be prophet in thy room. **(1 Kings 19:16)**

God practically participated in leadership succession of His people. The Bible is filled with so many instances of this. It is therefore important to always spend time in prayer and consultation with God in all cases of appointment and succession in order to protect our institutions and uphold their godly legacies.

A) GOOD GENERALS: ELIJAH AND ELISHA

So he departed thence, and found Elisha the son of Shaphat, who was plowing with twelve yoke of oxen before him, and he with the twelfth: and Elijah passed by him, and cast his mantle upon him. And he left the oxen, and ran after Elijah, and said, Let me, I pray thee, kiss my father and my mother, and then I will follow thee. And he said unto him, Go back again: for what have I done to thee? And he returned back from him, and took a yoke of oxen, and slew them, and boiled their flesh with the instruments of the oxen, and gave unto the people, and they did eat. Then he arose, and went after Elijah, and ministered unto him. **(1 Kings 19:19-21)**

Elisha was engaged at field work until he was unceremoniously called into the prophetic office by God through Prophet Elijah. It was noteworthy that Elisha did not hesitate to yield to the calling of God. In fact, he immediately slew a yoke of oxen and celebrated his send off party with his people to publicly signify his giving up his mundane pursuits for the work of the Lord. Throughout the Bible narration, we saw Elisha ministered to Elijah wholeheartedly.

And one of the king of Israel's servants answered and said, Here is Elisha the son of Shaphat, which poured water on the hands of Elijah. **(2 Kings 3:11)**

Can you imagine a successful businessman, stooping that low to serve a younger man? That was exactly what his honour for God brought Elisha to do. No wonder. His ministry was greater than that of his master. He was, in fact, the only prophet in the Bible who had a double portion of the anointing that operated on his master.

That is what a life of true service can bring on a man.

God, the ultimate rewarder, will judge everyone's act and heart and provide just a reward. There are great lessons to learn from Elisha.

Building an enduring relationship with your leaders

a) Take your spiritual leader as your spiritual father

And Elisha saw it, and he cried, My father, my father, the chariot of Israel, and the horsemen thereof. And he saw him no more: and he took hold of his own clothes, and rent them in two pieces. He took up also the mantle of Elijah that fell from him, and went back, and stood by the bank of Jordan; And he took the mantle of Elijah that fell from him, and smote the waters, and said, Where is the LORD God of Elijah? and when he also had smitten the waters, they parted hither and thither: and Elisha went over. And when the sons of the prophets which were to view at Jericho saw him, they said, The spirit of Elijah doth rest on Elisha. And they came to meet him, and bowed themselves to the ground before him. **(2 Kings 2:12-15)**

You can only receive from a man you dearly appreciate!

Though Elisha was quite older than Elijah, he nonetheless called him father. A father is someone you trust, obey, honour, admire and receive from. You do not contest, distaste or dishonour your natural father and still receive from them, do you?

God holds the office of fatherhood very important that it is hardly possible to see someone who dishonours his (biological or spiritual) father make it in life or ministry.

Honour thy father and thy mother: that thy days may be long upon the land which the LORD thy God giveth thee. **(Exodus 20:12)**

Honour thy father and mother; (which is the first commandment with promise;) That it may be well with thee, and thou mayest live long on the earth. **(Ephesians 6:2-3)**

You see, if you despise your father at home or in the Lord, it does not matter if the anointing upon him is raining over you like the ocean, you can not benefit from it. How much you receive from your leader will depend on how you see and esteem him. To receive from a man of God, first you need to respect and honour him!

And Jesus went out, and his disciples, into the towns of Caesarea Philippi: and by the way he asked his disciples, saying unto them, Whom do men say that I am? And they answered, John the Baptist: but some say, Elias; and others, One of the prophets. And he saith unto them, But whom say ye that I am? And Peter answereth and saith unto him, Thou art the Christ.
(Mark 8:27-29)

Jesus taught this mystery to His disciples while alive.
When it comes to receiving or being imparted by the man of God in your Church, what you see is what you get.
If you see him as your father, you will receive the blessing of a father from him. If you see him as your colleague or friend, you will receive the gift of a friend from him. If you see him as a vessel of God, your faith will connect to receive through him every divine blessing God has deposited in him for the Church. It is to you according to your faith. Do not allow familiarity to deny you of your blessing.
Many times, Satan will discredit men of God through sin or mistakes committed in public life and what you see next is their congregations taking off in droves. What an immature way of life!
If such a person genuinely asks for forgiveness from God and man, I know God has forgiven him or her. Now if God has forgiven His minister, what right do you have to still judge him or her guilty?
That is one powerful way the enemy uses to disconnect people from the anointed vessels of God. I have seen great ministries broke apart because of a minister's mistake. Though the gift of the Lord remains in such ministry, the accuser of our brethren swiftly cut off people of the Lord from benefitting from such anointing.

For the gifts and the calling of God are irrevocable. **(Rom 11:29** NASU)

Who is losing? We the body of Christ of course!
We lose for failing to practice forgiveness that we preach.
We lose for being cut off from the blessing God has deposited in His minister (Rom 11: 29) that fell under sin. We lose when such men waste their gifts and perhaps backslide from their services.
Do not get me wrong, I believe it is very wrong for ministers of God to entertain sins and all forms of immoral conduct in their lives.
That is very wrong and unacceptable. But if such things nonetheless happen, I insist that we exercise Christian mercy to recover a sinner from his sin. Throwing out dirty water with a baby is very wrong and two wrongs can never make a right!

b) Have an honourable view of your pastor

And when he was come into his own country, he taught them in their synagogue, insomuch that they were astonished, and said, Whence hath this man this wisdom, and these mighty works? Is not this the carpenter's son? is not his mother called Mary? and his brethren, James, and Joses, and Simon, and Judas? And his sisters, are they not all with us? Whence then hath this man all these things? And they were offended in him. But Jesus said unto them, A prophet is not without honour, save in his own country, and in his own house. And he did not many mighty works there because of their unbelief. **(Matthew 13:54-58)**

It is important how you see your leaders!
Do you see them as ordinary men though used of God or as ordinary men used by the mighty God to do the extraordinary?
Do you see your leader filled with the power of God or not?
The way you see him will determine what you get out of God's anointing deposited upon his life. Every where Jesus went and was received as a powerful man of God, the virtues in Him exploded to satisfy the various needs of the people (Matt 12:15). That situation changed as soon as He came to His own people in His own country. Though He still carried supernatural power of God in His being, He could not do any mighty work because of how they saw and received Him (Luke 4:23-27 ; John 6:42).

And he went out from thence, and came into his own country; and his disciples follow him…Is not this the carpenter, the son of Mary, the brother of James, and Joses, and of Juda, and Simon? and are not his sisters here with us? And they were offended at him. But Jesus said unto them, A prophet is not without honour, but in his own country, and among his own kin, and in his own house. And he could there do no mighty work, save that he laid his hands upon a few sick folk, and healed them. And he marvelled because of their unbelief. And he went round about the villages, teaching. And they said, Is not this Jesus, the son of Joseph, whose father and mother we know? how is it then that he saith, I came down from heaven? **(Mark 6:1, 3-6)**

The word of God already attached your prosperity to your prophet and pastor regardless of his age, status or look. It is to you according to how you see him now. As you relate and minister with her or him with love, your miracles of healing, blessing, breakthroughs and prosperity will be released in to your life.

Believe in the LORD your God, so shall ye be established; believe his prophets, so shall ye prosper. **(2 Chronicles 20:20b)**

That confirmeth the word of his servant, and performeth the counsel of his messengers. **(Isaiah 44:26)**

One reason it is necessary for you to see your leaders in correct light is the fact that fathers are meant to be our role models who not only show us exemplary leadership conducts but also offer us support for our sustenance. I pray that God will give you a true and perfect father, both in the natural and in the spiritual.

Your spiritual father will not only help you to grow in the Lord but will also provide for your spiritual sustenance as you move from one point of maturity to another. It is the same way that biological orphans (without fatherly guidance in life) have a tough time growing up perfectly that spiritual orphans suffer lack of spiritual guidance; protection and support that are needed to enrich their lives.

Relating correctly with your pastor as your spiritual father will allow him to speak the blessing and prosperity of the lord in to your life without limit.

The words that I speak unto you, they are spirit, and they are life. **(John 6:63)**

As you listen to his message directly or recorded, in addition to your regular study and meditation of the word of God, you will begin to see breakthroughs far beyond your wildest imagination.

God has given us all fathers to bless us.

Take hold of your blessing and never let it go!

c) Serve your leaders

But Jehoshaphat said, Is there not here a prophet of the LORD, that we may inquire of the LORD by him? And one of the king of Israel's servants answered and said, Here is Elisha the son of Shaphat, which poured water on the hands of Elijah. **(2 Kings 3:11)**

And certain women, which had been healed of evil spirits and infirmities, Mary called Magdalene, out of whom went seven devils, And Joanna the wife of Chuza Herod's steward, and Susanna, and many others, which ministered unto him of their substance. **(Luke 8:2-3)**

One scriptural way to receive from your spiritual fathers is to serve them. The Bible instructs that they that are taught in the word should minister back to him that taught him in all good things (Gal 6: 6).
If your well-being matters to your spiritual father that he focusses his entire being on it, you should be decent enough to support his livelihood too. As a member of the body of Christ, those who are labouring in the world should see it as their natural duty to support those that are labouring in the word of God.
That is how the whole body of Christ can grow well nourished.

> *We are fools for Christ's sake, but ye are wise in Christ; we are weak, but ye are strong; ye are honourable, but we are despised. Even unto this present hour we both hunger, and thirst, and are naked, and are buffeted, and have no certain dwellingplace; And labour, working with our own hands: being reviled, we bless; being persecuted, we suffer it: Being defamed, we intreat: we are made as the filth of the world, and are the offscouring of all things unto this day. I write not these things to shame you, but as my beloved sons I warn you. For though ye have ten thousand instructors in Christ, yet have ye not many fathers: for in Christ Jesus I have begotten you through the gospel.* **(1 Cor. 4:10-15)**

As the minister of God ministers to you the spiritual, it is your obligation to minister to his physical needs!

C) Relate closely with your minister

> *And Elijah said unto Elisha, Tarry here, I pray thee; for the LORD hath sent me to Bethel. And Elisha said unto him, As the LORD liveth, and as thy soul liveth, I will not leave thee. So they went down to Bethel.*
> ***(2 Kings 2:1)***

Elisha, despite the advice of Elijah, refused to be disconnected from his leader. No wonder, that journey ended up in his securing double anointing of what operated in the life of his leader.
Relationship is the birthplace of productivity.
The same way it takes a relationship between man and God for man to secure his anointing and same way deep relationship precedes procreation among partners does it require a close relationship between leaders and followers for impartation to take place. Lord Jesus Christ taught us this important principle when He made it clear that without a relationship with Him, we can do nothing. You see, it is good to physically relate with your spiritual father who in most cases should be your local pastor. Many times by the laying of the hands, God could through him impart you with great spiritual gifts.

> *Wherefore I put thee in remembrance that thou stir up the gift of God, which is in thee by the putting on of my hands.* ***(2 Timothy 1:6)***

It takes the dropping of Elijah's mantel on Elisha for the man of God to secure the double anointing of his master (2 kings 2: 13). God wrought special miracles by the hands of Paul in Asia that handkerchiefs or aprons were brought from his body unto the sick, and the diseases departed from them, and the evil spirits went out of them (Acts 19:11-12).

Leadership transfer

> *And it came to pass, when they were gone over, that Elijah said unto Elisha, Ask what I shall do for thee, before I be taken away from thee. And Elisha said, I pray thee, let a double portion of thy spirit be upon me. And he said, Thou hast asked a hard thing: nevertheless, if thou see me when I am taken from thee, it shall be so unto thee; but if not, it shall not be so.* ***(2 Kings 2:9-10)***

> *He took up also the mantle of Elijah that fell from him, and went back, and stood by the bank of Jordan; And he took the mantle of Elijah that fell from him, and smote the waters, and said, Where is the LORD God of Elijah? and when he also had smitten the waters, they parted hither and thither: and Elisha went over.* ***(2 Kings 2:13-14)***

Close relationship causes the gradual transfer of traits among people as a matter of fact. Quite often, couples begin to walk, talk and look alike by the sheer power of living together. Children naturally take the manners of their parents. In the spiritual also, you can be imparted by being around your spiritual father without being conscious of it.

Elisha got Elijah's anointing!

> *And he took the mantle of Elijah that fell from him, and smote the waters, and said, Where is the LORD God of Elijah? and when he also had smitten the waters, they parted hither and thither: and Elisha went over. And when the sons of the prophets which were to view at Jericho saw him, they said, The spirit of Elijah doth rest on Elisha. And they came to meet him, and bowed themselves to the ground before him.* ***2 Kings 2:14-15***

Both Prophets Elijah and Elisha performed the same types of miracles. They both increased widow's meal and oil as the only means of sustenance (1 Kings 17:14-16, 2 Kings 4:3-5), both revived dead boy after lying on him thrice(1 Kings 17:21-24; 2 Kings 4:32-36), both overcome drought through restored rains and healed water (1

Kings 18:41-45; 2 Kings 2:19-21) and both divided the river of Jordan by smashing the water with their mantels(2 Kings 2:8; 2 Kings 2: 14).

However because Elisha had the double anointing that was on Elijah's life, he was able to perform thirty two miracles instead of sixteen miracles performed by his master. That is what having intimate physical contact with your spiritual father can produce.

Serving your spiritual father increases you!

Being around a man of God will naturally impart upon you some of the anointing working in the ministry. When the Pharisees and Sadducees saw the boldness of Peter and John, after the ascension of Jesus and perceived that they were unlearned and ignorant men, they marvelled; and they took notice of them, that they had been with Jesus Christ (Acts 4:13.9). You may not know when it happens, but this spiritual mystery happens always be it by sheer relationship, laying of hands, teaching (John 6: 63) or exchange of mantels.

John the Baptist also got Elijah's anointing!

> *And his disciples asked him, saying, Why then say the scribes that Elias must first come? And Jesus answered and said unto them, Elias truly shall first come, and restore all things. But I say unto you, That Elias is come already, and they knew him not, but have done unto him whatsoever they listed. Likewise shall also the Son of man suffer of them. Then the disciples understood that he spake unto them of John the Baptist.* **(Matt. 17:10-13)**

Though John the Baptist and Elijah lived millennium apart and never had physical contact or relationship, they still shared the same anointing! You see, anointing transfer is a spiritual mystery that happens regardless of the distance of time, people or generation.

Yes, you do not need to physically relate with a person to secure his anointing but you must passionately desire the anointing, honour the carrier and relate with his ministry by all available means. That might be through the reading of books, listening to mesages and studying and practicing life principles of such a person. You need to covet the anointing deeply and honestly before it can be imparted to you.

If you take a look at John the Baptist, he lived his life exactly like Elijah. Though they lived generations apart, he lived the same Spartan life! Jesus in fact confirmed the similarity of the anointing between both men.

> *And he shall go before him in the spirit and power of Elias, to turn the hearts of the fathers to the children, and the disobedient to the wisdom of the just; to make ready a people prepared for the Lord.* **(Luke 1:17)**

> *For all the prophets and the law prophesied until John. And if ye will receive it, this is Elias, which was for to come. He that hath ears to hear, let him hear.* **(Matthew 11:13-15)**

A deep Bible study reveals the fact that John the Baptist operated in the same anointing as Elijah.

Both men lived in desserts (1 Kings 19:4; Mark 1: 4), ate strange animals (1 Kings 17:6; Matt 3:4), wore clothes made of camels' hair (2 kings 1:8; Matt 3: 4), fought ungodly leaders of their time (1 Kings 21: 18-20, 1 Kings 18: 20-24; Mark 6: 17-20, Matt 3: 7-10) and had their ministries challenged towards an end by adulterous women (1 Kings 19:3-16;Matt. 14: 6-10).

What about my anointing!

> *The words that I speak unto you, they are spirit, and they are life.* **(John 6:63)**

You can be anointed too!
The word you communicate with carries spirit and life!
God created the world at the beginning by calling out the light.
God still creates peoples' destiny and lives through His words spoken through men of God today. You see, the physical distance has no hindrance in the things of the Lord especially concerning your spiritual impartation and spiritual transfer. It is your heart desires and passionate acts towards the leaders and what they represent that will determine what you get from them. Before you realise, as you passionately and affectionately share a minister's vision, and passion, principles and doctrines, intentions and actions, you will begin to think and behave the same way he or she does.

So if for some reason, distance separates you from who you have taken as your spiritual father, distance needs not impair your relationship or your ability to receive blessing from him.

It is not always necessary that you meet somebody physically before he or she can impart you. It doesn't matter how far or close your spiritual father is. You can have a close relationship with him by seeking an audience with him for prayer and impartation sessions, regularly blessing him out of your own substance, listening to his messages, reading his books, supporting his ministry in cash and kind and communicating with him by all possible avenues.

Whichever way it takes, be it during the lifetime of the leader or after his demise, leadership transfer takes place in every godly and honourable relationship. In the case of Elisha, he secured a double portion of the anointing that operated in the life of Elijah.

> *And the spirit entered into me when he spake unto me, and set me upon my feet, that I heard him that spake unto me.* (**Ezekiel 2:2**)

> *The Spirit of the Lord is upon me, because he hath anointed me to preach the gospel to the poor; he hath sent me to heal the brokenhearted, to preach deliverance to the captives, and recovering of sight to the blind, to set at liberty them that are bruised.* (**Luke 4:18**)

While the relationship with men of God is an easy way to get anointed, you can directly be called and anointed by God too.

That is how many preachers themselves secured the anointing and leadership virtues operating in their ministries. Jesus Christ, for instance, was directly anointed by God to fulfil His earthly project.

If you ever locate your calling in the Lord, He will never let you go powerless without the anoniting (power of God) to fulfill your assignment. If He calls you, he will enable you to fulfill your calling. Faithful is He that calls you, who also will do it (1 Thess. 5:24).

Lessons from lifestyles of Elisha

a) To receive from a man of God, you need to operate in the same spirit with him

> *But Gehazi, the servant of Elisha the man of God, said, Behold, my master hath spared Naaman this Syrian, in not receiving at his hands that which he brought: but, as the LORD liveth, I will run after him, and take somewhat of him. So Gehazi followed after Naaman. And when Naaman saw him running after him, he lighted down from the chariot to meet him, and said, Is all well? And he said, All is well. My master hath sent me, saying, Behold, even now there be come to me from mount Ephraim two young men of the sons of the prophets: give them, I pray thee, a talent of silver, and two changes of garments. And Naaman said, Be content, take two talents. And he urged him, and bound two talents of silver in two bags, with two changes of garments, and laid them upon two of his servants; and they bare them before him.* (**2 Kings 5:20-23**)

> *But he went in, and stood before his master. And Elisha said unto him, Whence comest thou, Gehazi? And he said, Thy servant went no whither. And he said unto him, Went not mine heart with thee, when the man turned again from his chariot to meet thee? Is it a time to receive money, and to receive garments, and oliveyards, and vineyards, and sheep, and oxen, and menservants, and maidservants? The leprosy therefore of Naaman shall cleave unto thee, and unto thy seed for ever. And he went out from his presence a leper as white as snow.* **(2 Kings 5:25-27)**

Elijah's first servant before Elisha missed the leadership virtues upon his master. In fact the Bible refused to name him (1 Kings 18: 42-43). Elisha was later picked by God out of his business to serve Elijah.
Gehazi, the servant of Elisha chose to be a cheat and liar and ended up with leprosy instead of securing the anointing upon the life of Elisha. Though he was highly privileged, he lost his chance to greed and covetousness. God will prove you before you are approved for leadership in his kingdom.

b) **It takes great dedication, passion and desire to receive anointing from God be it direct or through men of God**

God may choose to directly anoint a man with leadership prowess for a particular office like in the case of John the Baptist but in most cases, like in the case of Elisha and the disciples of Jesus, you need to pay the price of service and closeness to your leader to be imparted.

c) **Leadership transfer is accessible at a cost**

> *Elijah said unto Elisha, Ask what I shall do for thee, before I be taken away from thee. And Elisha said, I pray thee, let a double portion of thy spirit be upon me. And he said, Thou hast asked a hard thing: nevertheless, if thou see me when I am taken from thee, it shall be so unto thee; but if not, it shall not be so.* **(2 Kings 2:9-10)**

Receiving mostly depends on the recipient than the giver!
Elijah here was telling Elisha that he can receive the leadership toga and anointing if he was ready to pay the price.
The disciples of Jesus Christ hanged around Him all the time in order for them to receive power transfer from their relationship with Him.
Elisha spent time with Elijah till the last minute he was carried away from his presence. He refused to quit even when encouraged to do so by Elijah himself (2 Kings 2: 6). You may be close to a man and

still fail to be blessed by the virtues and unctions in his life if you refuse to tap into them. Judas failed to tap into the anointing upon Jesus Christ although he was with Jesus always. Gehazi also missed the unction upon his leader despite serving under Elisha for long.

B) BAD BOYS: DAVID AND ABSALOM

Life Background

> *But in all Israel there was none to be so much praised as Absalom for his beauty: from the sole of his foot even to the crown of his head there was no blemish in him. And when he polled his head, (for it was at every year's end that he polled it: because the hair was heavy on him, therefore he polled it:) he weighed the hair of his head at two hundred shekels after the king's weight. And unto Absalom there were born three sons, and one daughter, whose name was Tamar: she was a woman of a fair countenance.* **(2 Sam. 14:25-27)**

Absalom was the third son of David.
After his pardon and return from exile for the murder of Amnon his half brother (who had earlier raped Absalom's sister) he began to plot his ascendance to the throne of his father (being the oldest surviving son after the demise of his two older brothers).

> God will prove you before you are approved for leadership in his kingdom.

Service orientation to others

One of Absalom's sources of failure might be the fact that he was raised up without a sense of loyalty or service to anyone.
As a prince, all he seemed to do is keep himself healthy- body and soul while he, like other brothers, enjoyed the goodness of the father. When Amnon his brother raped his sister, he withdrew to himself with nobody taking notice of this dangerous passivity that later incubated to murderous anger that led to the end of his half brother.

Human qualities

Therefore he said unto his servants, See, Joab's field is near mine, and he hath barley there; go and set it on fire. And Absalom's servants set the field on fire. **(2 Samuel 14:30)**

Absalom, like other children of David, was a spoiled brat swimming in excessive indulgence. All the children of King David were used to getting whatever thing they desire without any resistance.
Amnon though could have gotten his sister in marriage chose to rape and have her immediately rather than marry her officially.
Absalom saw nothing wrong in burning Joab's field only to get his attention. This type of poor reasoning and fearless conducts later led to his demise.
Absalom is an epitome of a spoilt upbringing. He grew up having no fear of God or his parents. He grew up to have no respect for the life of others. He had no honour for any position of authority.
It was no surprise that he grew up to become a villain whose life was cut short by the same army who would have protected him.

Relationship to leadership

a) Anger
Absalom's discontent with his father's handling of his sister rape did not dissipate with the murder of Amnon but rather grew from anger to contempt and from contempt to hatred. His criticism of his father's social handling of the family affair soon extends to include his official political conducts.

b) Fear of repercussion
With the death of his two brothers, Amnon and Chileab, Absalom suspected David might choose his beloved son, Solomon to succeed him (2 sam 12: 24-25). It was in order to prevent this situation that he began to recruit discontent people to join him in dethroning his father before he officially enthrones Solomon.

c) Disloyalty
Absalom fearlessly plotted to overthrow his own father.
He cultivated the habit of seating outside the court of his father to offer cheap support and promise to redress peoples' problems so

long they will in turn support his plans to usurp the power of his father. He did this purposefully to discredit his father and steal the heart of his subjects (2 Sam.15:6).

Leadership transfer

And Absalom said unto him, See, thy matters are good and right; but there is no man deputed of the king to hear thee.. Absalom said moreover, Oh that I were made judge in the land, that every man which hath any suit or cause might come unto me, and I would do him justice! **(2 Samuel 15:3-4).**

Absalom chose to use deceit and every ungodly means to steal the heart of the subjects of his father in order to dethrone him.
It is common in life that leaders are mostly engrossed with activities of administration thereby becoming quite distant from their people. In such a situation, it is not uncommon to see lower ministers whose positions offer closeness to these people to cheaply use the opportunity to turn the people's hearts against their leaders. That is an ugly and abominable thing to do - using your privilege to destroy the same man who has given you that privilege.

For rebellion is as the sin of witchcraft, and stubbornness is as iniquity and idolatry. **(1 Samuel 15:23a**

The gruesome means Absalom chose to accomplish the ungodly dethronement of his father was as bad, as the results it brought him.
Let us see some of the means Absalom employed to wrongly ascend the throne of his father.

a) Personality assassination

Absalom chose to discredit his father's personality by misleading people with his sweet talks and good looks promising to pay good attention to their judicial needs.

b) Scheming for leadership

Absalom started scheming to overthrow his father as soon as he was forgiven for the murder of Amnon (his own half brother). Absalom wittily played on Judah's (consisting of two out of the 12 tribes) jealousy of Israel, as the main headquarter of the merged kingdom of Judah and Israel. He not only selected Hebron, Judah's old capital as his headquarter for the revolt but also selected from Judah Amasa as his general and Ahithophel as his counselor.

c) **Dishonour of authority**

By Ahithophel's abominable counsel, Absalom slept with his father's concubines, at once committing his party to war for the throne (1 Kings 2:13; 2 Sam. 17: 4). If not for the intervention of God, Ahithophel's war counsel would have destroyed completely King David and his followers but God made way through the counsel of David's friend, Hushai to disrupt the good counsel of Ahithophel.

And Absalom and all the men of Israel said, The counsel of Hushai the Archite is better than the counsel of Ahithophel. For the LORD had appointed to defeat the good counsel of Ahithophel, to the intent that the LORD might bring evil upon Absalom. **(2 Samuel 17:14)**

d) **Destruction of life**

Many times, villains do not care for the loss of life and other drastic results of their action when they commit treasons. The church is not just about the organisation of people but also about the protection of their destiny. Many times when people revolted against authority, they break off from the body God has deposited their spiritual nourishment and starve themselves to death. Sometimes, such people will no more get the right opportunity to continue what God has begun in their lives. It is always very important to ask yourself the reason you are partaking in any revolt against your Church.
If you are comfortable in your Church and enjoy a good relationship with your Church leaders, then do not support any abasalonic group that is planning to disrupt peace in your congregation.

So the people went out into the field against Israel: and the battle was in the wood of Ephraim; Where the people of Israel were slain before the servants of David, and there was there a great slaughter that day of twenty thousand men. For the battle was there scattered over the face of all the country: and the wood devoured more people that day than the sword devoured. **(2 Sam. 18:6-8)**

Absalon's war did not just cause division among brethrens but it also leads to the unnecessary death of twenty thousand men.

1) **Death and aftermaths**

   And when Ahithophel saw that his counsel was not followed, he saddled his ass, and arose, and gat him home to his house, to his city, and put his household in order, and hanged himself, and died, and was buried in the sepulchre of his father. **(2 Sam. 17:23)**

Ahithophel hanged himself while Absalom was caught suspended on a tree by his hair locks. He was later slain by Joab (2 Sam. 18:9-11;2 Sam. 18:14-15.) Over twenty thousand people died in that war.

2) **Lessons from Absalonic lifestyles**

a. **Take cognizance of God**
It is a tragedy that sometimes, people try to use their personal will and power to do the things of the Lord. Absalom and his followers forgot that it was God who installed King David whom they were trying to overthrow by their own strength.
They completely forgot that nobody could prevail over God's plan.

b. **Every usurper should learn to honestly deal with pride**
Pride kills! The only claim Absalom had to the throne was for being born to King David's family. How could such a person suddenly believe he was better than his father? Quite often, people join an established Church and because they are given privileges to work close with the leadership of the Church or given the opportunity to lead a section of the Church, they would start believing that they are better than those they met there.
That is what foolish pride can do to ignorant and immature people.
Learn to humbly offer your service wherever you are privileged to serve. See everything as a grace of the Lord. Ministry is not about good looks or great oratorical skill, it is about the backing of God!

   Faithful is he that calleth you, who also will do it. **(1 Thess. 5:24)**

   Except the LORD build the house, they labour in vain that build it: except the LORD keep the city, the watchman waketh but in vain. It is vain for you to rise up early, to sit up late, to eat the bread of sorrows: for so he giveth his beloved sleep. **(Psalm 127:1-2)**

Why will you think of stealing, corrupting or disrupting a ministry you were not called to start? Why will you plot to pull down a ministry you knew nothing about when God called His servant to start? Some people just permit pride and bitterness to ruin their reasoning. Such madness or foolishness could only lead you to your disaster. Meddling in the work of God because of personal pride is a killer. Run away from it, lest the same source of your pride be the source of your fall. It was the same hair locks that Absalom prided himself over that hanged him on the tree till Joab and his men arrived and slain him (2 Sam 18: 9-15).

c. **Succession to a godly institution requires godly means**
Absalom woefully failed in his bid to take power from his father because he sought to do it in an ungodly way. Every time people try to scheme their ways to power, it fails sooner than later.
Ascending godly thrones requires godly means.

> *And Elisha died, and they buried him. And the bands of the Moabites invaded the land at the coming in of the year. And it came to pass, as they were burying a man, that, behold, they spied a band of men; and they cast the man into the sepulchre of Elisha: and when the man was let down, and touched the bones of Elisha, he revived, and stood up on his feet.*
> **(2 Kings 13:20-21)**

In the case of Elijah and Elisha there was peaceful hand-over with the successor gracefully receiving the blessing of the leader.
Gehazi, the servant of Elisha lost the chance to the leadership anointing of his master for failing to conduct himself in the honest way of the Lord. Gehazi died with leprosy instead of inheriting the double anointing on Elisha's life (2 Kings 5: 25-27).

CONCLUSION

And it shall come to pass in the last days, that the mountain of the LORD's house shall be established in the top of the mountains, and shall be exalted above the hills; and all nations shall flow unto it. And many people shall go and say, Come ye, and let us go up to the mountain of the LORD, to the house of the God of Jacob; and he will teach us of his ways, and we will walk in his paths: for out of Zion shall go forth the law, and the word of the LORD from Jerusalem. (Isaiah 2:2-3)

We are in the last days that God has predestined for excellent breakthroughs and success in His Church. One of the instruments God will use to uplift His Church in this end time is knowledge. The rain of His wisdom has begun to pour upon the body of Christ and is finding its way to every believer that will offer self as a vessel of honour for the use of our heavenly Master.

God's unchanging plan remains to recover mankind from the claw of the forces of darkness. The body of Christ is destined to lead all oppressed souls from darkness into the light.

This book is divinely inspired to break the body of Christ loose from every entanglement of ignorance that has been keeping the Church away from ascending her leadership position as a city set on a hilltop that cannot be hidden.

The Church is the salt and the light of the world!

Light destroys every form of darkness.

Light makes way for bright vision and clear speed.

Light empowers to fly at extra ordinary level.

The word of God deposited in this book has come to serve as a lamp for your feet and light unto your path. The living word of God in this book has come to revitalise and revive our dying world.

The seasoned word of God is coming your way today to untie you from every ungodly force inhibiting you from running your race with a focus on Jesus Christ, the author and finisher of our faith.

The Church is destined to call the shots to the world. We are not only expected to preach the living word to the dying world but also meant to display the true riches of hope, peace, healing, joy, love, eternal life and other godly provisions to the impoverished world.

But in the last days it shall come to pass, that the mountain of the house of the LORD shall be established in the top of the mountains, and it shall be exalted above the hills; and people shall flow unto it. And many nations shall come, and say, Come, and let us go up to the mountain of the LORD, and to the house of the God of Jacob; and he will teach us of his ways, and we will walk in his paths: for the law shall go forth of Zion, and the word of the LORD from Jerusalem. **(Micah 4:1-2)**

For the earnest expectation of the creature waiteth for the manifestation of the sons of God. **(Romans 8:19)**

The whole creation is still waiting for the manifestation of the sons of God. The whole heaven and earth are still waiting for you to take your place in the affairs of the world. You should realise that God has sent you, like everyone else, to fulfil a particular purpose in this world. You have a special purpose to play in God's corporate program for mankind. There is no one else like you in this world!

There is no other time for you to rise up to your responsibility than now. For you to live fulfilled, you will have to discover your calling, hone your skill, perfect your talents and put all your efforts in to impacting your generation. Our generation is waiting for great leaders who can selflessly serve their talents in order to improve our world.

Will you yield yourself to serve your generation today?

Will you satisfy the earnest expectation of creation to manifest your well processed potentials? Will you reach deep inside to unlock the floodgate into your heart and permit rivers of living water to flow out of your belly. There is surely more to you than the eye can see.

Greater is He that is you than he that is in the world.

You are destined to lead your people out of the pit that our human culture of ungodliness has dumped mankind. However to ascend your throne, you need to hone your gift till it becomes a skill.

You need to excel in your career until it becomes your calling.

Only then can you lead your people out of shame into fame.

Deliberate and meditate upon the revelations shared in this book. Most importantly apply everything you learn to improve your nation and generation. Arise and shine for your light has come!

May the leadership seed in you grow speedily and fruitfully to impact your generation with great blessing in Jesus' mighty name. Amen.

Other books available from Solomon Osoko:

ART OF TRIUMPHANT PRAYER
Power of Prevailing Prayer

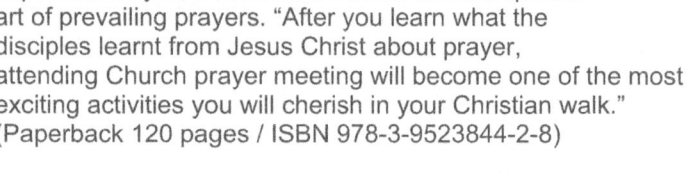

You can become all you want to be if all your prayers are answered. That is why it is very important for you to learn and master the triumphant art of prevailing prayers. "After you learn what the disciples learnt from Jesus Christ about prayer, attending Church prayer meeting will become one of the most exciting activities you will cherish in your Christian walk." (Paperback 120 pages / ISBN 978-3-9523844-2-8)

WALKING IN POWER:
Exercising Kingdom Authority

The realm of power is available for every believer of Jesus Christ. The power to heal the sick and prevail over the devil is made available to every Christian. However only believers dedicated to the work of the Lord can experience the power of the Lord. The simple reason for that is that the power of God is only made available to do the work of the Lord. Mouth without muscle makes you a mere charlatan. Leave that realm for theologians and religionists. You have talked of the power of God enough. It is now time you walk the talk.
The power of God is not for a joke but rather for yoke breaking! This is your time to embrace your destiny in Christ. It is now time to take your position among the blood washed, devil chasing, miracle working, heaven backed believers.

(Paperback 120 pages / ISBN 978-3-9523844-4-2)

FAITHFULNESS IN LEADERSHIP:
Discovering fruitfulness in Faithfulness

The rise and fall of every organization depend on its leadership. Smite the shepherd and the sheep will scatter!

There is no place where this truth is more relevant than in the Church of Christ where it requires the united efforts of a mature congregation and faithful leadership to fulfill God's purpose for His Church. Only rooted and well established people can bear fruits. Only a faithful leadership, conscious of its responsibility and focused on its calling can take its organization to the next level.

We need a culture of faithfulness to reap fruits of our labor. Remember that a big oak tree was once a tiny seed that refused to give up. Only finishers can be winners.

(Paperback 160 pages / ISBN 978-3-9523844-5-9)

MORE THAN CONQUERORS:
Victory Over Satan

Greater is He that is in you than he that is in the world. You have the Lion of Judah in you. Reveal Him and let Him roar!

Come along in this journey of revelation to see your enemy unveiled, exposed and disgraced. In this book, Pastor Solomon Osoko says, "Yes, you too can prosper in spite of the enemy. Now you can join the increasing numbers of believers prevailing over the enemy every day. Every man's mountain is his ignorance. The light of the word of God shared in this book is sure to place you far above every principality, power and opposition from the kingdom of darkness." You have suffered enough. Now you can prevail over Satan everywhere and every time. Now is your turn to triumph. Now is your turn to step into the realm of more than conquerors.

(Paperback 200 pages/ ISBN 978-3-9523844-3-5)

www.ingramcontent.com/pod-product-compliance
Lightning Source LLC
Chambersburg PA
CBHW031316160426
43196CB00007B/550